MUSIC IN THE ELEMENTARY CLASSROOM

Musicianship and Teaching

MARJORIE LATHAM HOFFER

CHARLES R. HOFFER

University of Florida

HARCOURT BRACE JOVANOVICH, PUBLISHERS

San Diego   New York   Chicago   Austin
London   Sydney   Tokyo   Toronto

ISBN: 0-15-564879-9

Library of Congress Catalog Card Number: 86-80753

Printed in the United States of America

COPYRIGHTS AND
ACKNOWLEDGMENTS

The poem "Who" on page 264 was written by Edith Savage and is from M. Val Marsh et al., *The Spectrum of Music*, Grade 6, copyright © 1980 by Macmillan Publishing Co., Inc. The poem "Everyone Sang" on page 286 is from *Collected Poems* by Siegfried Sassoon, copyright 1920 by E. P. Dutton Co., copyright renewed 1948 by Siegfried Sassoon; reprinted by permission of Viking Penguin Inc.

PICTURE CREDITS

Part I Opener: Charles R. Hoffer; p. 5: Barbara Lautner/Wichita Symphony; p. 23: Elizabeth Crook et al., *Silver Burdett Music*, Centennial Edition (Morristown, NJ: General Learning Corporation, 1985); p. 25: M. Val Marsh et al., *The Spectrum of Music*, Teacher's Annotated Edition (New York: Macmillan, 1983); p. 26: Charles R. Hoffer; p. 30: Talbot Studio, Bloomington, IN; p. 58: MMB, Inc., St. Louis, MO; p. 113: MMB; p. 148: Charles R. Hoffer; p. 194: Talbot Studio; p. 251: MMB, Inc., St. Louis, MO; p. 268: Talbot Studio, Bloomington, IN; p. 285: Ezra Stoller © ESTO; p. 285: Courtesy of Air France; p. 287: United Nations.

To Allan and Martha, ours by birth
and
Donna and Don, ours by marriage

Preface

An increasing number of colleges are combining the teaching of music fundamentals and music methods in a single course for future elementary school teachers. *Music in the Elementary Classroom: Musicianship and Teaching* has been written to meet the need for knowledge in both the subject matter and the techniques of teaching music. Much of the material has appeared, in somewhat different form, in *Teaching Music in the Elementary Classroom* by Charles R. Hoffer and Marjorie Latham Hoffer, published by Harcourt Brace Jovanovich in 1982. However, in this new book the emphasis has been shifted, some topics have been eliminated, and a new chapter, "Moving to Music," has been added.

By presenting the fundamentals of music in a series of boxed sections in close proximity to the related teaching suggestions, the book maintains the close bond between what is taught and how it is taught. Students who have already taken a course in music fundamentals may use the boxed material for review, or may omit it without detriment to the continuity of the teaching portion.

Part One discusses the value of music in the elementary school, the complementary roles of the classroom teacher and music specialist, and the factors to consider when planning music instruction.

Parts Two and Three describe practical methods for teaching music to children. These chapters explore the four basic music elements—rhythm, pitch, timbre, and loudness—through the activities of singing, listening, playing instruments, moving to music, and reading its notation. The music activities are viewed not as the main goal of music education in the elementary school, but rather as a means of deepening the children's knowledge of music, developing their performing and listening skills, and increasing their enjoyment of music.

Part Four contains suggestions for incorporating music into the study of the fine arts and social studies and concludes with a chapter on teaching music to special students.

Information in this book is presented for two general levels—the primary and the upper grades. Such a division recognizes the increments in music learning that should be achieved as children progress through school, yet it is flexible enough to accommodate the differences among classrooms and children. The placement of topics according to primary or upper grade levels corresponds in general to the appearance of those topics in current music series books and to conclusions drawn from research studies showing how children grow and learn.

Because the book does not assume that the reader has had prior music study, technical information is presented in such a way that it can be understood by nonmusicians. The suggestions for teaching music are varied and realistic. Teaching procedures are carefully described, and many are illustrated in dialogues that give insight into typical classroom situations. All chapters conclude with review questions and optional activities to involve the reader more fully in the topics being studied.

The book is eclectic in its approach to the various methods of teaching music. It owes no allegiance to a particular system, nor does it follow the curriculum sequence presented in any particular series of elementary music books. There is no way of knowing which series will be available to a beginning teacher, and such books are subject to frequent revision and replacement because of textbook adoption policies within a district or state. Nevertheless, the music series books offer significant help to the classroom teacher, and their use is strongly encouraged.

In short, *Music in the Elementary Classroom: Musicianship and Teaching* seeks to give prospective teachers a knowledge of music fundamentals and of the principles, procedures, and materials that will be useful in a wide variety of teaching situations.

We want to thank the following persons for their reviews of the manuscript: Marilyn Vincent of Ball State University, Linda K. Damer of Indiana State University, and Susan Tarnowski of the University of Wisconsin-Eau Claire.

Marjorie Latham Hoffer
Charles R. Hoffer

Contents

5   *Pitch Differences and Melody*   51

Concept of High and Low **52**   Melody **56**   Pitch and
Instruments **57**   Melodic Steps and Leaps **59**
Phrases **64**   Teaching the Notation of Pitch **66**   Orff and
Kodály Techniques **67**   Review Questions **71**
Activities **71**   Skill Practice **72**

6   *Timbre*   73

Teaching the Concept of Timbre **74**   Exploring Sound
Production and Timbres **75**   Basic Instruments and Voice
Types **76**   Sound Effects in Stories **78**   Review
Questions **81**   Activities **81**

7   *Dynamic Levels and the Combining of Musical Elements*   82

Loud/Soft Concept **83**   Gradual Changes in Dynamic
Level **84**   Accents **86**   Dynamic Level and Musical
Expression **88**   Putting the Musical Elements Together:
Performing **89**   Putting the Musical Elements Together:
Listening **90**   Review Questions **93**   Activities **93**

8   *Re-creating Music Through Singing and Playing*   95

Singing **96**   Playing Classroom Instruments **110**
Music Reading **115**   Review Questions **119**
Activities **120**   Skill Exercises **120**

9   *Creating Music*   121

The Value of Creativity in the Curriculum **122**
Adding Creative Elements to Existing Music **123**
Integrating Creative Activities with Other Arts **126**
Creating Original Music **127**   Review Questions **135**
Activities **136**   Skill Exercises **136**

10   *Moving to Music*   137

Fingerplays **138**   Guiding Early Movement Activities **139**
Action Songs **140**   Moving to Show Recognition of
Musical Elements **143**   Singing Games **143**   Folk and
Social Dancing **144**   Dramatizations **146**   Review
Questions **147**   Activities **147**

Part **IV** Other Aspects of Teaching Music in the
Elementary School   269

PART

I

Teaching Music in the Elementary School: Purpose and Structure

Part One presents fundamental topics that influence the teaching of music in the elementary school. As a basis for examining these topics, Chapter 1 considers the reasons for including music in the elementary school curriculum.

Because most schools designate a cooperative/complementary arrangement between music specialists and classroom teachers, the respective roles of these professionals need to be understood. The discussion in Chapter 2 seeks to clarify that relationship.

Chapter 3 describes fundamental guidelines which are derived from educational psychology and which form the basis for the teaching methods recommended in later sections of the book.

C H A P T E R

1

Why Is Music Taught in the Elementary School?

M usic is important in human life. All over the world people spend countless hours listening to music and performing it, and they spend vast amounts of money for instruments, records, and record-playing equipment. People dance, sing, play instruments, and create new tunes in every part of the globe. It is estimated that in America more than 30 million people play musical instruments regularly. More than 54 million people attend concerts of popular music, and 27 million attend concerts of classical music.[1] That is a greater number than attend sports events such as major league baseball and college football games.

Music has also been present in every age. The walls of ancient Egyptian buildings show people playing instruments and singing, and the Bible tells how David soothed King Saul with his music. In the Middle Ages a courtly gentleman was likely to serenade the lady of his choice, and competitive guilds were organized to reward excellence in music performance. The breadth and depth of mankind's interest in music are indeed impressive.

Why are music and the other fine arts so important? There are several reasons, but a most significant one is that music and other arts represent a fundamental difference between existing and living. Animals exist in the sense that they manage to survive. Humans live; they attempt to make life interesting, rewarding, and satisfying. Humans are not content merely to survive in a cave and grub roots for food. They notice sights and sounds and have feelings about them, and they find life richer because of these feelings and experiences.

People have always been looking at beauty in the world about them. They are fascinated by the shifting surf, the color of a sunset, and the shape of a flower. They create beautiful and artistic objects. They value paintings, symphonies, and poetry, and they seek artistic quality in their everyday surroundings—in their clothing, homes, furniture, automobiles. A wooden box could serve as a lamp table, and it would have the virtue of being far cheaper than a piece of furniture. But humans do not want to live with objects that are merely functional. The human spirit needs to appreciate and create things of beauty. This compulsion to reach beyond immediate needs is not a luxury; it is a basic element of being human.

Why Are Music and the Other Arts Taught in School?

The role of the school is to teach the subjects and skills that enable a person to function successfully in society. When mathematics, music, science, and other school subjects move beyond a rudimentary level, they exceed the teaching capabilities of most families. There are too many things to learn and they are often complex. It is no coincidence that every society that seeks to progress beyond the tribal stage has established a system of schools. This has happened because no better way has been devised to equip individuals to function in a society.

Schools are also needed to transmit the culture of the society to each generation. There is a wealth of music, art, drama, poetry and other forms of literature that young people would not be likely to know without instruction in school. Interpreting mankind's great cultural achievements is an important mandate for all teachers.

At first glance, the arts may seem to be an unnecessary component in the making of a productive citizen. School curriculums appropriately include subjects that are needed if one is to function in the contemporary world—reading, writing, arithmetic, and so on. But the concerns of most educators go beyond these subjects. They realize that giving children rudimentary skills is not enough today.

The notion that schools should be more than a training ground for the rudimentary needs of life has strong support. The American Association of School Administrators (AASA) has on three occasions gone on record in support of music and the other arts as necessary in the school curriculum. The first time was more than 50 years ago. Another statement was adopted in 1959. A portion of it reads:

> We believe in a well-balanced school curriculum in which music, drama, painting, poetry, sculpture, architecture, and the like are included side by side with other important subjects such as mathematics, history, and science. It is important that pupils, as a part of general education, learn to appreciate, to understand, to create, and to criticize with discrimination those products of the mind, the voice, the hand, and the body which give dignity to the person and exalt the spirit of man.[2]

A third statement of support by the AASA for the arts was adopted in 1973. It speaks explicitly against categorical budget cuts of "so-called 'peripheral' subject areas."[3]

In 1967 the Music Educators National Conference (MENC), which is the professional association of school music teachers in the United States, sponsored a symposium at Tanglewood in Massachusetts. Leaders from all walks of life met to discuss the role of music in American society. A portion of the Tanglewood Declaration issued at the conclusion of the Symposium reads:

> We believe that education must have as major goals the art of living, the building of personal identity, and the nurturing of creativity. Since the study of music can contribute much to these ends, *we now call for music to be placed in the core of the school curriculum.*
>
> The arts afford a continuity with aesthetic tradition in man's history. Music and other fine arts, largely nonverbal in nature, reach close to the social, psychological, and physiological roots of man in his search for identity and self-realization.[4]

IMAGINE
THE WORLD
WITHOUT
MUSIC.

Much has been written in recent years about nurturing the uniqueness of each child. Educators are saying not only that learning should move beyond the rudimentary and routine, but that each child should be encouraged to explore, express, and experiment so that he or she can develop potential abilities to the fullest extent. The artistic, aesthetic area is certainly one in which children should be given a chance to test their aptitudes and explore their interests. Music, art, dance, drama, and literature are recognized avenues for creative expression, and the schools are uniquely equipped to provide guidance and encouragement in such endeavors. When music and other arts are omitted from the curriculum, children are being deprived of a valuable part of their preparation for living today and in the twenty-first century.

Music as a Subject

Although music may provide greater opportunities for self-expression than most school subjects, it is a field of study—an academic discipline—like other subjects in the curriculum. It involves a body of information and skills with which every child should be familiar, at least to some degree. There are concepts related to the structure of music, as well as specialized techniques for performing and creating it. There is also much to be learned about the repertoire of music (called music literature) and about the syntactical patterns of the various types of music. It is a vast and varied field.

Like other subjects, music is learned through effort and concentration. Some people regard music primarily as an activity in which one participates for recreation. The pleasurable aspects of music are valid in many situations, but there is a difference between just singing through a song for entertainment and singing a song to gain a greater understanding of its musical properties. One is a pastime, while the other is a means of learning music. This is not to say that music should be only hard work instead of fun. Rather, it means that a person's enjoyment is heightened as understanding increases and skills are mastered.

Another characteristic of music as a subject is that many of its facets are unlikely to be learned by children outside the school. Popular music is heard virtually everywhere by children, so their familiarity with it is assured without formal instruction. The larger world of music, however, is less accessible to most children, so they are unlikely to learn about it unless they receive specific instruction.

Nonmusical Values of Music

Music has often been advocated for its contributions to reasoning ability, language arts, character, leisure activity, health, and so on. In the first part of this chapter, music and the other fine arts were cited as contributing to the quality of human life. The benefits of music are not confined to the art of music itself.

Transfer effects

If engaging in one activity causes behavioral changes in another area, the first activity is said to transfer to the second area. Does music instruction transfer to other areas of the school curriculum? If so, to which areas, and to what extent? One can read varied opinions about the transfer effects of music instruction. However, because research findings represent the best means available for securing solid information, this brief review is based on research results.

Several major attempts have been made to assess the results of arts instruction on general learning ability. In some cases, notably the Interdisciplinary Model Program in the Arts for Children and Teachers (IMPACT) and the Dallas "Learning to Learn through Music" program, positive results were achieved, but other data indicate that the enriched programs made little difference. Similarly mixed conclusions can be drawn about the claims for the transfer to general learning of the Kodály-Hungarian Singing School programs.

The area most likely to benefit from transfer of music instruction appears to be language arts. Two studies conclude that certain aspects of music instruction transfer to some aspects of reading achievement.

It has been known for some time that many stutterers sing without their usual hesitations. The likelihood that singing can improve some speech disorders suggests a positive transfer effect, but more research is needed in this area.

In the few studies that have been conducted to assess the connection between music study and skills in mathematics or social studies, little relationship has been found.

The limited amount of research on the effects of music instruction on self-concept and personality change has yielded inconclusive results. Generally, little difference is observed as the result of music instruction.

There is evidence of expanded chest and lung capacity when regular music instruction includes singing. Information is not available regarding other physical changes that may occur as a result of music instruction. In any case, the physical benefits of music study are small when compared to those of physical education and health instruction.

This discussion of the transfer effects of music instruction can best be summarized by citing the conclusions reached by Karen I. Wolff after her review of research on the topic.

> The weight of evidence gleaned from the research leads one to believe that there may be measurable effects of music education on the development of cognitive skills and understanding. This seems to be true for both general transfer, i.e., "learning how to learn," and specific transfer. Specific transfer is particularly apparent in its effect on performance in the language arts. . . .
>
> While it is true that most of the research related to the nonmusical outcomes of music education has produced positive results, the conclusions drawn generally remain unconvincing. This is due largely to obvious inadequacies in the experimental designs and also to the incomplete and equivocal descriptions of the experiments themselves.[5]

Attitude toward school

It has been demonstrated that a classroom program enriched by instruction in the arts provides a more interesting school environment for children and helps to reduce absenteeism. Advocates of behavior modification techniques have demonstrated the success of offering music as a reward for work completed in other areas of the school curriculum.

The reported influence of music and the arts in improving the outlook of children toward school should not be surprising in view of the long history of music in schools as a means of adding variety to classroom routines. In 1837, when Lowell Mason was finally given approval to institute music instruction in the Boston public schools, the subject was justified, by the Board of Education committee that evaluated the proposal, on the basis of its contributions to reading and speech. The committee also concluded that music provided "a recreation, yet not a dissipation of the mind—a respite, yet not a relaxation,—its office would thus be to restore the jaded energies, and send back the scholars with invigorated powers to other more laborious duties."[6] Music does add variety to the school day, although it certainly is not the only means of introducing a change of activity into the classroom.

Other values

Music therapy has demonstrated that the mind can respond to the evocative powers of music. The desire to use music for the release of feelings is stronger in some people than in others, but it is nevertheless a significant function of music, even for those who do not have serious emotional problems.

Music also offers many options for filling nonworking hours with constructive and interesting activity. While life expectancy is increasing, the average work week is decreasing. This means that leisure time is assuming a larger role in contemporary life. Music is an important avocational activity in most societies, including America. Participation may involve playing in a community orchestra, singing in a church choir, listening to recordings, or attending concerts. Again, music is not the only subject in the school curriculum that can enrich nonworking hours, but its avocational values are great.

The nonmusical benefits of music instruction must be kept in perspective. There are valid and supportable reasons for including music in the elementary school curriculum, apart from any nonmusical benefits. The additional benefits can be considered as "bonuses" arising from the music instruction that the schools should be offering anyway. The place of music in the elementary school does not depend on these benefits, but its position may be stronger because of them.

Implications for the Elementary School Music Program

The idea that music is a subject worthy of study rejects the view that elementary school music is primarily a training ground for musical organizations in the secondary schools. A good music program in the elementary school will of course improve the quality of the secondary school instrumental and choral groups. But that improvement is not a major justification for teaching music in the early grades. An elementary school music program designed to be of maximum benefit to the secondary school groups would not include the variety and types of activities that are usually recommended for children. Instead, it would consist of heavy doses of drill on specific performance skills such as music reading. Probably efforts would also be made to eliminate the less talented children from the instruction.

Music in elementary schools is more than a pleasant respite from the rigors of other instruction. It is a respected and time-honored field of study that should not be eliminated if time or money grows short.

For all of the reasons presented in this chapter, music should be a vital part of the curriculum of every elementary school classroom.

NOTES

1. *U.S. News and World Report*, Vol. 82, No. 20 (May 23, 1977), p. 63.
2. *Your AASA in 1958–1959, American Association of School Administrators*, Official Report for the Year 1958 (Washington: AASA, 1959), pp. 248–49.
3. "Curriculum Balance" (Reston, Va.: Music Educators National Conference, 1973).
4. Robert Choate, ed., *Documentary Report of the Tanglewood Symposium* (Reston, Va.: Music Educators National Conference, 1968), p. 139.
5. Karen I. Wolff, "The Nonmusical Outcomes of Music Education: A Review of the Literature," Council for Research in Music Education Bulletin No. 55 (Summer 1978), pp. 19, 21.
6. Edward Bailey Birge, *The History of Public School Music in the United States* (Reston, Va.: Music Educators National Conference, 1966), p. 43.

Review Questions

1. What objective evidence indicates that human beings value music and the other fine arts?

2. Why shouldn't the teaching of music be left to the family and to social institutions other than the school?

3. Name a few of the governmental and educational organizations that strongly support the inclusion of music in the elementary school curriculum.

4. Examine the photograph on page 5 that contains the words "Imagine the world without music." What is the message of that picture and that sentence?

5. Suppose that music has no nonmusical benefits. Should it still be taught in the schools? Why?

6. Does music training appear to have any transfer to other areas of the curriculum? What subjects and skills appear to receive the most benefits from music instruction?

7. How does music study seem to influence the attitudes of children toward school?

8. What nonmusical values other than transfer appear to accrue from music instruction?

Activity

Develop a ten-minute presentation on the topic "Why music should be a part of the elementary school curriculum." Assume that it is to be presented at a school board meeting. In preparing your rationale:

a. Determine what points you will stress.

b. Decide how you will make each point, using pictures, a lecture, a demonstration, or supporting statements.

c. Anticipate doubts and questions from the board members about providing adequate financial support for music in the elementary schools.

2

Who Teaches
Music?

Who is responsible for music instruction in the elementary schools? Under what arrangements is music taught? These questions are significant in determining the kind of instruction future classroom teachers and music specialists are given in their undergraduate preparation. If, for example, elementary classroom teachers almost never lead their classes in singing, then instruction in song-leading can be omitted from their music methods course. Because the roles of the classroom teacher and the music specialist are different, both future classroom teachers and music specialists need to be aware of the way in which music instruction is generally conducted "on the job."

Personnel Responsible for Music Instruction

Music specialists

Music specialists are teachers who hold certification in the subject area of music. Usually their undergraduate training has included special instruction in teaching music in elementary and middle/junior high school, as well as student teaching at these levels. In some universities, music education majors spend about half of their undergraduate program in the major area of music, taking courses in music theory, music history and literature, applied study on an instrument or in voice, music methods, conducting, and ensembles. Their subject-matter knowledge and performance skills are superior to those of most elementary education majors, who normally take only one or two courses in music.

Despite the expertise of the specialists, they seldom have sole responsibility for music in the elementary classroom. In actual school situations, they are able to spend only about 30 minutes twice a week with each classroom. They would like to meet each class more often, but the budget of a school district can seldom allow for the employing of enough specialists. Therefore, although their competence may be great, the time they have for teaching any one class is limited.

There are other limitations as well. Music specialists must operate on a strict schedule if they are to get around to all of the classes and schools for which they are responsible. This means that they cannot be flexible about the amount of time they spend or when they spend it. A classroom teacher may decide that two o'clock on Wednesday would be a good time for the children to sing some songs about pioneer life in the United States. But if the music specialist is scheduled with the class at nine o'clock on Tuesdays and Thursdays, the songfest will have to occur then, unless the classroom teacher can lead the singing at the desired time. Occasionally a music specialist can arrange a schedule change to accommodate a special event for a class, but that cannot be done often.

Furthermore, it is difficult for the specialist to integrate the music instruction with the social studies or language arts projects of a classroom that is not visited daily. It is not that the specialist is uncooperative, but it is hard for two busy teachers to remain in full communication about the current activities of any class. The problem is compounded by the number of classes for which the specialist is responsible. It is almost impossible for any specialist to devise a different plan for each of the several classes at all of the grade levels that are visited each week.

It is difficult for specialists, who usually see several hundred students each week, to know each child; it takes a few weeks just to learn their names. Again, it is not that the specialists care less about children than classroom teachers do. It is just the practical problem of dividing time and attention equitably among so many children.

Music consultants

A consultant is one who possesses expertise in an area and offers help on request. Music consultants are specialists who are responsible for helping teachers, usually those in the elementary classroom. The ratio of music consultants to children is generally much greater than that of specialists, who do the actual teaching. Although the teaching of children is not their main assignment, consultants are also strong in subject matter preparation.

In actual practice, some specialists who are designated as "consultants" are teachers, and others designated as "teachers" serve mainly as consultants. The terms are not applied consistently.

A continuing problem for consultants is that their advice is seldom requested, except by a few teachers who are already strong in music. The teachers most in need of help often do not realize that their efforts could be improved, so they are unlikely to ask for assistance. For this reason, consultants usually just offer suggestions and hope that they will be followed. Most consultants have no administrative authority, so they cannot require that their ideas be implemented. Their role is simply to share their subject matter expertise in an advisory capacity.

Often consultants are responsible for so many schools that they can have little personal contact with the teachers. Sometimes they can visit a classroom only a few times during the year. Written curriculum guides and memos containing suggestions and exhortations must take the place of personal contacts. Sometimes consultants organize inservice workshops for classroom teachers in the district. These sessions serve not only as a help to the teachers, but also as a device for coordinating music instruction within the district.

Music supervisors

A supervisor is more likely to work with music teachers as an administrator, and to serve as a liaison between music teachers and the central administration of the school district. The term is sometimes used interchangeably with "consultant."

Classroom teachers

Classroom teachers enjoy some advantages over music specialists in the teaching of music. They know their students better, and they can be more flexible about incorporating music into a particular learning situation. There is no problem about singing the songs of the pioneers at two o'clock on Wednesday if that seems best. Classroom teachers can integrate music with any area of the curriculum whenever they are so inclined.

Although the music preparation of most classroom teachers is much less extensive than that of a music specialist, the expedient of simply adding more hours of music to a college's elementary education program is not a viable solution. Someone once asked representatives from each academic area what they considered to be the *minimum* preparation that classroom teachers should receive in their particular academic discipline. When the recommended minimum requirements were totaled in terms of course hours, they amounted to more than 200 semester credits—the equivalent of seven years of college. A seven-year program is not a realistic possibility, of course, but the results of the survey point out the serious compromises that must be made in terms of the subject matter preparation of classroom teachers.

 It is not only a feeling of inadequate preparation that leads some classroom teachers to prefer minimal involvement with music teaching. They learn that it is hard to find sufficient time to plan for the many subject areas for which they are responsible. The subjects put off until last, both in teacher planning and in actual class time consumed, are often the "special" subjects like music. An imminent performance for parents or public is often a spur to intensive short-range work. But a balanced program of music instruction requires a sustained, varied, and long-range effort, and this requires a consistent investment of time.

It should not be assumed that the lack of organized music instruction is the fault of the classroom teacher. True, the curriculum statements of the school district may mandate a specific and rather sizable amount of time for music, and they may even include guidelines for course content and minimum music competencies for children at each grade level. But unless the principal or curriculum director makes clear that the district regards music as important in the education of children, and commends the music curriculum guidelines to the teachers, a sketchy music program may still prevail.

The Value of Mutually Supportive Teacher Roles

Arrangements for teaching music usually involve both the music specialist and the classroom teacher. Such combinations range from situations in which the specialist does little while the classroom teacher is responsible for most of the teaching, to situations in which the specialist does virtually all of the music instruction with little help from the classroom teacher.

It is difficult to obtain data about the various arrangements for teaching music in the nation's elementary schools. There are many variations from state to state, and a degree of confusion exists about the terminology that designates various teacher roles. Nevertheless, in most school districts the music instruction is undertaken as a joint venture between the specialist and the classroom teacher.

The combination arrangement has merit beyond its educational virtues. Economic factors also encourage it. Most educational institutions are hard-pressed financially, so they cannot hire as many specialists as they would like, and the involvement of classroom teachers becomes an economic necessity.

There is also the matter of released time for classroom teachers, as required in many states by regulation or by the master contract between the teachers' union and the school board. Teachers need some time each day to collect their thoughts and relax, away from the children. Since youngsters cannot be left unattended, other teachers must be instructing or supervising them while the regular teacher has released time. Special teachers fill this role automatically while teaching the children a legitimate subject. In some cases the impetus for hiring music specialists has come not from a desire to provide more music instruction, but from the need to cover for teachers while they are on released time.

Differences in the roles of classroom teachers and music specialists

Not only do classroom teachers and music specialists differ in training and competencies, but their assignments also differ. Music specialists are expected to devote their full attention to the education of children in one subject, while classroom teachers are expected to oversee many subject areas. Music specialists work at several levels within their academic discipline as it progresses from kindergarten through the higher grades, while classroom teachers must concentrate on the grade level at which they are teaching.

Basically, music specialists have the role of designer, and classroom teachers fill the role of technician or artisan. The two roles are analogous to those of a doctor (the expert in medicine) and a nurse (the technician), or an architect and a bricklayer. The expert/technician roles are complementary, not competitive. If carried out successfully, they lead to a better program of instruction in music than can be achieved by either specialists or classroom teachers working alone. The complementary nature of their roles can be summarized in this way:

Music Specialist	Classroom Teacher
Assumes a leadership role	Assumes a supportive role
Formulates objectives	Helps to achieve objectives
Makes plans	Implements plans
Introduces areas of study	Follows up areas of study

As an example of their respective functions, it is the specialist who decides if, when, and how hand signs should be taught, recorder skills should be mastered, and theme and variation technique should be introduced. The classroom teacher supports these endeavors by helping the children as they practice hand signs, review their recorder-playing skills, and listen to recordings of music that demonstrate theme and variation technique.

The attitude of classroom teachers toward music may be as significant as their ability to teach it. Children are quick to detect how their teacher feels about a subject. They get a clear idea when the music specialist enters the classroom and their teacher says with dismay, "Oh, it's not time for music *again*, is it?" They notice the positive attitude of a teacher who expects them to be attentive during music, who makes time for the music lesson despite the need for further academic work, or who presents a carefully prepared music lesson. Such actions influence the children's attitude toward music and indirectly affect how much they learn about it.

The teacher should convey a positive attitude not only toward the subject but also toward the children's efforts in music class. This includes praising the youngsters when they do well and seeing that they enjoy music; the instruction need not be tedious and unpleasant for learning to occur. An interested teacher can instill in the children an expectation of success in learning music. Success should not be gauged against an unrealistic standard of exceptional talent, but rather against the certain knowledge that almost all children can learn about music and perform it competently enough that it will enrich their lives. Such a goal surely justifies a positive outlook toward their accomplishments.

The need for cooperation

For the best results to be achieved, a cooperative relationship needs to be established between music specialists and classroom teachers. That is easier said than done, but it still should be accomplished. Part of the problem is the difficulty in finding time to communicate and discuss the music instruction. Music specialists may need to work with twenty or more teachers in two or more buildings. Because of their traveling assignments, they are not full-time members of any one building's faculty, so it is hard for them to attend faculty meetings or to see other teachers in the lunchroom or faculty lounge. These absences cause some building principals and other teachers to wonder about the loyalty and interest of the specialists, who in fact may be missing lunch each day in the rush to get to the next school. Sometimes music specialists must communicate by written memos, which tend to seem impersonal. Not all of the difficulties in communication can be fully overcome, but mutual understanding can help.

Classroom teachers have a right to expect that they will receive clear and reasonable suggestions for appropriate follow-up activities. The suggestions should be realistic in terms of what the children are likely to accomplish within the limited time available for follow-up. Music specialists have the right to expect that classroom teachers will remain with their classes during at least a portion of the music instruction. In this way the classroom teacher can gain some idea of what the children are learning in music, and can follow up more effectively.

Teachers working together in a spirit of good will and cooperation can accomplish more for the children's musical growth than one instructor working alone.

Review Questions

1. a. What are the advantages and disadvantages of having music specialists be responsible for all of the music instruction in the elementary schools?
   b. What are the advantages and disadvantages of having classroom teachers be responsible for all of the music instruction in the elementary schools?
2. What are the differences in roles between a music specialist and a music consultant?
3. In what ways are the interest and participation of classroom teachers important to the success of the music instruction?
4. a. If the benefits of a coordinated effort between the music specialist and the classroom teacher are to be realized, what roles need to be adopted?
   b. What conditions need to be met for a cooperative relationship to exist between the music specialist and the classroom teacher?

Activity

Find out the arrangements for music instruction in the elementary schools of a particular school district. (The districts near your college can be examined, as can your home school district.) Gather information on the following:

a. Who teaches music?
b. How much time for music does each classroom receive each week?
c. Is a curriculum guide or other information on teaching music available?
d. If a music consultant is employed, by what means does the consultant communicate ideas and suggestions to the teachers?
e. If music specialists are employed, how many children do they see each week? How many classrooms in how many schools?

CHAPTER

3

How Is Music Instruction Planned?

T he principles of good music teaching closely parallel those of successful teaching in other subject areas. The following guidelines may serve as a helpful checklist for the teacher during the various stages of planning and teaching music.

1. **Start where the students are.**   The principle of adjusting the content and methods of a class to the knowledge and interests of the students is a truism in education, but its application is difficult because of the differences that exist within any group of children. These differences are particularly noticeable in music, a subject in which some children receive private instruction outside of school. Nevertheless, the teacher must assess the various levels of ability within the class and plan the instruction so that it includes suitable learning activities and significant content.

2. **Provide experiences.**   Words cannot fully describe the fundamental aspects of music such as beat, pitch, tone color, loudness, harmony, and so on. Children can memorize a definition of "melody," but they will not understand it until they hear the concept in actual musical sounds. The value of providing experience before symbolization is clear in the language-learning process, and it applies to music as well.

3. **Use a multisensory approach.**   The more ways in which music is experienced, the more likely it is to be learned. Visual aids are helpful, and seeing an opera or ballet is better than merely hearing the music for it.

4. **Develop musical skills.**   Much of the skill-learning in music is simply the building of good habits such as careful listening, clear enunciation, and breath support in singing. Because no one can simultaneously concentrate on all of the musical skills needed to perform well, each skill should be isolated occasionally to reinforce the habit being developed. When good habits are well established, they will be maintained even in stress situations such as performing before an audience. There is no need to worry that the rendition will be mindless and mechanical; the good habits that have been built will help the performers to feel more confident, and will free their attention to focus on the musical qualities of their performance.

5. **Use the available time to ensure maximum learning.**   Any skill is learned more efficiently in several short sessions than in one long session. This is known as "distributed effort" or "spaced practice." For the teacher, this means that it is better for the class to leave something unfinished and to come back to it another day, than to overwork on it. Staying

on a problem until it is corrected—no matter how long it takes—often produces negative results, especially if the effort consists of dull and mechanical repetition. Using varied techniques for review is equally important. The maximum amount of time that should be spent on any one activity varies with the amount of concentration required, the age of the children, and their interest in the activity.

Throughout this book are short examples of classroom procedures that reflect teacher planning. The segments are set in small type and indented to indicate that they offer a *possible* approach to teaching the various aspects of music to children. The direct quotations are not a verbatim model for a new teacher to follow, but instead show the practical application of various teaching plans.

Assistance Available in Music Series Textbooks

This discussion of music textbooks is not a critique or evaluation. Rather it is an exploration of the many ways in which these books are designed to be helpful, especially to classroom teachers.

Three publishers currently market extremely attractive series of graded music books: Silver Burdett Company, Macmillan Publishing Company, Inc., and Holt, Rinehart & Winston, Inc.* The books are replete with color illustrations, and their content is carefully prepared with the help of expert consultants to ensure authenticity. Each music series includes a teacher's edition for each grade level, and sets of recordings of all the music presented in the books. The material should not be followed slavishly, but should be adapted to the needs of a particular class or school. The books contain more songs and activities than most classes can cover in a year, so teachers may choose what to include in their music classes.

Although books are not necessary for the teaching of music, they are helpful, for the following reasons.

1. They offer a selection of topics, songs, and activities that expert authors have compiled, so a teacher is spared the major effort of rooting around in search of songs and ideas for music instruction.

2. The books provide a minimum or "bedrock" program of music learning, which is especially helpful when no music specialist or district curriculum is available for the teacher's guidance. Often the book's content is organized around topics or units, and these provide a natural sequence for the music instruction.

3. The teacher's edition of each book suggests points to stress and questions to raise. Reference material is included, and musical terms are defined. Through the use of colored inks or explanatory material in the margins,

---

*See Appendix A for more complete information on these series.

the teacher's edition provides background information concisely and quickly.

4. Simple piano accompaniments for most of the songs in the book are included. The accompaniments are beyond the ability of a rank amateur, but students or teachers with a modest background in piano can play most of them.

5. The books include ideas for incorporating classroom instruments and orchestral instruments into the song accompaniments.

6. Pronunciation guides for all foreign language songs are included. Translations are also provided if they are not present as alternative verses of the song.

7. The recorded performances are of high quality. The instrumentalists employed for them are among the top performers available, because the rules of the American Federation of Musicians make it no more expensive to hire the best than to hire less able musicians. In the past decade there has been a trend toward recording children's singing on many of the songs. These performances provide an excellent model of good singing for the children to hear. Fine adult singers are also recorded for the albums. The musical arrangements of the songs are tasteful, interesting, and quite authentic, with folk instruments utilized when appropriate.

8. The books offer supplementary suggestions for extending the learning activities into other arts and other academic disciplines. For teachers familiar with the special music methods devised by Carl Orff and Zoltan Kodály, there are recommendations for incorporating those teaching techniques into the children's music experience.

9. The songs are indexed in several ways, according to title, type, country of origin, musical concepts, appropriateness for special occasions, and involvement of instruments.

To provide a clearer idea of the appearance of a teacher's edition and the help it can provide, two pages are reproduced here—one from the third-grade book published by Silver Burdett, and the other from the second-grade book published by Macmillan. In each example, the teacher's edition includes a reduced copy of the page from the student book. The teacher is told where to find an accompaniment part and a recording of the song. The lessons in each example are structured around particular concepts: form and duration, respectively.

On the page from the Silver Burdett book (opposite) the recommended materials and vocabulary are stated with utmost brevity, and the teaching procedures are kept simple. The strong visual aids in the children's book reinforce the music lesson and provide a logical extension into correlation with art.

In the Macmillan book (see p. 25), information at the top of the page tells the teacher the key and starting note of the song. Concise statements

MATERIALS: Record 4B, Band 8; recorder/bells

VOCABULARY: contrasting sections, ABA form

BASIC PLAN

1. Before playing the recording, tell children they will hear the song performed three times—vocal, instrumental, vocal. Then ask, "What makes the contrast between sections A and B in each performance?"
• Vocal: children sing section A; a man sings section B.
• Instrumental: cello plays section A; recorder plays section B.

2. Have children join in with the children's voices in section A on the recording.

3. Direct attention to the graphics on p. 88. Play the recording and ask children to listen for the form of the song.

Question: Which drawing shows the form of the song? (Circle, square, circle; ABA)

4. When they are familiar with the song, select children to sing the verse (section B) as a solo; others can sing the refrain (section B).

CIRCLES AND SQUARES

Shapes and letters can show form in music.

AB

ABA

Which set of shapes and letters shows the form of "Little David, Play on Your Harp"? To help you answer the question, listen to the recording.

Little David, Play on Your Harp

88

RESOURCE BANK

CLASSROOM CORRELATION: Art
Have children create their own visuals to show AB and ABA form. They can draw pictures (or find photographs) of animals, fruit, trees, flowers, etc. For example:
• orange-pineapple-orange (ABA)
• cat-dog-cat (ABA)
• sailboat-car (AB)
• bicycle-plane (AB)

SPECIMEN PAGE—*SILVER BURDETT MUSIC*

Source: Elizabeth Crook et al., *Silver Burdett Music*, Centennial Edition (Morristown, N.J.: General Learning Corporation, 1985).

of objectives, materials, and teaching procedures appear at the side of the page. Further information tells how handicapped children can benefit from the lesson, and offers ideas for correlating the song words with language arts instruction.

Planning the Music Class

Because the help given classroom teachers for music teaching varies in amount and type from one district to another, there can be no single best way for a teacher to plan the music instruction. The help from two sources—music specialists and music series books—has been discussed.

A third resource for assistance in planning is a curriculum guide. Many school systems and virtually all state education agencies publish curriculum guides for music. These are especially helpful to the classroom teacher because their suggestions are practical and stated in non-technical terms. The main complaint heard from state music consultants and school curriculum writing teams is that the fruits of their labor are not fully utilized. Perhaps the presence of a state curriculum creates concern about the loss of a teacher's individuality. This is a groundless concern, however, because a curriculum guide is not intended to be restrictive. On the contrary, it includes a wide range of workable suggestions that have been proved effective in a variety of situations. A beginning teacher will benefit by trying the ideas, adapting them as needed, and using them as a springboard for developing further ideas.

Procedures for planning a lesson

Good music instruction is based on a fundamental principle: *Every music activity should be designed to increase the children's understanding of music or to improve their musical skills.* It is not enough just to "put in time" singing songs or listening to recordings; the intent to further the children's education in music needs to be present.

Although no perfect plan exists for teaching, certain factors should be considered when planning for music instruction.

1. **Build on what has been learned in previous music classes.**   Begin by recalling what the children have done in music over the last week or two. Think about what they did well and did not do well, what they liked, what did not seem clear to them, and what they know that can serve as a basis for further learning.

2. **Choose two or three specific concepts or skills to teach in the lesson.**   The points to be learned should be stated in specific terms. An

Key: **F**
Starting Tone: **C** (5, sol)
Piano Accompaniment on page **P.A. 34**

RECORDING 2, SIDE A

WHOLE NOTES AND EIGHTH NOTES

Purpose: To introduce the whole note as a long sound, and the eighth note as a short sound.

Materials: Textbook, recording.

Motivation: Recall some nonsense song, or play some rhyming game. Do tongue twisters.

Exploration: Have the children:
1. Listen to the song. Read the words. Note that the colors have words that rhyme with them, such as "blue—glue"; "red—head." Find the line of the song with the nonsense words. [*Line 4*]

2. Sing the song.

3. Create new verses. Find new colors and make rhymes: "I won't wear green, 'cause it makes me mean." Look for unusual colors.

4. Read the text on the lower portion of p. 69. Look at the whole note and discuss its shape. [*Egg-shaped and hollow*] Look at the eighth note. Talk about its shape. [*Solid egg-shape with a line* (stem) *and a curved line* (flag).] Draw the notes, using large paper. Make the notes large. Find the whole notes and the eighth notes in the song.

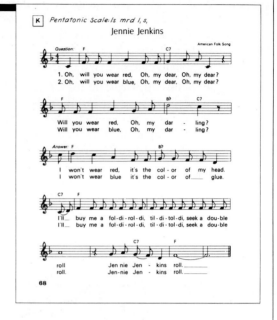

Mainstreaming Disabilities

Auditory: *Discrimination* (identifying long and short sounds) 1, 3   *Auditory-Visual Integration* (relating sounds to written symbol) 1, 4

Visual: *Discrimination* (identifying types of notes as written) 4, Extension   *Memory* (remembering differences in notes)   *Visual-Motor Integration* (drawing) 4

Motor: *Gross* (drawing) 4   *Fine* (singing, reading) 1, 2, Extension

Curriculum Correlation   In "Jennie Jenkins" there are several contractions. Ask the children if they can find them. "Won't" is the contraction for what two words? [*Will not*] "I'll" is the contraction for what two words? [*I will, or I shall*]
Ask the children what rhyming words are found in this song. [*Red, head; blue, glue*]

68

SPECIMEN PAGE—MACMILLAN *MUSIC*

Source: May Val Marsh et al., *The Spectrum of Music*, Teacher's Annotated Edition (New York: Macmillan, 1983).

objective such as "To learn about the music of Mexico" is too vague. An objective such as "To recognize, from hearing, the consecutive thirds found in Mexican music" is much clearer, and the children's success in learning can be evaluated more accurately.

3. **State the objectives for the class in terms of what the children should be able to do as a result of the instruction.**   Outcomes stated in such terms are called "behavioral objectives." Unless the children can provide evidence of how much they have learned, it is hard for the teacher to determine what should be taught in subsequent music classes. Some objectives can apply to skills: for example, "The class will learn to sing 'La Paloma' with accurate pitch and rhythm." Other objectives can apply to cognitive learning: for example, "Ninety percent of the class will be able to describe two characteristics of Mexican music."

4. **Select appropriate materials.**   A teacher who decides to stress the consecutive (or parallel) thirds in Mexican music can look through the books available and select a song that seems best for teaching that aspect. The music series books are a convenient resource, with their indexes arranged by activity (dances, singing games), song subject, country of origin, musical features, and so on. The teacher's editions offer further suggestions for instrument-playing and other activities.

5. **Decide how to teach the content.**   Suppose that parallel thirds in Mexican music is the concept that the class is to learn. There are several ways to teach this. If the class has sung a song with thirds, a review activity can emphasize the singing of that interval. Another approach is to examine the melodic features of Mexican songs and to add the notes a third below when they fit in a particular song. Recordings can be played, enabling the class to hear the sound of parallel thirds in a piece of Mexican music. If the children possess the necessary skills, they can play thirds on recorders or bells, or they can discover the interval for themselves by examining notation. All of these procedures are appropriate under the right circumstances. Knowing beforehand which of the several possibilities will be employed leads to more confident and more effective teaching.

   At least three types of activities should be included in a thirty-minute class period. Children, especially in the primary grades, tend to become restless, and consequently do not learn as much when they stay too long on one activity.

6. **Evaluate the success of each portion of the lesson.**   If the objectives have been stated in terms of what the children are able to do as a result of their learning, this step should not be difficult. Evaluation does not mean that a formal test must be administered. Evaluation can be simply the observation of a representative sample of the individuals in the class. If the first few children called on can respond appropriately to a review of the point being stressed, it is reasonable to assume that most of the others in the class have learned that point.

7. **When the preceding six suggestions have been followed, begin the next planning cycle.**   The results achieved in the preceding class should influence a teacher's decision to advance to the next step or activity, to reinforce a point previously covered, to try a different approach, or to spend more or less time on some aspect. Teaching and planning are a cycle. Each class period should relate to what preceded it and what will follow it.

   Before teaching a music lesson, the teacher should think through his or her plan and consider these questions:

   a. Will the points in the lesson be of reasonable difficulty for the class?
   b. Will the children experience music, or just talk about it?
   c. Will the teaching techniques involve several senses and different modes of presentation?
   d. Do the children have an adequate aural foundation for what they will be asked to learn?
   e. Will a special effort be made to help them apply what they have learned to other musical situations?
   f. If the learning involves skill acquisition, will the effort be spread out over a span of time?
   g. Will the learning be presented attractively, to encourage positive attitudes toward music?

Finally, will a balance among the guidelines be maintained? Good teaching means achieving the proper synthesis of the significant factors— the subject matter, the children's needs and interests, and an understanding of how people learn.

Review Questions

1. Which guidelines are violated by these teachers?
    a. Mary Finch plans for her class to learn note names and rhythmic values by filling out worksheets.
    b. Ralph Jones requires his students to memorize the definitions for musical terms before these concepts are experienced in the music.
    c. Shirley Mason introduces her class to rhythmic values by comparing the durations to portions of a pie: a whole note equals one pie, a half note is half a pie, and so on.
    d. Helen Andrews tells the children which of their songs should be fast and which ones should be slow. She believes the children are too young to arrive at their own understanding or make musical judgments on their own.
    e. Marshall Hill keeps his class working intensively on one song throughout the 30-minute period.
2. What are some sources of suggestions for teaching music in the elementary classroom?
3. Cite five ways in which the use of music series books can be helpful to the teacher.
4. Describe how the teacher's edition in a book series can aid the teacher.

Activities

1. Observe a music class in an elementary school, then respond to the following questions to determine how closely the guidelines in this chapter were followed:
    a. Were the points in the lesson of reasonable difficulty for the class?
    b. Did the children experience music, or just talk about it?
    c. Did the teaching techniques involve several senses or different modes of presentation?
    d. Did the children seem to have adequate previous musical experience for what they were asked to learn?
    e. Was a special effort made to help them apply what they learned to other musical situations?
    f. If the learning involved skill acquisition, was the effort spread out over a span of time?
    g. Was the learning presented attractively?

2. Select one song or other activity in the class you observed, and describe why it was well taught or how it might have been taught more effectively.

3. To the extent that elementary music series books and materials are available to you, examine and compare them, especially the teacher's editions, record albums, and other materials such as charts or tapes. In the teacher's editions, look for:
   a. classifications in the index
   b. outline of units or minimum program
   c. teaching suggestions, both general and specific
   d. piano accompaniments

Teaching Music in the Kindergarten and Primary Grades

Part Two contains specific techniques for teaching music. The presentation is divided into two general levels—primary and upper grades—so that reasonably detailed suggestions can be provided for teaching at each of the two levels. The teacher may adapt the procedures for specific grade or ability levels.

The teaching suggestions in Chapters 4 through 17 of this book are based on the premise that activities in the classroom should have an educational purpose. The organization of topics is designed to focus on specific aspects of learning. Intellectual understandings are classified into four basic elements of music: rhythm (duration), tone quality (timbre), pitch, and dynamic level. Skills are treated in chapters dealing with singing, playing simple instruments, creating, and moving to music.

The remaining chapters of the book contain realistic illustrations of possible teaching methods. These examples are only short segments, not complete lessons. They are intended to provide practical guidance in the initial stages of teaching music.

C H A P T E R

4

Basic
Rhythms

As is true of all the components of music, rhythm is impossible to describe fully in words. One can define *rhythm* as "the ongoing sense of motion that occurs as music progresses in time," but even this description is inadequate unless it is given meaning through the experiencing of rhythm. Rhythm is as basic as life itself, as fundamental as a heartbeat. To overlook this elemental nature of rhythm is to miss its essential character.

Every sound has at least four aspects: tone quality, pitch (highness or lowness), loudness, and duration (called rhythm when consecutive sounds are involved). Because rhythm is intertwined with the other components of music, a music lesson cannot deal exclusively with rhythm, but it can highlight that aspect. The challenge for the teacher is to help the children to sense rhythm as a driving force in music, and to produce rhythms precisely but not mechanically.

Not only is rhythm interrelated with other aspects of music; it is itself made up of different components: beat, meter, tempo, and so on. (These terms are explained in the boxed material on p. 34.) Helping children to understand these components through experience is an important goal in teaching music, and is the basis for most of the teaching suggestions that follow.

The songs and activities presented in this chapter are described with the help of music notation, but it is provided for the teacher's information, not for the children. Youngsters need to feel the rhythm in many musical situations before being asked to interpret its written symbols.

Experiencing the Beat

In music there are few examples of inherently logical learning sequences that need to be followed if learning is to be successful. To understand rhythm, however, children must first sense the beat, because that ability is basic to learning other aspects of rhythm.

Children usually require many experiences with the beat before they can sense it consistently and accurately. This awareness is not a skill that can be acquired in a lesson or two; it must be reinforced over a span of months. The review can be brief, and it can be integrated with the learning of other aspects of rhythm, but it must be emphasized persistently.

Rhythm, Beat, and Tempo

The words "rhythm" and "beat" are fundamental in music, but they are not synonymous. *Rhythm* is the more inclusive term and refers to the sense of orderly motion that occurs as music progresses in terms of time. The *beat* is the basic rhythmic device, the recurrent throb or pulse that makes a person want to tap or clap in time with the music.

The rate of speed at which the beats recur is called the *tempo.* Many different tempos are possible, ranging from very slow to very fast. Whatever tempo is selected for a piece of music, it is expected to remain steady unless there is a musical reason for changing it.

Judgments about tempo depend partly on how the performer perceives the music. The most helpful factor in determining an appropriate tempo for a song is to consider the mood or style of the music. In many songs, the most comfortable tempo approximates the rate of a normal heartbeat or a moderate walking pace.

Because the concept of a beat is so basic, the teacher should involve the children in discovering it. Here is one way in which this may be done.

"How many of you have felt your own heartbeat or taken your own pulse? If you haven't, do it now. Touch your throat with your fingertips on one side of your voice box and your thumb on the other side, like this. . . . Then press backward gently until you can feel the strong pulse in your throat. . . . Can you feel it? . . . Notice that it's very even and steady: throb, throb, throb. The beat in music is like that: in fact, it can be called a pulse, too."

How can children be taught to feel the beat in music? Like feeling the heartbeat, it is done through physical actions rather than through academic procedures. Gaining a feel for the beat seems to happen best when one just "rides along" with the flow. It seems to happen more easily in a group situation than in an individual lesson. There is something captivating about a group of people clapping or dancing along with the music, and children easily get caught up in the experience. When a child first demonstrates a sense of moving with the beat, *at that moment* the teacher should say, "There! Now you're feeling the beat of the music!" A relaxed atmosphere is also conducive to feeling the beat.

Some music educators advocate starting children in kindergarten and the primary grades with rhythmic experiences that involve the use of large muscles. Recent research does not support this advice.[1] Marching in time to music is a seemingly simple large-muscle activity. Nevertheless, dancing or marching with the beat is a skill that some adults never acquire, so it is unrealistic to expect all children to be able to do this. Rather, it appears that children execute rhythms more easily through speech patterns or by smaller muscle movements such as hitting sticks together or clapping. The Orff-*Schulwerk*, Kodály-Hungarian Singing School, and Dalcroze methods have recognized this fact, and emphasize small muscle movements and the chanting of rhymes.

Perceiving the Steadiness of the Beat

When children begin to sense the beat, they need to be made aware of its steady nature. Although the desire for beat regularity may appear to be a natural inclination, it probably is not. Like most human behavior, it must be learned. Much concentration is required to maintain a truly steady beat; some adults cannot seem to do this no matter how hard they try.

There are several ways to impress the steadiness of the beat on young children. It can be pointed out in the songs they sing and in the music to which they listen. It should be remembered, however, that listeners tend to take the beat for granted because they do not need to control it as does a performer.

The teacher may wish to bring a metronome into the classroom, preferably a wind-up model with a pendulum, because its movement can be seen. Clapping or chanting with the metronome will help children learn to maintain a steady beat. Youngsters may not believe they are rushing a tempo until they hear their deviations from the even ticks of the metronome. The simple routine of letting the children alternately listen to four ticks, then clap or tap four, is effective in helping them experience the steadiness of the beat.

Chanting short phrases is a further step toward establishing a feel of regular beat. Phrases for chanting can be derived from many sources: school cheers, rhymes, verses of songs, and lines made up by the teacher or the class. As the children become accomplished at reciting them, the class can be divided in half, with different phrases being simultaneously recited, or with a particular rhythm being chanted in staggered order like a round.

Further activity can be introduced by asking the children to make up their own chants and rhymes to reinforce their sense of a steady beat. Youngsters often devise their own rhymes when jumping rope or engaging in other play activity.

In these first experiences with group participation, the need for maintaining an even beat will be apparent to the children when they realize that an unstable beat creates confusion. A steady beat is necessary not only for the practical purpose of keeping the participants together, but also for the rhythmic drive that is required if the music is to sound vital and attractive.

This sense of vitality and intensity is achieved not through harshness and strain but through attention to the underlying rhythm.

The following lesson shows how a teacher can help the children to feel the steadiness of the beat.

> "Here's a song that I'm sure you'll like. It's 'The Bus.' If you know it already, help me sing it." [The teacher sings the first verse and a few children join in.]

THE BUS

2. The wheels on the bus go 'round and 'round . . .

3. The horn on the bus goes "Toot, toot, toot" . . .

4. The money in the box goes "Ding, ding, ding" . . .

5. The wiper on the glass goes "Swish, swish, swish" . . .

> "Good! Now, remember how you've been learning to feel the beat in music? Let's sing the song again and see if you can feel the steady beat. When you do, show us by clapping with the beat." [The teacher hums the starting pitch and indicates when to begin by making a motion of the hand or head, or by emphasizing an intake of breath. Because the children are inexperienced in group singing, the teacher also provides verbal cues like these, sung *in rhythm*, on the opening pitch: "Here's-our-note . . ." or "Rea-dy-sing . . ." The children start together and clap the beat as they sing "The Bus."]
>
> "Are the beats in the song even or uneven?" [Several students respond that the beats are even.]

Children enjoy acting out the words to "The Bus," even though the traditional motions occur not on every beat but in a "short short long" pattern beginning in the second full measure. Other actions are possible with a song such as this. The children can walk to the beat if they have succeeded in clapping accurately. They can chant the words with special emphasis on the syllables that occur on the beat, or they can tap the beat on simple rhythm instruments such as drums or triangles.

It is important to emphasize the beats and to recite the lines vigorously. Energetic speaking should not be confused with shouting or forcing the voice in an unattractive manner. Rather, each word should be sounded decisively, especially the syllables that coincide with the beats. Rhythmic precision is aided by having the children tap or clap the beats as they say the rhyme.

Tempo

When children can feel the beat and recognize its regular nature, they are ready to listen for the musical factor called *tempo*. Tempo can be experienced by the children, with the help of a metronome, in the following manner.

"The other day you took your own pulses by putting your fingertips on one side of your voice boxes and your thumb on the other. Do the same thing today, only this time, check the speed of your pulse.

"Jill, move your free hand to show us each time your heart beats. I'll measure the speed by adjusting this metronome to match it." [The teacher and class count the movements of Jill's hand.] "Now we have it: the speed measures 72 beats each minute. That's a nice, medium speed.

"Now, let's all stand up and run in place for about a minute. Pretend that we're jogging. Here we go!" [The class jogs in place.] "Okay, sit down. *Now* check your heartbeat. Is it faster or slower than it was before?" [The children report that their heartbeats are faster.]

"What does this have to do with music? Well, the speed of the beats—how close they occur one after another—is called *tempo* in music. I'll sing a song at two different tempos, and you tell me if the second version is faster or slower than the first."

Several procedures can be employed to direct the children's attention to the speed of the beats. One is to sing the same song at different tempos. The class can also listen to works of music that have different tempos. For example, the slow second movement of Haydn's "Clock" Symphony might be contrasted with the fourth movement, which has a quick tempo.

When the children are secure in their ability to recognize a steady beat, they can be introduced to music in which the tempos change noticeably during the course of one song or work. An example is the Hungarian *czardas*, in which the tempo of the music gradually increases until the dancers are supposedly no longer able to keep up. Another work that effectively demonstrates tempo change is Villa-Lobos' imaginative "The Little Train of the Caipira." The train is standing still at the beginning, then it starts up slowly, rolls merrily along, and finally winds down at the end of the journey.

It is important to stress to the children that *the speed of the beat is not the same as the speed of the notes*. Music at a slow tempo can contain short note

Note Values

A note is a printed symbol that serves two purposes. By its appearance it indicates how long a particular sound should last, and by its vertical position on a music staff it shows how high or low the sound should be. A note consists of an egg-shaped *head* that is usually connected to a vertical line called the *stem*. The note pictured below is called a *quarter note* and can be identified by its filled-in head and attached stem, which may point either up or down.

The duration of a sound in music is measured not by the clock but by the passing of consecutive beats. Although any type of note can be assigned to represent the beat, a quarter note usually represents a one-beat sound, as in this chart showing the relative durations of the most frequently encountered notes.

Whole note		usually lasts for 4 beats
Half note		usually lasts for 2 beats
Quarter note		usually lasts for 1 beat
Eighth note		usually lasts for ½ beat
Sixteenth note		usually lasts for ¼ beat

durations, and music at a fast tempo can consist of long, sustained sounds. Tempo refers to the span of time elapsing between the beats, not between the notes.

Long and Short Note Durations

In the following lesson the teacher uses the rhythm pattern of a song to show the difference between the number of notes on a beat and the beat itself. In the process, the children can observe that notes are of varying durations, and that these durations are judged in relation to the beat. The important point to be learned is not that the length of sound or silence is

The duration of a note is called its *value*. If the basic note values are arranged in order from longest to shortest, or vice versa, a 2:1 ratio is evident between each note value and the one next to it. Stated another way, each note value is twice or half as long as the adjacent note in the series. This 2:1 ratio for note values is basic to the understanding of rhythm notation.

The relationship among the note values is shown by the following chart. The arrows represent the passing of time, but they do not appear in actual music.

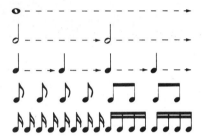

If two or more flagged notes occur consecutively, their flags are usually combined into a straight, solid *beam* connecting the ends of the stems.

Beamed notes are easier to read because they are visually grouped together to show more clearly where the beats occur.

referred to as "duration," but that the beat is the unit of time measurement in music.

The song "Are You Sleeping?" (p. 40) clearly illustrates the three common note/beat combinations: one note lasting for one beat, two notes lasting for one beat, and one note lasting for two beats. The song also establishes a strong sense of beat by featuring ten consecutive one-beat notes before any other note values are heard.

The teacher might introduce the idea of different note durations in this way:

"In music class on Monday you learned a new song, 'Are You Sleeping?' Today let's sing it again, while we clap the beat." [A few children are

ARE YOU SLEEPING?

uncertain in their clapping, but they make an attempt to follow their classmates or the teacher.]

"You did a good job of keeping your beats even, class. The beats have to be even because that's how we measure the passing of time in music. The beat helps us decide how much time should go by on the long or short notes."

"Now we'll just chant the words while we clap through the song again. We're trying to find out if the words and notes are always just as long as the beats. Think about it as we do the rhythms now."

[The children clap and chant with the teacher, who then invites their observations by questions like these: "Did our words always match our claps? Were some of the words longer than the beats we clapped? Were some of the words shorter?" The teacher helps the class to discover, for example, that there are two notes to a beat at the words "Morning bells are."]

The song "Are You Sleeping?" can also be used to help the class discover similarities among various rhythm patterns. The children can find out for themselves that in this song there are identical rhythms for each pair of consecutive phrases: the first and second ("Are you sleeping, Are you sleeping") the third and fourth, and so on. A few observant children may notice that the rhythm for the lines "Brother John" and "Ding, dong, ding" is the same. The class can also be divided to demonstrate different patterns, with some of the children sounding the pattern of "Morning bells are ringing" while the others produce the rhythm for "Ding, dong, ding." They can sound the patterns by clapping, tapping on a drum, hitting rhythm sticks together, or playing other rhythm instruments.

An excellent technique for making children aware of rhythms is to help them discover the patterns of words and names. Children are curious to find out what rhythm patterns can be made from their own names. Here is one way in which this can be done.

"Did you know that the name of every person in this class has a rhythm pattern? David, let's use your name as an example. It goes:

Da - vid *Smith*

"The name 'David' seems to divide into two notes in one beat, just like the 'morning bells' in 'Are You Sleeping?' The word 'Smith' is just one note, which takes up one beat. Let's all say 'David Smith' in a rhythmic way, with lots of energy." [The class chants the name and David seems pleased.] The teacher puts other children's names into patterns, pointing out that some names require three or four syllables within one beat,

Jen - ni - fer *Ar* - den   *Jer* - e - mi - ah *Hart* - man

and others require an "upbeat" because the first syllable is unaccented.

Di - *ane* *Rich* - ard - son.]

Sound and Silence

A good way to emphasize the continuity of the music during moments of silence is to let the children make decisive motions during the rests. In the song "If You're Happy," the teacher introduces the children to rests by

IF YOU'RE HAPPY

Traditional

If you're hap-py and you know it, clap your hands, (clap, clap) If you're hap-py and you know it, clap your hands, (clap, clap) If you're hap-py and you know it, then your face will sure-ly show it, If you're hap-py and you know it, clap your hands. (clap, clap)

Rests

A *rest* in music is a period of measured silence. Rests conform to the same 2:1 ratio found in note values.

Whole rest	▬	usually lasts for 4 beats
Half rest	▬	usually lasts for 2 beats
Quarter rest	𝄽	usually lasts for 1 beat
Eighth rest	𝄾	usually lasts for ½ beat
Sixteenth rest	𝄿	usually lasts for ¼ beat

To distinguish between the *whole rest* and the *half rest*, which are similar in appearance, it is helpful to remember that the half rest sits on the third or "halfway" line of the staff, and the whole rest hangs down from the fourth (next-to-top) line. One can also think of the whole rest as being "heavier" because it lasts twice as long, and therefore it hangs down from the line because of its extra "weight." The whole rest can also indicate an entire measure of rest, regardless of the number of beats in the measure. In such cases it is called a *measure rest*.

A rest is not simply a void or a stopping place in the music. Rests are musically significant because they help delineate the phrases and indicate aspects of performance style. Although there may be no sound for a particular moment in the music, the listener should feel that the flow of the music is continuing.

asking for silent action—moving the hands as if to clap, but not striking them together—during these intervals of "organized silence."

Another technique is to sing a song in which portions of the melody are replaced with actions or silence. "Bingo" is an example of this type of song.

"The song 'Bingo' doesn't tell us much about the dog, but we can make the music interesting by playing a game with his name. As you can see, I've printed 'BINGO' five times on the board, not in a line but one above the other, like layers in a cake. Before we play the game, let's review the song by tapping the beat as we sing."

BINGO

(For autoharp, transpose to F major)   American Folk Song

There was a farm-er had a dog, And Bin-go was his name-O. B-I-N-G-O, B-I-N-G-O, B-I-N-G-O, and Bin-go was his name-O.

"Here comes the game! We'll sing the song five times. Each time, exchange a clap for one letter in Bingo's name. The first time, clap for the letter 'B,' the second time for 'B' and 'I,' and so on. I'll help you by circling the letter that you're going to replace with a clap." [The class sings the song five times.]

"Now let's make it more tricky. Sing 'Bingo' five more times, but instead of claps, just think the notes *silently.* When you think of the letters of Bingo's name, keep your thoughts moving at exactly the same speed as the music. Keep that beat going evenly in your head."

Echo-clapping is an excellent means of teaching children to listen carefully to the interplay between sound and silence. Here is an example of how a teacher may do this.

"I'll tap out a pattern on the drum, and you tap it back to me with your rhythm sticks. Listen carefully, and start tapping when I give you the signal by nodding my head."

As the children demonstrate increased competence in imitating rhythms and rests, the patterns can be lengthened and made more difficult.

Meter

Children should gain a concept of meter and develop the ability to recognize and perform various meter patterns. The learning process is expedited if the children in their singing and playing are encouraged to emphasize the notes on the first beat by making them a bit louder.

In the following lesson the teacher points out the pattern of strong and weak beats, and introduces the children to the term "meter."

"You've been learning about the beat in music for several weeks now. Can you clap the beat to 'Eency, Weency Spider' as we sing the song?" [The class sings the song, clapping with vigor.]

EENCY, WEENCY SPIDER

Traditional

The een-cy, ween-cy spi-der went up the wa-ter-spout. Down came the rain and washed the spi-der out. Out came the sun and dried up all the rain, And the een-cy, ween-cy spi-der went up the spout a-gain.

"You made your claps nice and even, so they all sounded alike. But did you know that in music some beats are stronger than others, so they're sounded louder? And those strong and weak beats happen in a pattern. Sing 'Eency, Weency Spider' again while I clap the beats. But this time, listen to my clapping to see which beats are stronger." [The class sings the song while the teacher claps the beat, emphasizing the first beat of each measure.]

"This time sing 'Eency, Weency Spider' while *you* clap the beats. The pattern is STRONG-weak, STRONG-weak, so be sure to make a difference in the strength of your claps." [The class claps and sings the song, following the teacher's example by exaggerating the loudness and softness of alternating beats.]

"There's a word for the pattern of beats. It is *meter*. The meter of
'Eency, Weency Spider' is STRONG-weak, STRONG-weak. Each pattern has two beats in it, so we call it 'two-beat meter.'

"This time when we sing the song, keep on sounding the notes on
the first beat a little stronger than the others. Notice that I said a *little*
stronger. If you make too much difference, the song won't be smooth
and musical."

In addition to reproducing various meters and recognizing those performed for them by the teacher, the children should learn to recognize the
meter in music heard on recordings. The children can be directed to listen
carefully and then tap or clap the beat lightly. As they sound the beats, they
should try to determine what the metrical pattern is. Most marches feature
two-beat meter, and minuets by Mozart and Haydn are clear examples of
three-beat meter. Waltzes are usually not suitable for demonstrating three-
beat meter because their rapid tempos cause them to be felt as one beat per
measure instead of three, and tempo fluctuation (called *rubato*) is frequent.

Initially, the children should be introduced to only two- and three-beat
meter. When they are consistently correct in differentiating between those
two meters and performing them, they may move on to four-beat meter.
Although music with complex and unusual meters may be sung by young
children, the study of intricate meters should be delayed until the upper
grades.

The Notation of Rhythm

The experiences suggested so far in this chapter have involved the
"doing" of rhythm, rather than the reading of its notation. This arrangement has been deliberate, because experience with rhythm must precede
the symbolization of it, especially in the primary grades.

One successful way to introduce the reading of rhythm symbols is to
use "stick" notation. The main virtue of stick notation is its simplicity; all
distracting symbols are eliminated. At first the note values are limited to
quarter and eighth notes, for which stems and beams are sufficient. In stick
notation the quarter note is represented by a vertical line and the eighth
note by a vertical line with a horizontal beam connecting it to another eighth
note. Heads are unnecessary for the notes at this stage because both note
values would require identical filled-in heads, and the absence of pitch
eliminates the need for placing heads on a staff.

Often children are taught to say rhythm syllables in conjunction with
the stick notes. Although syllables can be introduced apart from notation of
any kind, learning the two together enables children to "name" a note value
and thereby reinforce the association between what they see and what they
hear. The use of rhythm syllables helps the children to recognize groups of
notes as identifiable units, in much the same way that young readers learn
to perceive letter-combinations as words.

Meter and Measure

There is a human tendency to perceive a succession of beats in patterns rather than as isolated, identical fragments. The ticks of a clock may be identical, but the mind tends to organize them into an orderly "tick tock" arrangement. In music, *meter* is the organizing of beats into patterns according to the heaviness or lightness of each beat. Most meter patterns are two, three, or four beats long, although other patterns are occasionally encountered. The first beat of the pattern is performed and heard more strongly than the other beats. For example, a three-beat meter is felt as BEAT beat beat, BEAT beat beat, and so on.

Because the phenomenon of meter is partially the result of human perception, it is somewhat subject to individual interpretation. For example, certain meter patterns can be thought of as containing two slow beats or four fast beats. This ambiguity affects one's feeling of tempo as well as meter; the speed of the beat can be perceived in more than one way, depending on one's inclination and the style of the music.

A *measure* (or *bar*) is the visual representation of meter. Each measure provides the notation for one meter pattern. Adjacent measures are separated by a vertical *barline*.

In most music the meter is indicated at the beginning by two

In fairness, it should be mentioned that some music teachers regard rhythm syllables as being redundant, because the children are taught a word system that later will need to be replaced with standard terminology. Furthermore, the syllables are of nonsense construction and therefore convey no inherent relationship among themselves. The conventional rhythm nomenclature ("two quarters equal a half," and so on) borrows from a number system that has its own logic.

There are several syllable systems, all of which work if taught consistently. The system most commonly used designates a quarter note with the sound "ta" and an eighth note with "ti" (pronounced "tee"). Here is an example:

Pattern in conventional notation:

Pattern in stick notation:

Rhythm syllables for the pattern: ta   ta   ti ti ta

numbers (or by symbols representing numbers) called a *meter signature* or *time signature*. Essentially the top number tells how many beats are in each measure, and the bottom number indicates what kind of note lasts for one beat. A "4" on the bottom stands for a quarter-note beat, a "2" for a half-note beat, and so on. The exceptions to this rule will be explained later in the book.

Many different note values are possible within a meter. A ¾ meter signature, for example, indicates that each measure contains three quarter notes *or their equivalent in other note and rest values.*

The first two notes of "If You're Happy" (p. 41) appear to form a shorter measure than is indicated by the meter signature. But when those notes are coupled with the incomplete final measure of the song, they produce the correct number of beats for one full measure. This is a common device in songs that are to be repeated through two or more verses; the meshing of the last and first notes into one meter pattern prevents a hitch in the rhythm when successive verses begin.

The presence of stressed and unstressed beats in a meter pattern has implications not only for the counting and notation of rhythm, but also for the way in which words are fitted to a melody. Each syllable of a song text needs to be placed with a sound that is similarly stressed or unstressed in the music. When important words are paired with important notes, the text and the music support one another to form a more effective phrase.

In the following lesson the teacher presents quarter and eighth notes in stick notation. At this stage, the two types of notes are not mixed in the same pattern.

"Today you'll learn a way to picture some rhythm patterns. First I'll draw a straight line that stands up. . . . This is a picture of a note that takes up one beat. Here's a pattern of four lines standing up. . . . This means beat-beat-beat-beat. Let's read what the picture tells us to do. For every note pictured by a line, say 'ta.' Rea-dy, go: 'Ta ta ta ta.'" [The class says the "ta"'s with the teacher.]

"Good! Now try to read the picture at a different speed, a little faster. The tempo this time is beat-beat. Rea-dy go: 'Ta ta ta ta.'"

The rhythm syllable "ti" is introduced in much the same way as the syllable and symbol for "ta." As in other presentations of new material, the teacher reviews previous learnings to provide the reinforcement that is often needed with children in primary grades.

The notation for rests can also be introduced in a simple form with a quarter rest represented by a Z-shape. As was pointed out earlier in this chapter, it is important to convey the idea of continued motion in the music during a rest. Since the syllables are being spoken, it is appropriate to have the silences also delineated by oral action, but not vocalized. A short puff of air on each rest, as if one is blowing out a candle, will help preserve the feeling of rhythmic continuity through the rest, and yet will ensure that it is silent.

In the initial stages of rhythmic reading, only one more note value is needed to complete a basic "vocabulary." It is the symbol for a note lasting two beats, most often represented by the half note. It can be the same in both stick and conventional notation. It is said "ta-ah," with the "ah" occurring on the second beat of the note.

The transition from stick to conventional notation is easy because of the similarity between the two types. All that is needed is the addition of heads to the quarter and eighth notes. When the children demonstrate that they understand stick notation, the change to conventional notation can be made.

There is a visual technique for helping children to understand the relative durations of the various note and rest values. In conventional notation every note and rest takes up approximately the same amount of horizontal distance; in that sense, they all appear to be about equal in length. To help the children associate a symbol with its relative duration, the teacher can try the following technique. It consists of drawing notes and rests on pieces of paper or cardboard of different lengths so that the piece of paper for the quarter note is twice as long as the piece for the eighth note, and the half note piece is twice as long as the quarter note piece. Short exercises in reading or computing note values can be solved by manipulating the slips of paper of various lengths. The technique is described more fully on pages 166–68. Whatever system is used, the rhythm combinations that are seen should also be performed in some manner, so that the children retain the association between symbol and sound.

The children will of course encounter more notational symbols than those introduced here. They will perform music involving compound meters, dotted notes, and more complex rhythms. In the primary grades their ability to hear and perform rhythm patterns will greatly exceed their ability to read notation. For this reason, much performance instruction is done by rote, and the children's inability to read notation does not hinder their ability to perform music.

NOTE

1. Edward L. Rainbow and Diane Owen, "A Progress Report on a Three-Year Investigation of the Rhythmic Ability of Pre-School Aged Children," Council for Research in Music Education, Bulletin No. 59 (Summer 1979). See also Ana Lucia Frega, "Rhythmic Tasks with Three, Four, and Five Year Old Children," Council for Research in Music Education, Bulletin No. 59 (Summer 1979).

Review Questions

1. Why is the experiencing of rhythm by students in the primary grades more important than a verbal definition of rhythm?
2. What are some teaching techniques for helping children to experience the beat in music?
3. How can chants and rhymes be used in aiding children to become aware of the steady character of the beat in music?
4. Describe some teaching techniques for helping children to gain an understanding of tempo.
5. How can a teacher present a phrase of a song to help children understand the different durations of notes in relation to the beat?
6. How can a concept of meter be developed in children in the primary grades?
7. Why is it necessary for children to have adequate experiences in music before they attempt to read music notation?
8. What is the advantage of stick notation in teaching the reading of rhythms?

Activities

1. Select a song with which to help your methods class become more aware of the beat. Decide the teaching procedures you will use to accomplish this.
2. Examine one of the music series books designed for first, second, or third grade. Select a song that illustrates the three commonly encountered rhythmic durations: one note per beat, two notes per beat, and one note for two beats. Teach a phrase of the song to the methods class and ask various class members to identify the different durations.
3. Set the names of some of the class members into rhythm notation.
4. Make up four short phrases of rhythm patterns. Clap each phrase for the class so that the group can echo your patterns.
5. Make up a rhythm that includes the three kinds of note values described in activity 2. Clap it for the class so that each individual can write it in rhythm notation.
6. In the music series books, find three songs that would be good for teaching two-beat meter to children, and three songs that would be helpful in teaching three-beat meter.
7. Find three songs (other than those cited in this chapter) that would be suitable for introducing young children to rests.
8. Create two rhythm phrases, each eight beats in length. Write them on the chalkboard in stick notation and lead the methods class in performing them by clapping and/or reciting them with rhythm syllables.

Skill Practice

1. a) Tap the rhythm of the notes of the songs in this chapter.
   b) Say the words to the songs *in rhythm* while tapping or clapping the beat.

2. Clap or tap a steady beat in the following measures, while saying the rhythm syllables "ta," "ti," and "ta-ah" for the appropriate note values.

3. Write in your own words a definition for the following music terms:
   a) beat
   b) rest
   c) rhythm
   d) note value
   e) tempo
   f) meter

5

Pitch Differences and Melody

P itch is extremely important in music. While there can be musical works without recognizable pitch levels, almost all music does involve pitch differences. This aspect of music forms the basis of melody and harmony.

Concept of High and Low

A concept of high and low must take into account the relative nature of the terms. Children tend to perceive a single sound as being high or low depending on where it lies in relation to their singing range. They need to learn that a given pitch is not automatically high or low; it is higher or lower than another pitch. In this music lesson the teacher is moving them from the narrow limitations of pitches heard in isolation and is stressing the comparative nature of pitch discrimination.

"For the past few music classes, we've been calling sounds 'high' or 'low' or 'medium.' Now here's a problem for you to solve. I'm going to play some notes on the piano, and you tell me how high or low they are. What should we call this sound: high, low, or medium?"

[The class responds that the note is high.]

"What about this sound: high, low, or medium?"

[The class says that the sound is low.]

"That was pretty easy. The first sound was much higher than the second. Now you'll hear two more sounds. Here's the first one: high, low, or medium?"

[The class, guessing the answer ahead of time, enthusiastically replies, "Medium!"]

"Now the next one. High, low, or medium?"

[The class hesitates, then a few children propose that the sound is medium.]

"Scott, the class says both sounds are medium. Does that mean those two sounds are the same?" . . . [If Scott answers incorrectly, the teacher plays the interval again and asks another child to compare the two sounds.]

"One sound is higher and one is lower, even though both of them are in the medium range. When we decide how high or low a sound is, our answer depends on the other sounds around it. A tall person doesn't seem so tall when he stands with other tall people. But when he stands with short people, he seems even taller. Sounds are like that, when we judge how high or low they are."

The echo-singing of two-note pitch patterns is one way to help children concentrate on pitch. The "cuckoo" interval, which in musical terms is referred to as a "descending minor third," is found in children's chants and games around the world, including the taunt, "Johnny has a girlfriend." It is the first interval introduced in the Kodály program, and is often utilized in the Orff-*Schulwerk* instruction. In the following lesson, the children imitate the "cuckoo" interval sung to them by the teacher.

"Today we're going to sing bits of songs back and forth. Listen carefully as I sing, then you sing the notes back to me. Do all of you know about the cuckoo? It's a bird that sings a short two-note call. Let's start by imitating the sound of a cuckoo. Listen to me first; I'll sing the cuckoo call two times."

Cuck-oo,   cuck-oo

"Now all of you sing the call twice." [The class sings the pattern.] "Good! I think some of you are ready to sing the cuckoo song back to me all by yourself. I'll go around the class and give a chance to as many of you as I can. Michelle, let's start with you. Listen carefully and sing back what I sing."

The Notation of Pitch

Pitch in music refers to the highness or lowness of a sound. Written notes, which indicate pitch as well as rhythm in music, are placed on a *staff* consisting of five horizontal lines and four spaces. The staff provides fixed reference points to show exactly what pitch should be sounded. In music the distance from one pitch to another is termed an *interval*.

The *clef* is a symbol placed on the staff to indicate the exact pitches assigned to each line and space. The range of musical pitches is wide, and the range of a staff is relatively narrow, so musicians have devised a system of clefs to show what portion of the total pitch range each staff is to represent. Unless there is a clef, the notes on a staff have no specific pitches, only relative positions.

The *treble clef* is the curving symbol seen at the beginning of each of the songs presented so far in this book. The inside curl of the treble clef curves around the second line, which is the note G. The other note names on the treble clef staff can be calculated from G. Every line and space is named for one of the first seven letters of the alphabet. The first note above G is A. The seven letters proceed in normal alphabetical order as the notes get higher, and in reverse order as they get lower.

If the interval is being repeated many times in succession, the teacher should change the pitch level occasionally. The continual use of the same pitches is tiring for both the teacher and the children.

The teacher can try other intervals on subsequent days. Intervals smaller than the "cuckoo" pattern are somewhat more difficult for children who have trouble discerning pitch differences. Intervals in which the notes are quite far apart are also difficult, not so much because they are hard to hear, but because children with a narrow singing range simply have trouble reproducing widely separated pitches. For variety, the teacher can play the pitch patterns on an instrument.

Simple games can be devised to help children become more aware of pitch levels. The teacher may:

1. Play or sing pairs of pitches and ask individuals to tell which pitch is higher.

2. Invite various children to "play teacher" by sounding the pairs of pitches and deciding whether the responses of their classmates are correct.

3. Sound an interval twice in succession. For the first hearing, the children should notice which sound is higher and which is lower. When the interval is repeated, they should show with their hands or other bodily movement which pitch is which. For example, for the low pitch in the second pair they might crouch or put their hands on their toes, and for the high pitch they might put their hands above their heads. Asking the children to close their eyes during this game encourages careful listening and discourages the copying of another child's motions.

4. Pass out six or eight bells (one to each child) in random pitch order, then invite the children to discover the relative pitch of each bell and arrange themselves in order from low to high.

Some songs are especially good for aiding children in developing a sense of pitch. In the song "Tony Chestnut," the opening four notes outline a chord, and the second portion of the first line is a descending scale. The actions that accompany the singing emphasize the play on words that is apparent in the construction of the boy's name: on the syllable "To(e)," bend over and touch the toes; on "-ny," touch the knees; on "chest," straighten up and touch the chest; and on "nut," touch the top of the head. On the words "Touch your fingers to the ground," wiggle the fingers while moving the arms and hands to the toes for the beginning of the next line.

The indexes in the teacher's editions of some of the music series books suggest other songs that reinforce the concept of pitch level through actions.

TONY CHESTNUT

Traditional

To - ny Chest-nut, touch your fin-gers to the ground, To - ny Chest-nut, way up high.

It is only a short extension of the high-low concept to the notion of melodic lines ascending or descending ("going up" or "going down"). In

"Tony Chestnut," the children can discover that the first four notes ascend and the next several notes descend. Simple pictures can be drawn and posted to provide visual reinforcement for the idea of pitch direction.

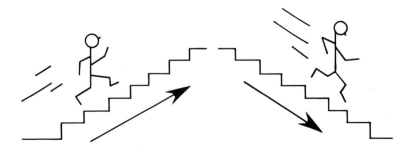

Melody

Children in the primary grades should be introduced to the standard terms for basic aspects of music, like *melody*. A verbal definition such as, "A melody is a cohesive series of pitches" is largely a waste of time for children at this age level, partly because the definition itself contains words that need to be defined. A knowledge of basic terms is valuable, however, because a word can say something more precisely and clearly than a description like "the bunch of notes that seem to belong together."

Here is how a teacher might help a class to understand what the word "melody" means.

> "The other day you learned a song called 'Tony Chestnut.' Let's stand up and sing it again, with the actions." [The class sings the song.]
>
> "Did you notice the direction in which your hands moved on the first four notes? You made them go higher because that's the way the notes sound at the beginning of this song. In what direction do the notes move on 'Touch your fingers to the ground'? Sing it and show me." [The class members move their hands in a downward direction.] "That's right, the notes get lower; they go down.
>
> "Since you're listening to the music so well, I think I'd better ask you to do something harder. Sing the song using only the sound 'loo' without the words. Then tell me if it's still the same tune. Think what your answer is going to be as you sing." [The class sings the song with "loo."]
>
> "Okay now. Did you still sing the tune for 'Tony Chestnut' when you didn't sing the words and just sang with 'loo?' . . . [The class responds, with some disagreement among the children about whether or not they did.]
>
> "You're both right, in a way. The words are needed if someone wants to know how the whole song goes. But a person who already knows the song would recognize what you were singing just from hearing the *melody* you sang with 'loo.'

"That word 'melody' is an important word in music. Every song has its own melody—its own special combination of high, medium, and low notes, with certain places where the tune gets higher, or lower, or stays the same. A string of pitches and its rhythm, when they seem to belong together, make a melody. The melody for 'Tony Chestnut' is what you sang with 'loo,' and it's the same no matter what words you put with it."

In the following lesson the teacher applies the concept of melody to instrumental music.

"Today we'll listen to music that features a very clear melody. But instead of being a song, it's a piece for four string instruments: two violins, a viola, and a cello. The melody is like a song, though, and it's sometimes played under the name 'serenade,' which is a certain type of song. Listen to it, then tell me whether the melody is in a higher or lower instrument." [The class listens to the second movement of the Op. 3 No. 5 string quartet attributed to Haydn.]
    "Who can tell me in which part the melody is played? Is is near the top, bottom, or middle of the pitch range?" [The class notices that the melody is in a high range.]
    "So that you can see for yourselves how song-like this melody is, I'll play a little bit of the recording again so you can learn the tune, and then we'll sing the first few notes of it. Listen." [The teacher plays about a minute of the work.]
    "There, now. Can you remember that tune? Let's sing the melody with 'loo.' Here's the starting pitch. Rea-dy, sing." [The class sings the first two measures of the quartet theme.]

Here is one way in which a teacher can emphasize the sense of cohesiveness that is necessary if successive pitches are to be perceived as a melody.

"I'm going to sound some pitches on the bells, but I'll do it without looking or thinking." [The teacher strikes random bars in no recognizable rhythmic or melodic pattern.]
    "Is that the kind of melody you'd like to sing?" [The consensus is "no."] "No, because the notes don't seem to fit together. It's a bit like this class right here. You belong together; you do things together. You're not just 25 children who got thrown into a room to ignore one another. The notes in a melody have something to do with one another, and that's what makes a melody sound good, instead of just being a bunch of scattered notes."

Pitch and Instruments

Most of the melodic instruments that are played by children in the primary grades are of the simple keyboard type. Although they do not have keys to be depressed as on a piano, the bars on the xylophone, metallo-

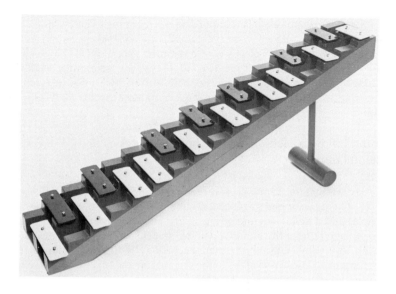

phone, and similar instruments are arranged with the pitches in the same horizontal pattern. This creates a problem for many children. After getting accustomed to describing pitches with "high/low" words and actions, they are now told that "high" is to their right on the instrument they have in front of them. In other words, the terms for vertical alignment are now employed for horizontal alignment.

One aid in overcoming this inconsistency is a simple xylophone instrument called the Step Bells, shown above. The pitches on it follow the horizontal keyboard arrangement and ascend from left to right, but they do so with each pitch raised in stair-step fashion. In this way, children are better able to relate the vertical and horizontal aspects of pitch arrangement. If Step Bells are not available, a metallophone or other xylophone-like instrument can be propped up on a table or hung on the wall so that the bars are viewed vertically.

In this lesson the teacher encourages the children to notice certain facts about pitch and the instruments.

> "Julie, would you please take the mallet and strike each bar on the Step Bells? Go from the one nearest the table up to the one that's highest off the table." [Julie plays the bells in ascending order.]
>
> "Class, what was the order of the pitches that Julie played? Did they move from high to low, or low to high?" [The class reports hearing the low-to-high direction.]
>
> "That's right: low to high. Kevin, you try the bells this time. Start with the bar highest off the table and play them in order moving toward the table top." [Kevin plays the Step Bells in descending order, and the class notices the high-to-low direction.]

When the children understand pitch relationships on the Step Bells or on a vertically positioned instrument, they can move on to instruments that have the keyboard arrangement on a horizontal plane. The transition can be aided by having the children discover that high and low pitches can be determined by their placement to the right or left, and by the relative length of the bars, with the longer bars being lower.

Children enjoy preparing water bottles to produce different pitches. Thin-sided glass containers, such as ordinary drinking glasses, produce a clear tone, but using them increases the risk of spilling and breaking. Bottles with caps are safer and prevent evaporation. The set should be matched in size and construction so that the orderly gradations in water levels can be observed.

To prepare the set, the children can put varying levels of water into the bottles, tapping them frequently to be sure each pitch relates properly to others in the lineup. (The teacher may prepare the bottles ahead of time, or may just experiment to find the appropriate water levels and then mark each bottle with a line to aid the children when they fill the bottle later. Either type of help reduces the amount of mess and confusion.) There may be as few as three bottles—tuned to *do, re, mi* or to *sol, mi, la*, depending on the songs being sung by the class—or as many as eight, tuned to the steps of a major scale. It is visually helpful to add different food colorings to designate bottles. This helps the children locate specific notes as they play, and points out any melodic pattern the teacher may want to emphasize.

As an outcome of their work with water bottles, the class should observe that more water in a bottle produces a lower pitch when the container is tapped. Older children can learn that this happens because the water, by touching the glass, keeps it from vibrating as fast as it would if empty. The opposite situation prevails if someone blows across the top of a water bottle: only the air column is vibrating, so more water makes a shorter air column, producing a higher pitch.

Some of the songs in the music series books have optional parts for instruments. These can contribute to the children's understanding of pitch and melody, but they should not be allowed to consume too much class time. The children's singing should have first priority, and classroom instruments are limited in their ability to enhance this skill. Bell-like instruments are pitched in a higher octave than the voice, and their percussive tones do not provide as good a model for singing as do instruments like the flute or violin, which can sustain sounds. Although classroom instruments are not the best aids for developing pitch discrimination and vocal tone, they do provide variety within the music class, and introduce the children to the vast and rewarding world of instrumental music.

Melodic Steps and Leaps

As children grow in their understanding of melody, they should begin to notice the relative closeness of pitches to one another. Intervals of a whole or a half step are referred to as being a *step* apart. Larger intervals are described as *leaps*. In the following lesson, the teacher helps the class

The Keyboard; Sharps and Flats

Because pitch itself is intangible, a visible representation of pitches is useful, and the piano keyboard provides this. The keyboard is also the basis for the arrangement of notes on certain simple melody instruments, such as the tuned metal bars called "bells."

The black keys of the piano are arranged in groups of twos and threes. All white keys are identified in relation to these groups of black keys. For example, every C on the piano is a white key to the left of a two-black key group; every F is a white key to the left of a three-black-key group. The white keys are named from left to right with the letters A to G.

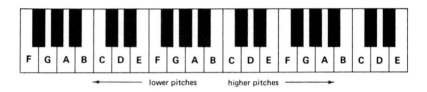

Some notes require a modifying symbol in addition to the letter name. The following three symbols are placed on the staff to the left of the notes they modify. (When spoken or written with letters, the order is reversed so that the symbol occurs last.)

Sharp   (♯)   Raises the pitch one *half step*, which is the smallest pitch difference possible on the piano.

Flat   (♭)   Lowers the pitch one half step.

Natural   (♮)   Cancels a sharp or flat previously applied to the note, and indicates that the pitch is neither raised nor lowered.

The sharp of any white key on the piano is the black key touching it on the *right*. The flat of any white key is the black key touching it on the *left*. If there is no black key on a given side, the nearest white key in that direction is the sharp or flat.

Every black key has two names—one including the term "sharp," and the other including the term "flat." For example, the key called D sharp (because it is to the right of D) is also designated as E flat (because it is to the left of E).

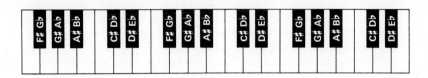

Middle C is the C nearest the middle of the piano keyboard and is also the note that occurs midway between the staffs of the two most common clefs: treble and bass. The *bass clef* is pictured below the treble in the next example. The two dots are part of the bass clef sign, and they occur above and below the particular line known as F. The pitches of the bass clef can be determined by counting in either direction from the F line, or by proceeding downward from middle C. In fact, using the position of middle C as a guide, a person can look at any note on either staff and find on the piano the exact note it represents.

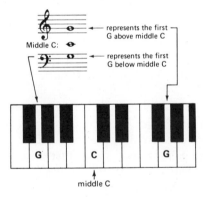

Middle C is too low to be placed within the bounds of the treble staff and too high to be placed on the bass clef staff. Such a note is written above or below the staff with the aid of *leger lines*, which are short horizontal lines that extend the range of the staff. They are the same distance apart as the staff lines. Some notes, such as those shown below, require more than one leger line.

to decide whether an interval is a step or a leap. The song is shown on page 64.

> "Last week you learned a song called 'The Little Chickens.' Let's sing it again today to see how well you remember it. Here's the starting note. Rea-dy, sing." [The class sings the song.]
>
> "That's good. Now we're going to find out how far one note is from the next one. Listen to the first five notes of 'The Little Chickens' as I sing them slowly. As you listen, decide if the notes are 'next door' to each other, which is a *step*, or if they're farther apart than that, which is a *leap*." [The teacher sings the first five notes, then helps the class to discover that they move up by step.]

Intervals

An *interval* is the distance from one pitch to another. To calculate the distance between two notes, a person may apply a "1" to either note and count by step to the other, including the final note in the tally. The count is by alphabet letters, not half-step spacings. For example, the interval of G up to B is a third, counted G A B; it is not a fifth as one might assume from counting each half step: G G♯ A A♯ B.

A whole step or a half step is called a *second*, not only because the two notes in either pair are named for consecutive letters of the alphabet, but also because they are on an adjacent line and space of the staff. Counting lines and spaces instead of letter names is an equally effective way to identify intervals. Again, the number of lines and spaces in the total must include both the upper and lower notes of the interval.

Interval names are not fractions, so the designation of "a sixth" does not mean "one-sixth" of anything. Nor do the names function as ordinal numbers, as in "the sixth item in a series."

Interval names stay the same whether the two sounds occur separately or together, and the presence of a sharp, flat, or natural does not change the basic name of the interval. It is possible to add qualifying words that indicate the number of half steps encompassed by a given interval, as in the term "minor third" (p. 53) which describes the "cuckoo" interval more specifically than does "third" alone. But for children, a simple counting procedure to define the basic span between any two notes is sufficient.

Here are the intervals above the note G:

"So we have five notes, each one a step away from its neighbor. What about the notes on the words 'chickens'?" [The teacher sings the two notes which happen to be the "cuckoo" interval or descending minor third. The class discovers that the interval is a leap.]

The teacher can proceed through the song, asking the children to decide whether various intervals form a step or a leap. Variations of this procedure include playing the intervals on an instrument, asking the children to sing or play the intervals, and showing by hand motions the relative distance between steps and leaps.

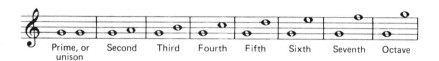

Prime, or unison   Second   Third   Fourth   Fifth   Sixth   Seventh   Octave

The *octave* is an interval of eight notes extending from one tone to the nearest tone of the same name. An octave is the most consonant or best-matched interval in music, because the higher of the two tones vibrates exactly twice as fast as the lower tone, causing the two sounds to blend so well that one seems to duplicate the other.

An *inversion* is produced when either the upper or lower note of the pair is moved to a different octave, making it appear that the original interval has been inverted or turned upside-down. For example, C up to E is a third,

but E up to C (its inversion) is a sixth:

The sound of most intervals can be remembered by associating each with a particular song. For example, "Bingo" (p. 43) opens with a fourth, and "Hush, Little Baby" (p. 103) begins with a sixth.

LOS POLLITOS ("The Little Chickens")

Mexican Children's Song

Los   pol - li - tos   di - cen: pi - o, pi - o,   pi - o,
Hear   the   lit - tle   chick - ens   peep - ing, peep - ing,   peep - ing,

cuan - do   tie - nen   ham - bre,   cuan - do   tie - nen   fri - o.
when___   they   are   hun - gry,   when___   they   are   cold.___

Phrases

Phrases in music are like phrases in language: they are a grouping of sounds or words that are intended to stand together as a single idea. On a printed page of language, phrases are marked off by commas, semicolons, and periods. In music, stopping places are also delineated with varying degrees of finality, primarily through the choice of notes and chords at the phrase endings. If a song is well written, the phrases of the text and of the music will coincide.

Here is one way to help children become aware of logical groupings in music. (The song "All Night, All Day" is presented on p. 105.)

"I don't know if any of you have tried it, but it is nearly impossible to sing a whole song without stopping to take a breath. Even if you could do it, it wouldn't be worth it, because you'd have to race through the song with no expression at all. Let's sing 'All Night, All Day' all on one breath. Sing as far as you can then drop out. Take just one breath at the beginning, now: 'All night, all day . . .'" [All sing the song as far as possible on one breath.]

"We didn't sound too good, did we? And it wasn't very comfortable to feel as if we were going to pass out near the end. Music has places where it seems right to take a breath at that moment. The music and the words just seem to make more sense if you pause at certain places.

"See if you can find those places that seem right for taking a breath. I'll sing a bit of 'All Night, All Day' and stop for a breath, and you tell me if I stopped in the right place." [The teacher stops after the first note, to the amusement of the class. Later pauses occur after "night," "day," "watching," "my," and so on, while the children indicate whether each spot seems like the right place for a pause.]

"You're getting good at noticing where music has sensible places for a short break. In music, the sections that should *not* be split up are called *phrases*. When you pause or breathe only at the logical breaks between sections, you are *phrasing* the music, and that makes it sound better."

Noting the similarity of phrasing in speaking and in singing helps to reinforce the concept.

> "Phrases in music are like phrases in speech. You've been phrasing ever since you learned to talk—and you didn't even know you were so talented! When you talk, you don't run all your words together or say them all in the same way. Remember when you learned about patterns in rhythm? You discovered that people don't talk like a machine 'with-all-sounds-ex-act-ly-a-like.' You make certain sounds stronger or lighter, and you group them in certain ways so that other people will understand what you mean."

Another way to make children more aware of musical segments is to print the words on the board and mark off the phrases with over-arching lines:

All night, all day, Angels watching over me, my Lord.

The options available in even this short example indicate that judgments about phrase length are subjective and open to interpretation. There is no single right way to analyze every phrase.

When the children have had experience in analyzing phrases in vocal music (which has words to provide clues), they can try to identify the exclusively musical phrases in instrumental works such as the Haydn string quartet discussed on page 57.

Children in the primary grades should learn to notice whether phrases are alike or different. In the song "Tony Chestnut" (p. 55) the children can sing the song and then decide how many phrases there are and whether the phrases are the same or different. If the children hear two long phrases, further analysis should elicit the observation that the two phrases are identical until the halfway point, and then they differ.

Children should also begin to sense the statement-answer phrase pattern that appears in many songs. In this construction, one phrase seems to present the first half of a musical statement, and the second phrase seems to respond to it with a certain degree of conclusiveness. This pattern is apparent in "All Night, All Day" and "Tony Chestnut." Sometimes the statement-answer idea is a bit more difficult to find, as in "The Little Chickens." In the first two measures the pitch level quickly ascends five notes, while for the last six measures it gradually descends in an overall stepwise manner that can be traced by examining the first pitch in measures 3 through 8. In fact, the class can capitalize on this basic descending line by turning it into a counter-melody to be sung along with the main tune:

Peep, peep, (etc.)

The important point for the children to learn in comparing phrases is that there is a *musical* logic that undergirds the organizing of musical ideas.

Teaching the Notation of Pitch

As in the learning of rhythm, the children's understanding of pitch can be furthered through the use of visual symbolization, if the instruction is based on prior aural experience. The teacher should introduce the reading of music symbols only after the students have demonstrated a solid aural comprehension of pitch.

The initial efforts to teach symbolization need not start with conventional notation. Rather, the use of one- and two-line staffs, with notes placed in relative positions around those lines, has been found to be a successful introductory system. Here are two examples of simplified pitch notation.

The first example utilizes a one-line staff, which is sufficient for melodies that have only a three-note range. A two-line staff is preferable if the melody contains five adjacent pitch levels. The clef sign, bar lines, and meter and key signatures are missing because they are not necessary at this point, and their absence reduces the number of distractions. Here is how a teacher might introduce the graphic symbolization of pitch.

"You've been reading pictures of rhythms for quite a while. I think you're ready to look at drawings of different pitches. First, let's start by putting down two lines that run along together sideways. One step is the distance from a line to the next space, or from a space to the next line. With two lines, we can show five steps."

"Now I'll put some notes on the lines and spaces, and you tell me how far apart the notes are, and whether the sound moves higher or lower. Here's an example." [The teacher draws a note head under the bottom line and another slightly to the right, bisected by the bottom line.]

"This interval moves up a step, doesn't it? It will sound like this." [The teacher sings an ascending whole step on a neutral syllable, establishing the pitch according to the first two notes of a major scale. Another note is added in the space above the second note, and the class observes that it is higher by one step.]

"Very good reading! The hard test is to see if you can play on the bells the notes that I put on the board." [The teacher draws two more notes: one on the upper line and another on the space above it.]

"Tim, here are five bells, arranged by step from lowest to highest. That means the bell on your left is the sound for the lowest space note on the board. First play all your notes in order from low to high as I point to them on the board." [Tim plays the notes.] "Good. Now I'll point to two notes on the board and you play them on the bells."

The children should sing each pattern after hearing it on the bells, then they may try to sing directly from the notation, which is more difficult than singing by imitation or playing the pattern on an instrument. The children may be invited to come to the board individually to draw or point to notes for the class to perform.

At this point, no attempt should be made to combine rhythm and pitch in the notation exercises. The children may be seeing complete notation in the songs they sing from their books, but they are not trying to sight-read that music. As they become more proficient at reading, the stick notation discussed in Chapter 4 can be presented in conjunction with a two-line staff. Note heads are necessary, of course, if pitch is to be reproduced accurately from the printed symbols.

Orff and Kodály Techniques

The Orff-*Schulwerk* and the Kodály-Hungarian Singing School methods are educational approaches that have been undertaken by many American music specialists. To be implemented fully, each system requires specialized knowledge and training. An introduction to these methods is warranted, however, because classroom teachers should be prepared to follow up the activities and procedures previously started by music specialists, and to give the children additional practice in the techniques. The full scope of the two systems will not be explored here; only their respective approaches to the development of pitch discrimination will be cited.

Both Orff and Kodály use the movable *do* system and begin the work on pitch with the "cuckoo" interval—the descending minor third. Songs are selected to feature this interval, and children practice specifically to sing it accurately. Often the pitches are assigned the syllable names of *sol* for the higher pitch and *mi* for the lower. Numbers may also be used for this purpose, but they are not advocated by specialists in either of these methods.

The next syllable to be taught is *la*. With just these three pitches it is possible to create a surprising number of simple songs. The pattern is featured in many songs such as "A Tisket, A Tasket." (see p. 68.) The children

A TISKET, A TASKET

Singing Game

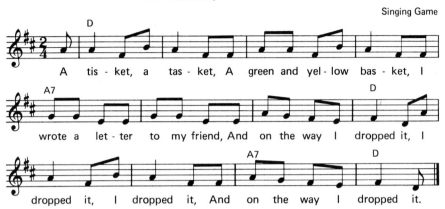

A tis - ket, a tas - ket, A green and yel - low bas - ket, I

wrote a let - ter to my friend, And on the way I dropped it, I

dropped it, I dropped it, And on the way I dropped it.

can sing the song while the teacher points to the three notes that have previously been put on the board. If the children have access to the complete notation of the song, they can find the three special notes in the longer version.

The next pitch to be added is *do,* which greatly expands the song possibilities. The addition of *re* completes the *pentatonic* (five-tone) scale that is featured in both the Orff and Kodály approaches. The syllables *fa* and *ti* do not appear until later because each creates a half step with a neighboring note of the scale, and this sets up a more rigid expectation of key center.

The Kodály method employs hand signs, in which a different hand position represents each syllable. The signs for the most frequent syllables are shown on page 70. The syllables *fi, si,* and *ta* are *chromatic* (half-step) alterations that sometimes occur in a key. They are indicated by accidentals in the notation because they represent a departure from the prevailing key signature.

The purpose of the hand signs is to provide a physical, kinesthetic reinforcement of the relationship among various pitches. Many music specialists, however, adequately indicate pitch level by simply moving a horizontal hand either up or down, without changing its appearance. This procedure is helpful to the children and easier for the teacher, because much time needs to be invested in learning the hand signs before a person feels fluent and comfortable with them.

In the following lesson, the teacher integrates practice on the melodic pattern *sol-mi-la-sol-mi* with a phrase from "A Tisket, a Tasket."

"Now that you've been singing the syllables *sol, mi,* and *la* for a while, you can make them into a phrase of five syllables going in this order: *sol, mi, la, sol, mi.* I'll sing *sol* again. Just follow my hand so we can all stay together on our tune." [The teacher leads the class in singing the five pitches.]

Pitch Syllables

The song "Do Re Mi" from the musical *The Sound of Music* is based on the seven Latin syllables traditionally applied to pitches in music: *do re mi fa sol la ti do*. (In all of the pitch syllables, *i* is pronounced "ee" and *e* is pronounced "ay.") When heard in this basic order as a scale, adjacent syllables are a whole step apart except for a half-step spacing between *mi fa* and *ti do*.

There are two systems that use those syllables. One is called *fixed do*, and it establishes a specific syllable for a specific pitch, no matter what the key of the music. This system requires not only the seven basic pitch syllables, but also ten more to provide two names for each of the five black keys, as shown in the boxes below:

C	C♯	D	D♯	E	F	F♯	G	G♯	A	A♯	B
do	*di*	*re*	*ri*	*mi*	*fa*	*fi*	*sol*	*si*	*la*	*li*	*ti*
C	D♭	D	E♭	E	F	G♭	G	A♭	A	B♭	B
do	*ra*	*re*	*me*	*mi*	*fa*	*se*	*sol*	*le*	*la*	*te*	*ti*

The other system is called *movable do*. It assigns *do* to whatever note is step 1 of a major key. A problem arises, however, when the music changes key and the original pitch for *do* is no longer the key center. There is also the matter of what to do about songs in minor keys. After trying to establish in the children's thinking that *do* is always the keynote, the music teacher must either say that *la* is the keynote in a minor key, or introduce the half-step syllables to accommodate the special interval patterns of minor scales.

The extent to which pitch syllables aid in music reading is debated among music educators.

"Good! Have you sung a song in the past week that uses those syllables just as we want them?" [The children discover that the pattern appears three times in "A Tisket, A Tasket."]

"Let's sing that song, but instead of singing the regular words when you get to those three places, sing the syllables. I'll sing it for you once. Notice that I'm singing syllables for these three sets of words: first, 'A tisket, a tasket,' then 'a green and yellow basket,' and finally 'I dropped it, I dropped it.'" [The teacher sings the song with syllables through the word "basket," with text through the first "I dropped it" phrases, and with regular text to the end.]

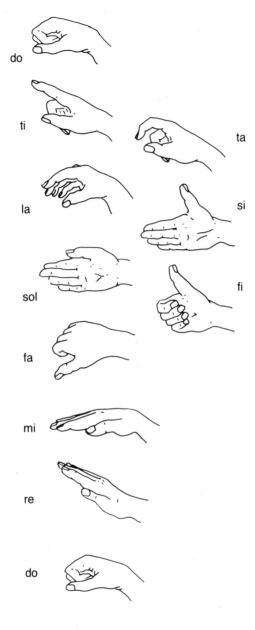

Curwen-Kodály Hand Signs

The procedures in the foregoing lesson may vary depending on the musical experience of the children and the preferences of the teacher. Hand signs can be presented, notation can be drawn on the board, and syllable songs can be created by the class. It is important, however, that the children realize that the pattern on which they are focusing is not just an isolated exercise. Attention to melodic patterns should derive from, and revert to, actual music.

Review Questions

1. Why are definitions of words like "pitch" and "high" of limited value to young children?
2. Describe four teaching procedures for helping children to gain a better understanding of high and low pitch.
3. How can a teacher help children to transfer their vertical high-low concept to the horizontal high-low arrangement found on keyboard-type instruments?
4. Suppose that several first-graders are having trouble telling the difference between steps and leaps. Describe a teaching procedure that might improve their ability to do this.
5. Describe three techniques for helping children to become aware of phrases in music.
6. What are the advantages of a one- or two-line staff in the initial stages of reading music notation?
7. (True or false?) Pitch syllables imply particular interval relationships between the notes.
8. With what two pitch syllables do both the Orff and Kodály approaches begin?

Activities

1. a. Plan a three-minute lesson in which you help the class to gain a better idea of high and low pitch.
   b. Plan another three-minute lesson to help the class apply an understanding of high and low pitch to a simple instrument such as the bells or xylophone.
2. From one of the music series books, select two songs—one that contains melodic movement primarily by step, and one that contains many leaps. Plan how you would use the songs to help the children gain a better understanding of steps and leaps.
3. Referring to the two songs you selected for the preceding project, decide how you would help children in a primary class to recognize the phrases in these songs. Identify the aspects of phrasing that you would point out to the class.
4. Get together with another class member and practice sight-singing short and simple melodic patterns, with syllables, from songs selected at random from music series books.

Skill Practice

1. Practice saying the pitch names in the following excerpts. Next, say the pitch names for the same duration as the note values, while clapping a steady beat. Then play the exercises on the bells or piano. Finally, sing the exercises on a neutral syllable.

2. Name the basic intervals in each excerpt of Practice Exercise 1.

3. Assuming that the note F is *do*, write the pitch syllable names for a) and b) in Practice Exercise 1. Then sing the two lines with the correct pitch syllables.

4. Name and play the following notes on the bells or piano:

5. Looking at the chart of Curwen-Kodály hand signs on page 70, form each sign at an even pace, moving from the bottom of the chart to the top and proceeding downward again. Then sing a scale with pitch syllables, starting with any comfortable pitch as the lower *do*. Finally, sing the same scale while forming the hand signs.

C H A P T E R

6

Timbre

E very sound, every person's voice, and every type of musical instrument has a unique tone quality. The musical term for the quality of a sound is *timbre*, which is usually pronounced in the French manner as *tăm*-bur. Along with pitch, rhythm, and loudness, timbre is one of the four basic elements of music.

Teaching the Concept of Timbre

Until they are made aware of the subtleties of tone quality, most children are only vaguely conscious of this element of music. One way to draw their attention to it is to compare timbres on a same-different basis. Here is how this can be done.

> "Today let's notice the quality of the sounds we hear. We'll do it by playing a game. On the table in the back of the room there are several rhythm instruments. Todd, why don't you go back there by the table. Look over the class to make sure no one is turning around and watching you. Then play two different sounds, one after the other. You can play them on different instruments or on the same instrument. Then call on someone in the class to tell if the qualities of the two sounds were the same or different." [Todd plays several pairs of sounds, each time calling on a different child to say whether the timbres were alike or not.]

The game can continue as other children take turns producing sounds that are available around the classroom: tapping or scraping against flower pots, window shades, the chalkboard, glass items, and so on.

Children should learn to distinguish between sounds with different timbres and sounds with the same timbre that are different in pitch. When children first hear two different pitches on a melodic instrument, they may respond that the sounds have different qualities. Here is how a teacher might clarify the situation.

> "I'm going to play two notes for you on the bells. Listen and tell me if they have the same tone quality." [The teacher plays the notes G and E descending.]
>
> "Troy, was the tone quality the same each time, or was it different?"
>
> "It was different."
>
> "You heard that *something* was different between the notes. Let's discover what it was. You heard these notes. . . ." [The teacher repeats

G E.] "It's the *pitch* that's different. Was the second note higher or lower than the first one, class?" [The class indicates it was lower.] "Sure, it was lower. That means the pitch was different. But the tone quality was the same. Here's a hint to help you the next time you want to compare sounds: If different notes are played on the same instrument with the same sticks, the quality will be about the same."

Another way to stress the uniqueness of timbre is to ask the children to identify, without looking, the voice of a child who is speaking. To prevent identification of the voice by its location rather than by its timbre, the teacher can ask the children to stand in a circle but face outward. The teacher then stands in the center of the circle and taps a child on the shoulder to say a word or phrase in a normal manner. The children should not try to fool one another by disguising their voices, because that destroys the point of the activity.

"We're going to try to tell who is talking just by listening to that person's voice. You're standing facing away from one another so that you won't be able to guess the voices on the basis of where the people sit in class.

"Each person will say the same thing. If I tap you on the shoulder, say 'Do you know my voice?' Don't try to change the way you normally speak. Let's practice the words together once, so you won't get mixed up if you have a turn. The words are 'Do you know my voice?' All together now, 'Do you know my voice?'"

[The teacher taps various children on the shoulder, and class members guess which child has spoken. The children return to their seats, and the teacher explains what has been demonstrated by the activity.]

"You see, you can recognize people just by hearing their voices, even though they're saying the same words. Why can you do that? Because each person in the whole human race has a somewhat different quality of voice. You don't get mixed up at home listening to your mother, father, brother, or sister speaking, even when they're in a different room, because they each have a quality all their own. The word for quality of sound is *timbre*."

For a variation of this game, the children divide into teams. The winner is the first team to guess, without looking, the identity of every speaker on the other side.

Exploring Sound Production and Timbres

Children can learn much about timbre by allowing their natural curiosity to function in exploring instruments. Because of its large size and easy availability, the piano is a logical instrument on which to begin exploring the nature of sound. Children can try the following activities:

1. They can feel the vibrations by putting their hands lightly on the piano's soundboard or on the strings after pitches have been sounded.

2. They can observe that the lower strings are thicker and longer than the shorter and higher strings.

3. They can watch the strings moving like a blur as they sound, especially the larger, lower strings that vibrate more widely. (String vibration can also be easily seen on a large string instrument such as a cello, string bass, or guitar.)

4. They can see that the felt hammer that strikes the string must immediately leave it if the string is to sound freely.

5. They can hold down the sustaining pedal—the one farthest to the right—while they tap the strings with different objects such as a pencil or a triangle beater.

Basic Instruments and Voice Types

Children in the primary grades should learn to recognize basic instruments and voice types. The process is not difficult, because they are likely to have some knowledge from their preschool experiences and from watching television. The basic instruments may be considered to be piano, violin, clarinet, trumpet, and snare drum; the basic voice types for this level are the male (bass-baritone) and female (soprano). The teacher should continue to stress that each instrument and voice has its unique timbre. The recognition game described earlier can be varied by playing recordings of instruments and asking the children to identify the instrument by name and picture. Instructional packages on musical instruments are available to assist teachers in this effort. (Appendix A contains a list of sources for these materials.)

At about the third-grade level, children can begin to compare families of instruments according to their methods of tone production. The most basic groupings are the winds, in which the player blows breath through the instrument; the strings, in which the player bows or plucks the desired note; and percussion instruments, which the player strikes, shakes, or scrapes. In addition to recognizing instrument families, children at this age should be able to identify such individual instruments as trombone, organ, cello, flute, oboe, and timpani.

Children should understand that the way in which an instrument is played also alters its timbre. They can discover this fact for themselves by experimenting with classroom instruments. Here is an example of how such experimentation might be conducted.

"I'm going to pass out three different types of sticks for the metallophone. Karen, here's one that has a hard head. Daniel, this one is medium, and Melissa, here's a soft one. The three of you go to the metallophone and take turns striking any bars that you wish. The rest of us will compare the tone qualities that we hear when the different types of sticks are used."

Similar changes can be observed on the autoharp when the children play with different picks—one that is felt and another that is plastic, for example. There is even a difference in sound when the angle of the pick strumming the strings is altered. Drums produce a slight change of timbre when struck at different places on the drumheads, or with different parts of the hands.

A good way to encourage children to investigate timbres and types of instruments is to ask them to make simple instruments at home from inexpensive articles they find around the house: a piece of old garden hose, empty cereal cartons, tin cans, bottles, pie pans, combs, and so on. A few guidelines should be given to prevent the experience from becoming an exercise in junk collecting. If the instrument is of the percussion type, it should have a clear and easily heard tone, plus the capability of withstanding repeated striking or shaking. If the instrument is of the wind or string type, it should be capable of producing at least three distinct pitches with a reasonably clear timbre.

Here is a list of simple instruments that can be constructed with the help of a teacher or parent.

DRUM—Remove both ends of a gallon can. Cut two circles from a tire inner tube, making them somewhat larger than the ends of the can. With a paper punch, make holes about 2½ inches apart around the edges of the rubber circles. With leather strips, lace the heads onto the drum by running the strips back and forth between the two circles.

TRIANGLE—On a steel rod about 18 inches long, measure 6 inches from each end and bend the rod in a vice until the ends nearly touch, forming a triangular shape. Attach a cord to one corner of the triangle, and hold the instrument by the cord when playing. Use a large nail for a beater.

SAND BLOCKS—Cut two wood blocks about 3" × 5" × 1". Attach a knob to the large side of each block. Cut two pieces of heavy sandpaper large enough to cover the side of each block opposite the knob, and long enough to fold over onto the ends of the block. Attach the sandpaper with thumbtacks or staples. To play, hold each block by its knob and scrape the rough sides together to produce a brushing sound.

MARACAS—Wash two empty half-pint milk, yogurt, or cream cartons. Place dried beans or metal nuts inside and staple the top closed.

RHYTHM STICKS—Cut dowel rods, about ⅜-inch thick, into lengths of about 14 inches.

The children should be prepared to answer questions about the instruments they make.

1. Can the instrument produce both high and low sounds? If its pitch is limited, is the range basically high or low?
2. Does the sound tend to be loud or soft? How much variation in loudness is possible on the instrument?

3. Can one sound be held for a while if desired?
4. Can notes be played on the instrument one right after another in rapid succession?
5. Does the sound have a "ring" or is it dull?
6. Is the timbre especially suitable for a certain type of song?
7. Is the instrument more appropriate for playing a tune or for accompanying?

Children may be invited to discover that certain songs suggest a particular voice quality. Songs in the music series books, for example, sometimes require the youngsters to imitate animal sounds ("peep, peep") or other tonal effects such as the howling of the wind ("oo-oo-oo"). These words or sounds are attempts to infuse a special timbre or tonal effect into the music.

Songs about instruments are helpful because they imply certain tonal characteristics. The "German Instrument Song" concludes with a simple instrumental part of four pitches. Of the five instruments mentioned in the song, a set of bells can play the notes of the instrumental part in the first verse. The next two instruments can also play their respective verses as written, with the recorder assuming the role of "pipe." Chords are suggested for the fourth instrument—the autoharp—which is not at its best when played melodically. The drum, which cannot play pitches at all, is given an independent rhythm part to add interest to the song. If no instruments are available, the children can make up sounds and words for those parts, as the teacher has them do in this class.

> "We don't have all the instruments mentioned in the song, so we'll just have to make the instrument sounds ourselves. What would be a good sound or word for the bell? Matthew?" [Matthew suggests "ding," and that seems acceptable to the other children.]
>
> "All right, let's say "ding' for the bell. Who has an idea for the fiddle? Vicki?" [Vicki suggests "zing," which seems to satisfy the other children.]
>
> "That's a good sound, and it rhymes with 'ding' for the bell. Now, what about the pipe to blow on? Michael?" [Michael suggests "toot," which doesn't please some of the other class members.] "What other sound might work for the pipe? Cheryl?" [Cheryl suggests whistling the notes for the pipe.] "How many of you prefer 'toot'? . . . How many prefer whistling?" . . . [The class favors whistling.]
>
> "Okay, let's sing the first verse with 'ding' for each note of the bell, the second with 'zing' for each note of the fiddle, and the third with whistling for each note of the pipe."

Sound Effects in Stories

Children in the primary grades like to add sound effects to stories that they know, and this helps to increase their consciousness of timbres.

GERMAN INSTRUMENT SONG

English words by Tulla Statler

German Folk Song

1. If I had a bell to play a tune on, If I had a bell, oh, how I'd *ring.*

(Instrumental)

2. If I had a fiddle, fiddle, fiddle,
   If I had a fiddle, how I'd *bow.*

3. If I had a pipe to play a tune on,
   If I had a pipe, oh, how I'd *blow.*

4. If I had an Autoharp to play on,
   If I had an Autoharp, I'd *strum.*

5. If I had a drum that I could play on,
   If I had a drum, oh, how I'd *beat.*

6. Now we have a tune to play together,
   Now we have a tune, oh, how we'll *play.*

From Bennett Reimer et al., *Music*, Book 3. Words copyright © 1974 by Silver Burdett Company.

For example, "Jack and the Beanstalk" could be "orchestrated" in the following way:

Jack climbing up	—— ascending pattern on bells
Jack climbing down	—— descending pattern on bells
Giant	—— large drum or low notes on piano
Hen cackling	—— castanet
Harp	—— autoharp
Chopping beanstalk	—— woodblock
Beanstalk falling	—— cymbals and drums

As the children gain experience in associating "effects" with a story, the teacher can move on to more sophisticated music.

Many compositions feature timbres by associating them with a story. Prokofiev's *Peter and the Wolf* includes a part for a narrator, who tells how a boy with the help of some animal friends captures an angry wolf. Various instruments play tunes specifically associated with the characters: Peter, Grandfather, a duck, a cat, a bird, some hunters, and of course the wolf. The music is imaginative and charming. On the first hearing the children can concentrate on the story, because they will be interested in the outcome. On subsequent hearings they should concentrate on the tonal qualities of the instruments that are associated with the characters—the clarinet with the cat, the bassoon with Grandfather, the strings with Peter. The oboe, which represents the duck, has a nasal quality that somewhat resembles the sound of that animal. The oboe also has a plaintive quality, which Prokofiev must have thought appropriate for the story, since the duck gets eaten by the wolf.

Timbres are not always associated with objects, animals, and personalities, of course. Children should also experience abstract music that consists of tonal effects. Otto Luening's "Sonic Contours" is a composition of flute sounds recorded on tape and then manipulated in several different ways to create an interesting musical work. It is not performed in the usual sense of the word, with musicians re-creating and interpreting the composer's ideas. Instead, the final tape is heard exactly as Luening created the different sounds. His short piece contains no meter or other conventional characteristics of music, but it is fascinating to hear, with tune fragments and reverberations that are attractive and enjoyable. If music truly is organized sound, such works qualify as music.

A good combination of tonal effects and conventional music is Carlos Chavez's *Toccata for Percussion Instruments*. In this work, Chavez successfully exploits rhythms and the possibilities offered by the variety of percussion instruments.

Timbre is an important component of music. To help children appreciate its potential, the teacher needs to employ a variety of procedures through which they can discover and experience timbre in music.

Review Questions

1. Why is the same-different comparison a good teaching procedure for children in the early grades of elementary school?

2. How can children be taught to discriminate between differences in timbre and differences in pitch?

3. Describe a game that can be played to encourage children to listen for differences in timbre.

4. What aspects of sound can children learn from exploring a piano?

5. Name four basic instruments that children in the primary grades should learn to recognize by sight and sound.

6. How can children learn that the manner in which an instrument is played often affects its timbre?

7. Describe two instruments and explain how they can be constructed by the children and/or the teacher.

8. What are four questions that can be asked about the timbre of an instrument, especially one that is homemade?

9. In what ways can the activity of singing contribute to children's increased awareness of timbre?

10. Name three works that are especially effective in encouraging youngsters to listen for timbre.

Activities

1. Try out the same-different listening game in class by having various class members strike objects around the room.

2. Select an instrument, other than the piano, that is often available in the elementary classroom, and explain what can be learned about sound and timbre with that instrument.

3. Develop a lesson in which the children learn about the basic groups or families of instruments. Encourage the children to discover for themselves the basis for the groupings.

4. a. Make an instrument and bring it to class.
   b. Explain how your instrument could best be used in an elementary school music class.

5. In an elementary music series book, find a song that is especially suitable for helping children become aware of timbre. Describe how you would teach the song to help the children understand this aspect of music.

6. Listen either to Luening's "Sonic Contours" or to a movement of Chavez's *Toccata for Percussion Instruments.* Plan how you would teach about the timbres and tonal effects in the musical work you have selected.

C H A P T E R

7

Dynamic Levels and the Combining of Musical Elements

I n music, the relative strength of a sound is referred to as its *loudness*. Although radios and television sets are regulated by a knob to control "volume," that is not the preferred term in music. It has been replaced by *dynamic level*, which refers to the degree of loudness.

Loud/Soft Concept

The difference between loud and soft music is perhaps the element most easily recognized by children in the primary grades. They may have trouble sensing the beat or discerning differences among pitches, but seldom do they find it difficult to distinguish between contrasting dynamic levels.

Although loud/soft difference may appear to be the most obvious element of music, this aspect of music can be very subtle. It is largely responsible for the nuances that create effective phrasing and convey the performer's musicianship. It is true that children approach loudness in music in a more basic way, but the more they notice changes in dynamic level, the more they will understand and enjoy music.

Even in kindergarten, the children's attention can be directed to this element of music. For example, the youngsters can perform simple rhythm patterns at different dynamic levels. If the class is clapping a series of quarter notes, the children might be told to clap four of them loudly, four softly, and four loudly again. To ensure that differences in dynamic level are achieved, the children can be asked to use the entire hand for loud clapping and one finger against the palm of the other hand for soft clapping.

As they become more adept in their ability to switch levels, the youngsters can change from loud to soft more frequently: two loud and two soft, then one loud and one soft. They can also learn to achieve gradual changes, even if the terminology for gradual changes has not been introduced. A clapping game might be devised by asking the children to get gradually softer by clapping four times with four fingers in the other palm, four times with three fingers, then with two fingers, and finally with one finger. The pattern can also be reversed, of course.

It is not necessary to introduce the traditional dynamic markings in the primary grades; that can be done later. In fact, songs in the music series books for younger children often do not contain dynamic markings. They may include an oblique reference to loud/soft considerations by proposing that a song be sung "gently" or "vigorously," but these terms have as much to do with style as they do with dynamic level.

Some songs by their nature suggest certain treatments of dynamic level. The "Echo Carol" refrain contains repeated phrases that sound more effective when the second phrase of each pair is sung softly, like an echo. To ensure that the echo portions will be softer than the rest of the song, the teacher can choose two or three reliable singers to perform the echo part. The echo effect is more apparent if the small group is positioned away from the rest of the class.

Here are other techniques that can be tried to help children become more sensitive to dynamic levels.

1. Ask the children to determine which classroom instruments are essentially loud and which are soft. For example, the rhythm sticks and maracas may be considered to be soft, while the drum is loud. The children should experiment with different ways of playing the instruments, to learn the extent to which each can produce loud and soft sounds. They will discover, for example, that hitting a drum with a wire brush produces a softer sound than hitting it with a stick.

2. Say chants or rhymes at different dynamic levels.

3. Suggest that the children display pictures of things that produce loud noises and things that are soft in sound. A diesel railroad engine and a large dog barking are examples of loud noisemakers, while a cricket and a small bird make soft sounds.

Gradual Changes in Dynamic Level

Although few songs in the music series books include dynamic markings, subtle changes in level can be noticed when the music is performed expressively. Most music would be quite uninteresting if performed at the same dynamic level from beginning to end, and the phrasing would be less effective. To determine where nuances might be appropriate in a song, the class should examine not only the words but the melodic line. The highest notes in a phrase are often the most important and are approached with more intensity. Conversely, notes that dip especially low tend to convey a sense of relaxation and can be sung a little more gently, if the words of the text support this interpretation.

The song "Tony Chestnut" (p. 55) is well adapted to gradual changes in dynamic level that conform both to the melody and to the bending and rising physical gestures of the song.

"Tony Chestnut, touch your fingers to the ground;

Tony Chestnut, way up high."

ECHO CAROL

2. Born is the Child, in manger small,
   Whom God hath sent to save us all.
   O sing with joy, etc.

3. Go you this night, and you will find
   God's Son so pure, so sweet and kind.
   O sing with joy, etc.

4. He has been sent from God above;
   He brings to man the gift of love.
   O sing with joy, etc.

5. If you will keep him in your heart,
   Never will joy from you depart!
   O sing with joy, etc.

The teacher may need to remind the class that the terms "high" and "low" in music refer to pitch, not to dynamic level—a common misconception among children who assume that "high means loud" and "low means soft." In "Tony Chestnut" the teacher can differentiate between the concepts of pitch and loudness by pointing out the feeling of expansion and growth as the body stretches upward with the music, and the feeling of shrinking as the body moves downward. This emphasis links the selection of dynamic levels to body feeling rather than to pitch levels, and helps to preserve the distinction between loudness and pitch.

There are numerous examples of gradual changes in dynamic level in recorded instrumental music that can be played for the class. Villa-Lobos'

"The Little Train of the Caipira," mentioned in Chapter 4, is a good example. Another is the "Bydlo" ("Peasant Cart") from Mussorgsky's *Pictures at an Exhibition*. The ponderous sounds of the cart increase in loudness over a long span of time, then subside in the same way.

Accents

Some notes tend to be stressed because they occur on the first beat of the measure, but other notes can also be emphasized. An accent is the technique by which this emphasis is most often accomplished.

On a page of music, the accent mark looks like the letter "v" turned counterclockwise on its side. Although it resembles a decrescendo in shape, it applies to only one note; it is not elongated to span several notes in succession. The shape of the accent shows how it should be performed: the

---

Dynamics

The terminology for dynamic levels in music includes these basic Italian terms and abbreviations:

pp (pianissimo)	means "very soft"
p (piano)	means "soft"
mp (mezzo piano)	means "moderately soft"
mf (mezzo forte)	means "moderately loud"
f (forte)	means "loud"
ff (fortissimo)	means "very loud"

Terraced dynamics occur when each phrase of the music maintains a consistent dynamic level, with abrupt changes of loudness occurring only between the phrases.

A gradual change of dynamic level can be indicated by either words or symbols:

crescendo	or ⊲	means "gradually louder"
decrescendo or *descresc.*	or ⊳	means "gradually softer"
diminuendo or *dim.*	or ⊳	means "gradually softer"

Indications of dynamic level are relative, not absolute, because a person's impression of loudness and softness depends on the context in which the sounds are heard.

BOOM DALI DA

Slowly

Israeli Folk Song

Boom da-li da, Boom da-li da, Boom da-li, da-li,

Boom da-li da, Boom da-li da, Boom da-li, da-li,

very fast

Boom da-li, da-li, Boom da-li, da-li, Boom da-li, da-li,

Boom, ha! ha! Boom da-li, da-li, Boom da-li, da-li,

Boom! Da - li, da - li, da, Boom!

beginning of the accented note is abruptly loud, with an immediate decrease of loudness. The effect is a quick "jab" of sound.

The song "Boom Dali Da" contains several accented notes. Here is how the teacher might introduce them.

> "Listen while I sing you a new song. Don't worry about the strange words; just listen to the way I sing the *music* differently on some of the notes. When I finish, tell me in what way those notes were different." [The teacher sings "Boom Dali Da," performing the accents with exaggerated emphasis. The children observe that certain notes are punched out more than others.]
>
> "Good for you! I really gave those notes a poke. It's called an *accent* in music. The song is in your books. Let's look at it. . . . Do you see a sign we haven't talked about before?" [Some class members notice the unfamiliar marks.]
>
> "Right; those signs that look like a 'v' on its side are the accent marks. As we sing the song and you come to an accent mark, give that note a quick punch with your voice. Here's a hint to help you: keep the other notes smooth and whispery. Then when you come to the accent, the sound will seem to pop out without a lot of effort. Pretend you're trying to scare someone on that note, like a surprise on Halloween. Don't shout, though."

On another day the teacher might review the learning of accented notes in this manner.

"In music yesterday we learned 'Boom Dali Da.' Let's sing it again today to make sure that you know it. Show me, by your singing, how much you remember about accented notes." [The class sings the song, observing an occasional accent.]

"Is it coming back to you now? We'd better sing it again, because I missed hearing the Halloween effect. You didn't scare me! Maybe Halloween isn't your favorite holiday. What other holiday might fit the loud surprise notes?" [Greg suggests the Fourth of July, and the class sings the accents more explosively.]

"Much better! Now is there some way we can make these notes even stronger than we can with our voices alone?" [Shauna suggests clapping or playing a percussion instrument on the accented notes.]

"Good idea, Shauna. Let's all clap *once* on each accented note. Don't forget to sing as you clap; we shouldn't let a clap take the place of singing."

Dynamic Level and Musical Expression

Although children do not have strong enough voices to produce a wide range of dynamic levels, they can still make small differences and perform music expressively. They should try to make a difference not only between a vigorous song and a lullaby, but also between various phrases within a song. This is called *expression*, or *interpretation*, and even slight nuances help to make the music more effective.

Children should learn from their earliest school music experiences that loudness in itself is not an indication of vocal mastery. In an effort to duplicate a popular style, they sometimes force their voices, resulting in a tone that is strained and unnatural.

Some children (and teachers) seem to regard boisterous singing as evidence of youthful exuberance and enjoyment. While it is true that one of the objectives of a music class is to get the children to sing with enthusiasm, sheer loudness is not the best measure of their interest. In fact, their enjoyment in their music-making will increase as they learn to appreciate musical nuance and realize that they can contribute in less obvious ways to a musically satisfying result.

Occasionally a teacher will encounter particular children who sing noticeably louder than the rest of the class. These individuals may not realize they are louder, either because they are not listening or because they are overly zealous in wanting to demonstrate their singing abilities or their familiarity with the song. Occasionally a child will even appear to be singing more loudly than the others to get attention, sometimes with a conspicuous lack of pitch accuracy. Whatever the reason for this disparity in individual levels of loudness within the group, the teacher should take steps to correct the unevenness, not by criticizing the child who is louder but by emphasizing the need for a blended quality within the group, to make the music sound better.

Children may need to be reminded that soft singing should not result in diminished mental alertness. When the music is soft, inexperienced singers sometimes relax to the point of inattention and lose a certain amount of vocal control, to the detriment of the tone quality. A feeling of energy (not strain) must be maintained through the soft passages so that the music conveys a sense of direction and optimum tone quality at every dynamic level.

Putting the Musical Elements Together: Performing

Studying the various aspects of music is important, but putting them together creates music. "Boom Dali Da" (p. 87) contains several features that represent an integration of musical elements.

1. The tempo changes from slow to fast, creating the effect of a meter change from three beats per measure to one beat per measure. In fact, the quarter-note beat speed in the first six measures can be regarded as the dotted half-note beat speed from measure 7 to the end. This triples the pace of the song while keeping the beat speed constant. The children can observe this by tapping at one rate from beginning to end.

2. The melody is interesting, partly because the song is in a minor key and the seventh step of the scale is raised. In the faster section, one-measure patterns are repeated a step lower, giving the music a feeling of continuity and drive.

3. The phrases are of unequal length, creating a feeling of imbalance and surprise. The slow segment consists of three measures that are repeated exactly. The fast section presents phrases of four measures, then three, then six. The total of nineteen measures is an unusual length for a song.

4. Because the text consists of repeated nonsense syllables, no meaning is lost if they are replaced with new words created by the class. The sudden tempo change may suggest a twist within narratives invented by the children for this tune.

5. The absence of story-telling words, the shifts of mood, and the inclusion of accents only on the strong first beat of a measure suggest that this is a dance tune. The children can make up their own steps and motions to convey their interpretation of the music.

6. The song is an excellent one for adding simple instrumental accompaniments. There is the "boom" sound to suggest a timbre, and the tempo change is extreme enough to divide the song into two segments, each of which can have a different instrumental treatment. On a melodic instrument, the note C will blend with every measure of the song except at the

first dotted half note; the D♭ and C will clash there momentarily, but will resolve in the next measure. By considering the note F as an option, in addition to the C, the children can devise their own two-note harmonizing part.

7. The fact that the song is an Israeli folk tune makes it a useful bridge to the study of another culture.

Seldom is a teacher likely to cover all seven features of this song with a class. Such instruction would require several class periods, and while "Boom Dali Da" is a nice song, enough is enough. The ideas can be pursued in other songs that are equally good. The purpose of the endeavor is to help children see that rhythm, pitch, timbre, and dynamic level all combine to form a unique musical work.

Putting the Musical Elements Together: Listening

Often people turn on a radio or record player and insist that they are "listening" to it as they study or talk to friends. Providing oneself with music as a sonic background for other activities is not listening as musicians use that word. Listening means giving the music undivided attention, keen concentration, and contemplative thought. For this reason, music instruction in the elementary school should include experiences that help children listen to music in a more mentally active and analytical way.

Unfortunately, several factors in American society work against the idea of careful listening. First, music is so pervasive in our culture that no one can pay careful attention to all of it. The sounds emanating steadily from business establishments, radio, television sets, and record players provide so many aural stimuli that people find it hard to listen selectively. They simply fall into the habit of "tuning out" many of the sounds that they hear every day. Second, popular songs are generally short and simple. Art music (or what is often called "classical music") tends to be longer and more complex, requiring more concentration. Third, people expect much of today's popular music to be performed loudly. They are not accustomed to noticing music that does not capture their interest through sheer strength of sound. Fourth, much popular music does not present the sophisticated manipulation of sound that is a feature of art music. For these reasons, the idea of listening analytically is foreign to most children and adults.

It is not possible to change society and significantly reduce the amount of music that people hear each day. What is practical, however, is to teach children to listen to different types of music in different ways. Much of the music they hear on the radio or in the supermarket can be given only cursory attention because it does not contain subtle or sophisticated organization. To appreciate music that is carefully crafted, however, the listener needs to give undivided and concentrated attention to the sounds, because there is a depth of expression and compositional skill that cannot be encompassed in one hearing. Such music has a quality that invites examination and discloses new facets with repeated hearings.

Listening is a skill that is developed. That is why children in a music class should be given many opportunities to listen as well as to perform and create music. In fact, the ability to listen is basic if the experiences with performing and creating are to be musically satisfying for the children.

How can children be helped to listen more effectively?

1. Direct them to listen for something specific in the music. Asking youngsters simply to "listen" is too vague a request. They should know ahead of time what features they are expected to notice, as in this example:

   "Here's a piece of music written a long time ago by a man named George Frideric Handel. He composed it for the king of England to listen to as he sailed on the river near his castle in London. The musicians floated along nearby on boats and played the music 'live' for the king to enjoy. That's why the music is known to this day as the 'Water Music.'

   "First listen to the music straight through, so that you'll get an idea of how it goes. At the end, be ready to tell how fast you'd say the music is." [The teacher plays the "Allegro deciso" or thirteenth movement of the *Water Music Suite*. After hearing it the class decides that the tempo was fast.]

   "That's right. The name of this section has 'allegro' in it, which means fairly fast. I'll play the opening part again so that you can learn the opening theme." [The teacher plays the first 20 seconds of the piece twice.]

   "This time I'll let the music go to the end. Close your eyes and listen to whether or not that opening theme comes back. When we're through, I'll ask you if it came back."

   The above example consumes probably the maximum amount of time that should be spent on listening in any one period. On subsequent days the children can discover the syncopated rhythmic figure in several measures of the melody, the fact that sections of the orchestra seem to answer one another, and so on.

2. Limit the number of features that the children are expected to notice in a single hearing. It is better to select fewer aspects and examine them more thoroughly. Kindergarten and first grade children may be able to attend to only one feature at a time. It is good teaching procedure, however, to present the music again and ask the youngsters to notice one or two additional characteristics.

3. Direct the children's attention to musical features. Program music—instrumental music that has nonmusical ideas associated with it—is attractive to children because it suggests images that are familiar to them. Children need to realize, however, that instrumental music cannot truly "tell a story." Only words, which can be sung in a song, have the capability to relate a specific message. Instrumental music can offer only

general impressions. They are so general, in fact, that almost any story can be made to fit a particular instrumental work. When children become preoccupied with attempting to identify certain events in the music with the story or program, it is likely that they are not listening to the work as a piece of music. Furthermore, they are apt to assume that all instrumental music is incomplete, and therefore uninteresting, unless it serves as a backup for song words or narrative events.

If program music is to be played for the class, the teacher might present it with an explanation similar to this one.

> "Today we're going to hear a short piece called 'Circus Polka.' This piece, written by Igor Stravinsky, is not trying to tell us any details about the clowns and animals and trapeze artists. Instead, Stravinsky is giving us his impressions of a circus. The piece may remind you of a circus, but you won't be able to say, 'Now he's telling us about the lion trainer,' or 'There's the music about cotton candy.' Let's listen to the meter of the music. Is it in twos or threes?"

In the preceding example, the teacher has encouraged the children to listen to a program work for its musical qualities, and not for its "story."

4. Play a particular work enough times so that the children become familiar with it. Think of it not only as a means of illustrating compositional features to the class, but also as an artistic experience in itself. The children should hear it often enough to recognize it, remember it, and enjoy it as one of "their" pieces. This is not to say that a work should be repeated until the children tire of it. Rather, the listening repertoire should be varied in number of selections and frequency of appearance. In this way, each listening event will reflect a balance between freshness and familiarity.

What musical selections are best for listening experiences in the primary grades? In general, the pieces should be short enough to be heard within a class period. Extending the listening over several days is possible but not as effective. Children at this age level respond more favorably when the music presents a feature that they can hear rather easily: the second movement of Haydn's "Clock" Symphony, Stravinsky's "Circus Polka," Bach's "Sheep May Safely Graze" from the *Birthday Cantata*, and similar works. Teachers should not assume that twentieth-century works are too difficult or too dissonant for children. Youngsters are in fact receptive to electronic music and other contemporary styles. Most of the music series books designed for use with the primary grades suggest several selections that are appropriate for listening.

Many children have record-playing equipment of high quality in their homes. For this reason, and also so that the music may be rendered adequately, recordings should not be played on inferior equipment at school. Cheap record players and equipment in disrepair are worse than nothing. Each elementary school should purchase at least one quality set of components that can be attached to a cart, rolled from room to room, and locked up when not in use.

Experiences with rhythm, pitch, timbre, and dynamic level, as well as with the skills of performing and listening to music, are all necessary if children in the early grades of elementary school are to establish a solid foundation for their further education in music.

Review Questions

1. (True or False?) Songs in the elementary music series books usually recommend specific dynamic levels.
2. What instruction can be given to help the children exaggerate the difference between loud and soft clapping?
3. When the class is singing a song with echo effects, what can be done to ensure that the echo phrases will indeed be softer than the rest of the song?
4. Describe three techniques to help the children notice differences in dynamic levels.
5. Describe how an accented note should be performed.
6. Why is it difficult for children in the early grades of elementary school to produce extreme differences in dynamic level when they sing?
7. What are some of the causes for the habit of not listening carefully?
8. List four guidelines that should be followed to help children learn to listen to music more fully and accurately.
9. Why should the "program" or "story" associated with program music be de-emphasized when children are learning to listen to music?
10. What are some characteristics of musical works that are especially appropriate for listening by children in the primary grades?

Activities

1. From one of the music series books, select a song that would be suitable for making children more aware of dynamic level, and decide what teaching procedures would be effective in presenting the song.
2. Using twelve consecutive quarter notes, plan two clapping patterns—one simple and another more advanced—that emphasize changes in dynamic level.
3. Find a song that contains some accented notes and is appropriate for children in the lower grades of elementary school. Plan how you would teach the children to notice the accents and to observe them in performance.

4. Referring to the song you selected for either activity 1 or activity 3, select at least two other aspects of music that could be taught through that song.

5. Select a recording of an instrumental work that would be enjoyed by children in the early elementary grades, and prepare to present it as a listening lesson.
   a. Decide which features of the music you want the children to notice.
   b. Decide the steps by which you would present the music to the class.
   c. Estimate how much time would be needed to teach the features you have selected.

8

Re-creating Music Through Singing and Playing

Music teaching shares this basic principle with other areas of the elementary school curriculum: Experiences are the foundation on which intellectual understandings are built. The performance of music through singing and playing instruments, therefore, is a necessary beginning for an education in music.

Intellectual concepts in music and experiences with music must be closely coordinated if the learning activity is to be of value. The performance of music provides the basis for lasting understandings, and such understandings, in turn, help children to perform music better. For this reason, it should not be assumed that children must spend the first several months learning to perform and create music before they can move on to understanding what they have been doing. The relationship should be a reciprocal one, with technical skill and musical insight each contributing to the other.

Most music experiences involve performing or listening to music previously created by someone else. That body of music is large almost beyond comprehension. It includes the folk, art, and religious music of all cultures in all historic periods. Because of this diversity in styles and media (both vocal and instrumental), insight is increased if the children can develop enough skill to re-create the music with some degree of satisfaction.

In this book, as in the elementary classroom, the fundamental skills are considered to be singing, playing simple instruments, and, to some extent, reading music notation. The development of music skills in the early grades is not primarily for the purpose of enabling children to render music faultlessly. Instead, the skills of singing, playing, and reading music are a *means* to greater understanding. Certainly performance skills in music should be developed as fully as possible, given the time available for instruction and the abilities of the class. But the main concern is to see that children learn about the music and enjoy it, rather than that they demonstrate an advanced level of singing or playing.

Singing

Singing is the basic means of performing music in the primary grades. Every child has a voice that he or she has been using for talking, and sometimes singing, by the time music instruction begins in kindergarten or first grade. No financial outlay is required to possess this means of making music, and technical problems are few because there are no fingerings or other overtly mechanical procedures to learn. Perhaps most important, the voice is an extremely personal means of expression. It displays a sensitivity to emotion and a responsiveness that are difficult to achieve on an instrument. Words are usually sung with a melody, and this contributes further to the expressiveness of singing.

Children's voices

It is traditional to describe the quality of children's voices with words like "light," "free," and "clear." These words are as good as any, although none truly describes the quality of the sound. Children at the ages of five through eight are not big enough physically to produce a full, rich tone; they do not have the vocal mechanism or breath capacity for it. To sing more loudly, they must "force" the quality of their voices and produce a distorted sound that is often out of tune. The result is a quality closer to shouting than to singing. If continued, such singing can injure the voice.

Unfortunately, there are not many good examples of children's singing to emulate. The best source appears to be provided by the elementary music series books (see Appendix A), which have accompanying recordings that contain songs sung quite well by children. It is this tone quality that children should attempt to copy, rather than the forced style that is heard so often in popular music.

When properly produced, the singing of children gives an impression of being "floated" out, not forced. It is as though the breath being used for singing would support a feather fluttering a few inches away from the mouth. To achieve this, children need to stand or sit erect when they sing. Standing is an excellent way to attain the straight spine that allows for sufficient breath. The breath should be inhaled as if it is being directed to the area below the rib cage, so that the wall of the abdomen moves *out* as the breath is taken *in* and slowly moves in as air is expelled. The expansion needed for the breath comes not from puffing up the chest or raising the shoulders but from moving the diaphragm down toward the waistline.

The mouth should be quite open. Some teachers maintain that the teeth should be far enough apart to allow two fingers aligned vertically to be inserted between the upper and lower teeth. The actual height of the opening varies according to the word being sung. Except for the wall of the abdomen, there should be little tension, especially in the throat. The attention of the singer should be on maintaining a steady flow of air, not on manipulating the voice box. The idea should be to sing *through* the larynx, not *with* it.

The range of most children's voices extends approximately from middle C to the C an octave higher, although many children encounter difficulty in singing around G or A above middle C. Some children force their voices in an effort to sing higher or lower than their comfortable ranges, but such singing should not be encouraged. As the children mature and learn to sing better, their ranges slowly expand. For many children and adults, a range of about one octave is the usual limit for comfort and pleasant sound.

Even young children can appreciate the difference between singing and talking. The vowels are sustained in singing, but not in speaking. In fact, the vowels in singing should be regarded as being connected to one another in a continuous "stream" until the conclusion of a phrase. This point may need to be worked on in a variety of songs over a period of weeks. One simple procedure is to sing the song or phrase on a neutral syllable instead of with the words. When the flow of singing tone has been achieved, the song should be sung with words and with the same stream of sound. If a steady flow of sound is not achieved, the result is a chopped style in which each syllable is separated briefly from the next. The result is a puffing or panting effect.

OLD MACDONALD

American Song

1. Old Mac - Don - ald had a farm, Ee - i - ee - i -
2. Old Mac - Don - ald had a farm, Ee - i - ee - i -
3. Old Mac - Don - ald had a farm, Ee - i - ee - i -

o, And on that farm he had some chicks,
o, And on that farm he had some ducks,
o, And on that farm he had some pigs,

Ee - i - ee - i - o. With a chick - chick here, and a
Ee - i - ee - i - o. With a quack - quack here, and a
Ee - i - ee - i - o. With an oink - oink here, and an

chick - chick there, Here a chick, there a chick, ev - 'ry-where a chick- chick,
quack-quack there, Here a quack, there a quack, ev - 'ry-where a quack-quack,
oink - oink there, Here an oink, there an oink, ev - 'ry-where an oink - oink,

Old Mac - Don - ald had a farm, Ee - i - ee - i - o.
Old Mac - Don - ald had a farm, Ee - i - ee - i - o.
Old Mac - Don - ald had a farm, Ee - i - ee - i - o.

Selection of songs

The songs in the music series books are graded and carefully selected, but a teacher can be flexible in borrowing music recommended for another grade level. There is room for disagreement among reasonable people as to whether a certain song is better for one grade or for another.

Although there are no exact criteria to employ in making grade-level distinctions, four general factors appear to determine the placement of a song in the music series books. One is the length of the song. Young children are more likely to lose interest when the song is long, so most of the material suggested for this age level is short.

A second factor in determining an appropriate grade level is the amount of repetition in a song. If lines or phrases are repeated, that condition makes learning easier. An example of such a song is "Old MacDonald," in which the response "Ee-i-ee-i-o" appears after each phrase of the text. The children can learn the nonsense phrase quickly and then chime in on it as the entire song is sung by the teacher. Also, the remainder of the song presents only a limited number of musical ideas. "Old MacDonald had a farm" and "On that farm he had some chicks" are sung to the same melody. The "chick-chick" segment is sung almost entirely on one note.

The song "John the Rabbit" features a two-word refrain that stays on

JOHN THE RABBIT

the same pitch and appears six times. The children can join in on the "oh yes" statement with emphasis and feeling.

A third consideration regarding the selection of songs for children is the text. If possible, it should involve something that the children have experienced. It is for this reason that many of the songs in primary grade music books deal with topics of the home, school, and adult occupations that are readily visible in the community. The words in the text should also be understandable to the children. Long, complicated words should be avoided, unless they are vital to the humor of the text—a use epitomized by "supercalifragilisticexpialidocious."

A fourth factor in song selection is the degree of musical complexity. Singing in parts is seldom attempted before the third grade, so songs that depend for their effectiveness on two or more simultaneous melodic lines are best introduced in the later grades. A good preparation for part singing is the experience of performing rounds.

Rounds

A *canon* or *round* is a song in which the same music is sung by different sections of the class starting at different times. Only certain songs can be sung as rounds, but several are included in the music series books. A round is notated like any other song, except for the inclusion of numbers indicating when the second and subsequent groups of singers should start in relation to the progress of the first group. A round can be repeated as often as desired, but traditionally the melody is sung as many times as there are sections participating.

"Good Night" is a typical round. It has three lines, so it will sound best when performed by three groups of singers. The second group starts at the beginning of the song when the first group starts the second line, and

GOOD NIGHT

Old English Round

the third group begins when the first group gets to the third line. The rendition of a round is balanced, with the first group singing the first line alone at the beginning, and the last group singing the last line alone at the end.

The techniques for teaching a round are similar to those for teaching any other song. However, three points should be kept in mind by the teacher. First, the children must know the song thoroughly in unison, and be able to sing it without teacher help, before they attempt it as a round. Second, the youngsters must hold the tempo steady when they sing it as a round. Despite the potential distraction caused by different entrances and exits, the experience is not a race to see who can sing fastest. Third, the children should not cover their ears in an effort to eliminate the sound of other groups. The musical appeal of a round is the harmony that is created automatically as the groups proceed through different portions of the song at the same time. Blocking out the singing of other people negates the point of the class effort, and makes it harder for those children to stay together with their respective groups.

If the class has little experience in singing rounds, the teacher may sing the second part alone while the entire class sings the first part. Or the teacher may sing one part while playing another on the piano with the children. (The teacher may have to practice this double skill alone before the class, and then remind the children to "match the piano part, not my voice.") When the class is first divided, it is better to try only two parts at a time, even on a three-part round. As their experience increases, the children will be able to handle more parts.

The children assigned to begin a round must be especially stable and independent so that they can keep singing as the teacher directs the entrance of the second group. Generally the teacher should assign a larger proportion of reliable singers to the first group, because a round is most likely to break down as the first group enters its second section unaided. Once the round is underway, with the first two groups singing steadily, success is more likely.

Singing by the teacher

Many classroom teachers are reluctant to sing for their students. This hesitancy is seldom due to an actual lack of singing ability, especially among those teachers who had some music training as a part of their undergraduate preparation. Of course this background does not ensure that they will sing as well as a music major who has had years of special instruction in voice. But there are four facts that should be remembered by every classroom teacher who needs encouragement in singing. First, a singer with an operatic quality is not needed in the elementary grades. In fact, an overly mature voice quality complete with full vibrato is not the most suitable model for children because it is too different from the way they sound when they sing. Second, the children don't compare a classroom teacher to some fine soloist. Such models are so infrequent that they are not part of the children's frame of reference. Youngsters are satisfied when the song is sung accurately with a pleasing voice quality. Third, practice by actually "doing" will produce improvement in the teacher's singing as well as in the children's singing. Gradually there will be greater ease in singing, better tone quality, and wider range. Finally, and most important, a teacher's willingness to sing with the children shows them that music is to be shared and enjoyed by people of all ages.

Sometimes teachers prefer to use the piano or a simple instrument such as a set of bells to teach a song. This is acceptable only if the teacher's singing is poor. The tone quality of an instrument differs from the quality of a voice and therefore is not the best example for children to copy. Also, percussive instruments such as the bells and the piano do not sustain pitches well. Their tones begin to fade immediately after being sounded, so they do not produce the continuous stream of sound that is desirable when singing. Finally, children find it more difficult to locate the correct pitch from most instrumental sounds than from most singing voices, a fact that is especially true of bell instruments that sound one or two octaves higher than the voice. An instrumental rendition is better than nothing, but the teacher's singing is the more desirable option.

Teaching songs from recordings

Students in music methods classes often ask, "What about teaching songs from recordings? Isn't that just as good as singing, especially since I'm not a very good singer?" The answer is usually "no." A rendition of a song "live" by the teacher is better for teaching children than is a recording, for the following reasons:

1. Because the teacher is presenting a live performance for the children, it has a greater impact on them than merely hearing a recording. Children have many opportunities to listen to recordings, but seldom do they hear a song sung "in person" just for them.

2. The teacher can start and stop at the ends of phrases and isolate places that need work. It is impossible to locate exact places on a tape or a long-playing record. A song learned from a recording must be mastered by hearing the complete song again and again.

3. Many elementary classrooms do not have sound-reproducing equipment of a quality that does justice to the fine recordings that accompany the music series books. The abilities of recording artists may fail to come through because of inadequate equipment.

4. The accompaniment on a recording may make it more difficult for the children to learn the melody of the song. However, in some stereo re-

cordings it is possible to emphasize either the melody or the accompaniment by moving the balance knob to make one channel predominant.

If a recording is used in the teaching of a song, the learning may be aided if the teacher first introduces the song words. This can be done by visual means if the children are old enough to read. Presenting the words before the children listen to the recording will allow them to devote more of their attention to the music when it is finally played for them. It is best if they do not sing along with the recording the first time it is played. When they do sing with the recording, they should sing softly enough so that they can continue to hear it.

The recordings in the music series albums are helpful not only as aids to teaching songs and as models of singing for the children to imitate, but also as sources for instrumental sounds. The accompaniments for many of the recorded songs are played by excellent musicians and acquaint the children with a variety of instrumental tone colors. Such an accompaniment is rarely possible in the elementary classroom except on a recording.

Introducing a new song

It is a good idea to introduce a new song by promoting those aspects that are most likely to attract the interest of the class. Some thought in the text may be especially appealing. In the following lesson the teacher builds on the children's interest in babies.

> "Today we're going to learn a song that a mother might sing to her baby to help it fall asleep. I'll bet that some of you have little brothers and sisters who have trouble falling asleep sometimes. Maybe your mother sings to them to help them feel sleepier."

HUSH, LITTLE BABY

American Folk Song

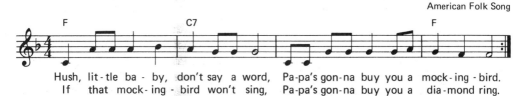

Hush, lit-tle ba-by, don't say a word, Pa-pa's gon-na buy you a mock-ing-bird.
If that mock-ing-bird won't sing, Pa-pa's gon-na buy you a dia-mond ring.

A song may be introduced by first teaching the children a repeated portion of it. For example, in the song on page 105, the words "All night, all day" are sung to exactly the same music each time the phrase appears. The words "Day is dying in the west" and "Sleep, my child, and take your rest" are sung to the same melody, which is merely a more elaborate version of the first four half notes.

In other cases the children might first learn the words and then say them as expressively as they can. Or they might start by listening to a recording of the song. On other occasions they might learn part or all of a song on the bells or some other simple instrument prior to singing it.

Procedures for starting a song

The teacher does not usually conduct children when they sing in a classroom situation. Since the purpose of the singing is to learn about music rather than to prepare for public performance, conducting is not necessary. In addition, conducting suggests a formality that is out of place when the group is small and the children can easily hear voice directions. There is also the practical problem that is encountered when children try to read words and music from a book while watching a teacher's conducting motions.

To help the class start singing a song together, it is best to follow a consistent verbal routine. The particular words involved are not crucial. What matters is that the same routine be followed consistently so that the children become accustomed to it. Before starting to sing a song, they need to know the pitch of the first note, the tempo, and when to start. The pitch can be given by humming or singing the first note on a neutral syllable, or by sounding the note on a bell or piano if necessary. The teacher then sings or speaks *in the tempo of the song* a phrase such as "Rea-dy, sing" or "Rea-dy, go." These directions are usually given on the two beats before the song starts. If the song begins with a pickup note of less than one beat, the music starts at the appropriate moment after the signal. Here is an example of one such beginning.

Procedures for teaching a song

There are several effective ways to teach a song. The choice depends on the nature of the song and the interests and abilities of the children and teacher. In the primary grades, most songs are taught by rote. That is, the teacher sings the song or a phrase of the song while the children listen, and then they attempt to sing it. The procedure is repeated until the entire song is learned. The length of the phrase sung for the children depends on their abilities and on the difficulty of the music. If a song is quite short, it may be sung without interruption. Longer songs are usually broken into phrases.

For example, the song "All Night, All Day" is probably too long to be learned in one segment. The teacher may find it helpful, however, to sing the entire song for the children at first, to give them an idea of how it goes. The rote teaching begins when the teacher sings "All night, all day" (if the children are young and inexperienced) or "All night, all day, angels watching over me, my Lord" (if the children are older and more experienced). The phrase is sung twice for the children before they attempt to sing it themselves. When that phrase is learned satisfactorily, the teacher moves on to the next phrase and repeats the procedure just described. With each new phrase, the previously learned phrases are included at least once in the children's response. At this point the song may be set aside for the rest of the period. It can be refined on subsequent days.

Most of the work toward improving the children's singing of a particular song is done "on the spot" without prior planning. The teacher hears what the children sing, and takes that as a basis for deciding what points in the song need attention. The teacher needs to be analytical enough to detect errors and to know how to correct them. The extent to which a classroom teacher is able to do this depends on his or her training and ability in music. Most classroom teachers improve this skill simply by repeated efforts.

ALL NIGHT, ALL DAY

Here is how one teacher attempts to identify and correct the places at which the children are not singing accurately.

> "Your tone quality was just right that time. But there's one thing we can improve. We didn't all get the third note right. It's the one after 'night.' Listen while I sing the first three notes very slowly. . . .
>
> "Now, while you sing the same notes, hold your hand in front of you like a shelf, like this, and move it up and down as you think the pitch of the note goes. If you think a sound goes up, move your hand up. If you think a sound goes way up, move your hand way up toward the top of your head. Show me with your hand where you think your voice should go. Rea-dy, sing. . . ."

Teaching expressive interpretation of a song

Another aspect of the class effort that may need attention is the expression with which a song is sung. Determining the best tempo and style for a song requires an examination of the text and music. For example, "Hush, Little Baby" (p. 103) is a lullaby, so the tempo should not be rushed, nor should the tone quality be harsh and loud. The children should be encouraged to offer their opinions as to the most appropriate style and expression for a song. Here is an example of how this might be done.

> "In 'Hush, Little Baby' let's pretend that we're singing to a real baby. Joel, should we sing the song loudly like this?" [The teachers sings the song boisterously.] "Or should we sing this way?" [The teacher sings softly.]
>
> "Eboni, should the song go fast like this?" [The teacher sings a phrase at a rapid tempo.] "Or should it move gently like this?" [The teacher sings at a leisurely tempo.]

When the teacher asks for an opinion from the children, it is good to reach general agreement on the point of interpretation. If a child seems mistaken in a choice, a bit of probing—"Why do you think so?"—may uncover a different way of thinking about the song. The teacher should not pass judgment by saying the answer is right or wrong, but should merely ask other children for their ideas, in the hope of securing a more fitting response. If none is given, the teacher should demonstrate an alternative to let the class see its merits. Providing a choice, as the teacher did in the preceding example, helps the children arrive at an appropriate decision. Children may not know what certain words—like "fast," "light," or "pretty"—mean in terms of a song. They need to hear different speeds and styles in order to understand what the descriptive words mean.

The recordings that accompany the book series can serve as examples for appropriate style. In fact, that is one of the values of these recordings. The children should listen carefully to how the song is performed before they sing along with the recording. As with so many other aspects of music, performing with the proper expression is—at least initially—a matter of listening and imitating. It is impossible to describe verbally all the subtleties of how a song should be sung. Most songs, even those that appear to be simple, are too complex to be explained by words that attempt to describe the many nuances of rhythm, tone color, and dynamic level.

Helping out-of-tune singers

Many children in kindergarten and first grade seem unable to sing in tune. In fact, one study estimates that 36.6 percent of children in first grade experience some problem in singing accurately on pitch.[1] The problem gradually disappears for most children, so that by the end of sixth grade that percentage has dropped to about 10 percent. It is encouraging to observe that with music instruction the difficulties with out-of-tune singing are greatly reduced as children progress through school. Less encouraging is the fact that in the meantime they may be acquiring a negative attitude about their musical interests and abilities. Like adults, children tend to dislike activities in which they do not do well, and to enjoy activities in which they can achieve.

Why do children so often have trouble singing on pitch when they enter first grade? There are several reasons.

1. Many parents do not sing to their children as infants. Research data indicate that the amount of music activity in the home has much to do with the child's music capabilities on entering school.[2] Children who have had a limited music background simply need time and experience to gain the ability to sing on pitch.

2. Some children have not yet gained the concept of high and low pitch. They do not understand what they are to do with their voices.

3. Some children seem unable to pay attention well enough to learn a song. It is performed for them, but they fail to concentrate when listening or trying to sing.

4. Some children have not learned the muscle movement necessary to make their voices change pitch accurately. They tend to drone within a narrow pitch range because they are unable to get the voice to sing higher (or occasionally lower).

5. Some children cannot hear the difference between pitches. True monotones—those who are unable to distinguish between pitches at all—are rare. It is true that some people hear pitch more accurately than others, but almost everyone can learn to carry a tune.

6. A few children have vocal problems, such as nodules on the vocal cords, that prevent them from singing well. The nodule condition can be corrected with therapy and/or surgery. If a teacher suspects nodules on a child's vocal cords—a condition manifested by a persistently husky voice

quality—the child should be encouraged to sing only very softly, or to stop singing altogether, until a medical examination can be conducted.

7. A few children demonstrate good pitch discrimination except when they themselves sing. Apparently they lack the normal aural feedback of their own voices. Many of these children can eventually succeed in instrumental performance.

What can be done to help out-of-tune singers? First, they should never be given the idea that something is seriously and irrevocably wrong. After all, most such children will eventually overcome the problem. Children who have trouble carrying a tune should not be singled out in front of their peers. The teacher should not bend over them and sing into their ears, nor should the youngsters be asked to sing in front of the group or to remain silent because their singing doesn't "contribute to the class." If they volunteer to sing alone, they should be encouraged to do so. But the teacher should not mislead them by saying, "That's fine!" when in fact their singing is poor. It is more productive and honest to offer such comments as, "I'm glad you volunteered to sing for us," or "Your words were clear and easy to understand." Even in first grade, children can sense when their singing is faulty. The attitude of the teacher should be, "Let's work to make it better."

Probably the best way to help out-of-tune singers is to work with them privately or in a small group. This can take place during recess or lunch period, so long as the children do not regard the sessions as punishment.

Music specialists differ somewhat on how to help non-singers. Some teachers believe the first step should be to help these children discover what it feels like and sounds like to be in unison with a given pitch. That is what the teacher in this example is trying to do. In this case the teacher sings the pitches, but they may also be played on the piano.

"Peter, sing what you think is your best note—the one that feels most comfortable for you and sounds best to you. When you find it, hold it while I sing that same note. . . .

"Okay. Now listen carefully to how it sounds when you and I are exactly together on that note. The two sounds seem to agree. Try it again." . . . "That's the idea." . . . "Now let me sing the note again and you match it." . . . "Better. Do it again. . . .

"Now let's move up one note from the pitch that we've been singing. Think of moving your voice up just a short step."

If the child is able to move up a step and match pitch, then another note, perhaps the next step higher, can be attempted. Sometimes it helps if the child rather than the teacher plays the note on the piano. Also, the child may find that putting a hand over one ear helps focus attention on his or her own voice.

Other music specialists have observed that children in the first grade seem to have two types of voices, a "chest" or "speaking" voice and a "head" or "singing" voice. The "singing" voice is about five notes higher than the "speaking" voice. After the children learn to recognize the difference between the two voices, they can be encouraged to use the singing voice for music. A teacher might say to a child who is droning in a chest voice, "That's your speaking voice; now try it with your singing voice." Either the pitch-matching procedure or the "singing-voice" procedure appears to work when applied consistently.

After the sensation of unison pitch-matching or using the singing voice has been experienced, other techniques can be tried.

1. Ask the child to imitate a siren by gradually raising and lowering the pitch level of his or her voice. This promotes the concept of changing pitch level without requiring the child to match exact pitches.

2. Invite the child to indicate with his or her hands the approximate pitch level of what is being heard or sung. One pattern can be sung to the words "Bounce my ball." As the words are sung, the child makes a bouncing motion with his or her hands, palms down, but with the height above the floor regulated by the relative pitch levels. A wide interval, even an octave, works well in this routine because the rhythmic flow gives a feeling of energy and momentum, and the sudden leap in pitch encourages vocal flexibility.

Bounce   my   ball!

3. Give the out-of-tune singer extra practice on the echo patterns that are sung in music class to help all children sing pitches more accurately. (See p. 53).

4. Tape record the out-of-tune singer during these practice sessions if the child does not become self-conscious. Listening to oneself on a recording makes self-evaluation more objective.

5. Suggest that the out-of-tune singer make up a short tune to sing. Sometimes a child who sings on only one pitch will make up tunes that require singing on a variety of pitches.

6. Ask the child to imitate the sound of a cuckoo—the descending interval found in so many children's songs around the world.

7. Invite the out-of-tune singer to pick out familiar tunes at the piano or on the bells. These instruments provide visual and physical reinforcement of the distance between pitches.

Some children may need special help for several months. Some may achieve the unison sensation once or twice, only to lose it by the next day. Patience is needed to help the children who find it hard to sing on pitch. The efforts at helping them are well worth the teacher's attention, however, because their outlook toward music in later years will benefit from early correction of singing difficulties.

Major Scales

A *scale* is a series of pitches that move up or down according to a specified pattern of intervals. Eight-tone scales are the most common, and they can be built on any note, which then becomes the *tonal center, tonic, key center,* or *keynote.* Consecutive numbers are often assigned to the notes or *steps* of a scale to show the relationships that occur among them. Here is a scale built on C:

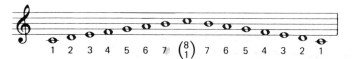

When eight-tone scales are written on the staff, there must be a note on every line and space between the low and high keynotes, so that every alphabet letter is represented in the scale. For example, there cannot be a G and a G♯ in the same scale, because then some other letter would be left out entirely. An eight-tone scale has only seven different letters because the eighth step has the same name as the first.

A *major scale* reveals this pattern of whole and half steps:

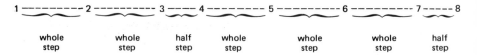

| whole step | whole step | half step | whole step | whole step | whole step | half step |

The eight consecutive notes produce only seven intervals, since two sounds are necessary to produce any one interval.

A scale can also be pictured as a flight of stairs. The steps of a major scale are not of equal height, however, because the distance between 3–4 and 7–8 is only a half step.

The arrangement of whole and half steps can be experienced easily by playing a C major scale on the piano. There is no black key

Playing Classroom Instruments

Instrument playing is included in elementary music classes so that the children can learn to supplement and enrich a song, not so that they can gain technical facility for its own sake. Instrumental activity is time-consuming, requiring assignment of instruments, instruction in their use, and taking turns so that several children can share the experience. Time

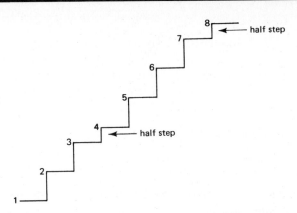

between the adjacent white keys of E–F and B–C, indicating that those two sets of white keys are tuned only a half step apart. When C is step 1 of the scale, those two half step intervals occur between steps 3–4 and steps 7–8, producing the interval pattern for a major scale.

An ascending major scale is present in the bracketed portion of "The First Noël," and a descending major scale is evident in the opening phrase of "Joy to the World."

D is the keynote in each of these carols, and two sharps (F♯ and C♯, shown to the right of the clef sign) enable the pitches to conform to the major scale pattern. Their presence causes the half steps to occur between steps 3–4 (F♯–G) and 7–8 (C♯–D).

seems to be in short supply in most elementary classrooms, and must be allocated carefully. Nevertheless, experience with instruments is of sufficient value to warrant the extra time and inconvenience that this type of activity entails.

In kindergarten and first grade, much of the instrument playing is done by the teacher. Gradually the children are introduced to playing short phrases and easy parts on an instrument. The guideline to follow in select-

Classroom Rhythm Instruments

Rhythm instruments produce no specific pitches. The rhythm instruments used most often in the classroom are listed below according to the manner in which their tone is produced.

Instruments that are shaken:

Maracas—Rattles, often in pairs, that are shaken to produce the sound of moving pellets.

Sleigh bells or jingle bells—Small spherical bells attached to a strap or frame and shaken.

Tambourine—A skin or membrane stretched across a wooden hoop rimmed with metal discs that produce a jangling sound when the instrument is shaken, struck on the center with the knuckles, tapped with the fingers, or played with mallets.

Instruments that are scraped:

Guiro (*Gwee*-roh)—A notched gourd scraped with a stick.

Sandblocks—Flat metal or wood surfaces over which sandpaper is stretched to create a scratching sound when two are rubbed together.

Instruments that are struck:

Castanets—Two small wooden cup-shaped pieces struck together against the leg or palm of the hand, or held in one hand and tapped together by the fingers, or (if attached to a handle) struck together by a whip-like motion of the player's wrist.

Claves (*clah*-vays)—Two cylindrical wooden blocks, one of which is supported lightly in the hand and struck with the other block.

Coconut shells—Two hollow half-spheres that can be struck together on their open ends, hit singly on a flat surface, or struck on the outside with a mallet.

Cymbals—Large metal discs struck together, or suspended singly and hit with a mallet or brush.

Drum—A skin or membrane stretched over a frame and struck with the hand or a beater.

Finger cymbals—Two small metal discs struck against each other on their edges to produce a high-pitched bell-like sound.

Rhythm sticks—Two dowel rods that are hit against each other.

Temple blocks and wood block—Wood blocks struck with a mallet to produce a hollow, resonant sound.

Triangle—A three-sided suspended metal frame struck with a beater to produce a clear metallic tone. The impression of a continuous sound is achieved by repeated strokes, in rapid succession, alternating between the adjacent sides of an inside corner.

1. Alto Metallophone
2. Alto Xylophone Diatonic
3. Soprano Xylophone Diatonic
4. Cymbal, 14"
5. Rotary Timpani, 20"
6. Rotary Timpani, 16"
7. Tambourine, 12"
8. Cymbals, 8"
9. Hand Drum, 14"
10. Hand Drum, 12"
11. Hand Drum, 13"
12. Box Rattle
13. Sleigh Bell Wristlets
14. Finger Cymbals
15. Sleigh Bell Spray
16. Tubular Woodblock
17. Bell Spray
18. Woodblock
19. Castanet
20. Claves
21. Soprano Glockenspiel Diatonic
22. Alto Glockenspiel Diatonic
23. Alto Xylophone Diatonic
24. Triangle, 6"
25. Triangle, 8"

ing or creating instrumental parts for primary school children to play is: *Keep it simple.* At first, only one or two instruments should be played at the same time.

An example of how instruments can be worked into music instruction can be seen through the song "Are You Sleeping?" (See p. 40). The song is in the key of F. That pitch can be sounded on the first beat of each measure throughout the song. If the child playing the instrument senses the beat clearly, he or she can think (and even say softly), "Play, rest, play, rest," and so on. If that procedure does not work, the teacher can point to the child each time the note is to be sounded. Several different instruments can sound the note F for "Are You Sleeping?", including bells and piano.

The suggestion in the preceding paragraph—that the teacher direct the child each time a note is to be played—is typical of the amount and type of help that needs to be given when children first begin to play instruments. Much of the teacher's attention will need to be devoted simply to keeping the player on the beat so that an incorrectly played part does not confuse the singers. To limit the amount of distraction, it is important that the class have the song learned thoroughly before an instrumental part is added. Also, it is often necessary to take a minute or two of class time to let the instrument player practice the part, even though that part may seem extremely simple to the teacher.

The teacher should give each child an equal opportunity to play the instruments. This means that the less musically able youngsters, as well as the talented children, must have a chance to play. It is advisable to select the more able students to perform the part the first time or two it is played. This gives the class an idea of how the music should sound, and helps the other children learn the part so they can play it better when their turn comes.

Some children have started to take piano lessons by the time they are in first or second grade. These children should be given the opportunity to play with the class. Such an activity reinforces what they have learned, demonstrates to the other children the practical advantages of piano study, and contributes to the music class. Even children not studying piano can be taught to play a simple one-finger part like the one-note repeated accompaniment suggested for "Are You Sleeping?" (p. 40).

The song "All Things Bright and Beautiful" (p. 115) moves essentially by step, making it relatively easy to play as well as to sing. The same song sounds good with a descending scale—one note per measure—played on the bells.

Despite the presence of eight different notes, the part is relatively easy because each note is played "in order." One child might play all eight notes,

ALL THINGS BRIGHT AND BEAUTIFUL

Words by Cecil F. Alexander   William Tyndale

1. All things bright and beau - ti - ful, All crea - tures great and small,
2. Cold wind in the win - ter, The pleas - ant sum - mer sun,

All things wise and won - der - ful, The Lord God made them all.
Ripe fruits in the gar - den; He made them ev - ery one.

Music copyright © 1966 by Gulf Music Co. Used by permission.

or eight children might be invited to play one note each. Bells are more appropriate than a sustained vocal sound for this scale passage, because in several measures the initial note clashes with the chords implicit in the last half of the measure. Again, the children may need to be given a clear signal for each note they are to play. The scale pattern may also be played so that the notes occur in ascending order as an introduction, coda (ending), or interlude between verses.

Music Reading

Music reading refers to the ability to look at music notation and reproduce it in sound. This skill is not essential for the performance of music, but it is a valuable aid and a desirable outcome of music instruction in the elementary school. When children can read music, they can learn new songs more quickly and more independently, with less help from the teacher. The ability to read music expands the child's opportunities for participating in music and enjoying it.

Learning to read music is similar to learning to read language, in that both skills require the development of sound/symbol associations. A child learns that a dog is a particular type of animal and that a certain vowel/consonant combination of sounds stands for that animal. Later the child

Classroom Melody Instruments

In contrast to rhythm instruments, melody instruments produce definite pitches. The melody instruments used most often in an elementary classroom are:

Glockenspiel and bells—Metal strips arranged in keyboard fashion and slightly upraised from their supporting frame so that they can vibrate freely when struck with a mallet. In a set of resonator bells, each bar is mounted on a separate hollow block which can be removed from the set for individual use.

Xylophone—Similar to the glockenspiel except that its bars are of wood and are mounted on resonating devices.

Recorder (and songflute, flutophone, Tonette)—A wind instrument with finger holes that can be covered in various combinations to alter the length of the air column and thereby change the pitch.

Piano—A keyboard instrument capable of producing 88 pitches, each sounded by the action of a hammer hitting against strings.

In addition to the piano and autoharp, the following string instruments are appropriate for accompanying singing because they can produce several notes simultaneously.

Ukulele and guitar—Strings stretched on a hollow wooden body for resonance, and plucked or strummed with the fingers.

learns that the letters d-o-g, when combined, are a visual representation of that sound and concept.

Reading music notation is more complex than reading language, however. Music notation indicates both pitch and rhythm, and offers some idea as to how the music should be performed. Most of these directives are written in a nonverbal code that uses symbols peculiar to music. Song words are divided by hyphens when they are more than one syllable long, and are placed below the staff of music. This placement requires the eyes to move up and down, as well as laterally from left to right.

Music reading, even in the best school music programs, is taught for much less time than the reading of language, perhaps because the advantage of music reading in the world outside of school is not nearly as evident as is the need to read words. Children see adults read newspapers, books, and signs much more often than they see them read music. Even then, with large amounts of skilled instruction and a high level of reinforcement by society, many children have trouble learning to read language well. Therefore, because of the greater difficulty of music reading and the lesser amount of time and importance given it, it is not surprising that few children in the primary grades possess the ability to read music.

Teaching music reading

When does instruction in reading music begin? In a way, it begins when the child first hears music, just as learning to read begins when a child first encounters speaking. Aural experience is the basis for a successful reading effort in both music and language.

Direct instruction in music reading usually begins in a limited way in the first grade, when the children are shown selected notation symbols in large print, as well as illustrated material in books. As with reading language, intensive efforts must wait until there has been sufficient development of the eye muscles to allow for focusing on smaller print.

Some "primer" type music books are available for children in kindergarten and first grade, but books are not usually placed in the children's hands until second grade. In no sense are second graders expected to *sight-read* the music; that is, to perform it unaided on first encounter, solely by observing the notation. Rather, the books contain the song words, which many of the children can read, as well as the notation. The presence of the notation acquaints the children with its appearance and gives them an impression of how the system represents pitches and rhythms.

There is an additional complication in music reading, however. Music reading involves understanding relationships as well as learning fixed meanings. The notes E and G on the staff are fixed designations and can be identified rather easily by someone with a rudimentary knowledge of note names. It is harder to sense an interval in terms of sound and to reproduce the two pitches accurately. Music notation also presents relationships in its rhythm values. A child may be able to identify a quarter note at sight, but useful reading will not occur until the child can interpret that symbol by reproducing a sound of the proper duration in the context of a given meter and tempo.

Music reading can be taught through singing or playing simple instruments, or both. The voice requires less technical skill development on the part of the children than do most instruments, because in singing there are no keys to push down or bars to strike. When singing, however, the children do not have the benefit of the fixed pitches found on most instruments. Nor do they have the additional reinforcement of the physical sensation of spatial distance that occurs when they produce an interval on a keyboard-like instrument.

As with most skill-learning, frequent practice is necessary if children are to develop their ability to read music. The eyes must learn to move efficiently, the mind must learn to interpret the symbols quickly, and the

Major Key Signatures

The *key signature* is the group of sharps or flats placed after the clef at the beginning of the staff. Every flat or sharp in a key signature applies to its particular note throughout the piece, unless it is later cancelled with a natural sign. The key signature indicates the tonal center of a composition.

The key of C major requires no sharps or flats. The other major keys can be identified as follows: if the signature contains sharps, the last sharp to the right is step 7 of the major scale, so the keynote is one half step above that sharp. If the signature contains flats, the last flat to the right is step 4 of the major scale, so the keynote can be located by counting up to step 8 or down to step 1. If there is more than one flat, the major keynote will have the same name as the next-to-last flat in the signature.

The key signatures for all major keys are illustrated below. An examination of the chart will show that sharps and flats do not appear in the same signature. Furthermore, the order in which flats appear in a signature is the reverse of the order in which sharps appear. From left to right in a key signature, the order of sharps is F♯, C♯, G♯, D♯, A♯, E♯, and B♯; the order of flats is B♭, E♭, A♭, D♭, G♭, C♭, and F♭. The order of flats is easy to remember because the first four spell the word "bead." An acronym for the order of sharps is: Fat Cows Get Drowsy After Eating Breakfast.

ear must learn to anticipate the sound that is intended by the visual code. There is no magic process in learning to read music, nor is there only one way in which it can be accomplished. Any one of several different approaches will do the job, if it is practiced persistently. Once a system for music reading has been started, it should not be mixed with other systems. Consistency of approach will reduce the amount of confusion for the children.

Skills are acquired gradually, not in one or two large breakthroughs. The teaching of music reading in the primary grades is the beginning of a process that will extend over several years, and the amount of music reading skill eventually achieved will vary from one student to another. Most people can detect some meaning from looking at notation, but almost no one can read difficult music flawlessly.

NOTES

1. A. Oren Gould, *Finding and Learning to Use the Singing Voice: A Manual for Teachers* (Washington, D.C.: Office of Education, OEC 6-10-016, 1968).
2. Ibid.

Review Questions

1. Why is singing the basic means of performing music in the primary grades?
2. What is the approximate range of children's voices in the first and second grades? What are the characteristics of their voices?
3. What types of song texts are especially suitable for children in the primary grades?
4. Describe the movement of the abdominal wall when a person is singing correctly.
5. Why is an operatic voice not especially appropriate as a model for children?
6. For teaching purposes, why is a live vocal performance of a song preferable to a rendition on the bells? to hearing the song on a recording?
7. What are the basic procedures for teaching a song by rote?
8. Approximately what percentage of all children entering first grade can be expected to have trouble singing on pitch?
9. What are some reasons for pitch problems in children's singing?
10. Cite five techniques for helping children learn to sing on pitch.
11. What musical instruments are most likely to be available in primary grade classrooms?
12. In what ways is learning to read music similar to learning to read language?

13. At what grade level are music books usually made available to the children?

14. What are some reasons for the fact that reading music is more difficult than reading words?

15. Why is it desirable for children to start learning to read music in the primary grades?

Activities

1. Examine one of the music series books designed for first, second, or third graders. Select one song to teach to the methods class. Decide what steps you will take to ensure that the class will learn the song easily and sing it well.

2. Practice the procedures for singing. Referring to the song you selected for activity 1, decide how you might teach the methods class to sing better by applying the principles of good vocal technique to specific aspects of that song.

3. Select one round from a music series book designed for a primary grade. Learn the round, then teach it to the methods class.

4. Work with another class member and learn his or her song. Sing it to the best of your ability and let your partner offer suggestions for improvement. Reverse roles and repeat the procedure.

5. Select another song, one for which you can introduce a simple instrumental part. (The index of a music series book will help you locate such arrangements.) Teach the song to the methods class, then select students to play the instrumental part.

6. Evaluate the performance of two songs sung by the methods class.

Skill Exercises

1. Practice playing these exercises on the bells or piano.

2. Sing the music examples above on a neutral syllable while playing them on the bells or piano.

9

Creating Music

C reativity is a troublesome word because it is used in many ways. Sometimes it is intended to define the tangible result of a monumental effort, like writing a novel or composing a symphony; sometimes it implies only that an idea or product is original to a given person. At times it seems to be merely a synonym for "different."

Difficult though it may be, it is necessary to devise a definition of creativity for use in this book. A short, practical definition is: "a thought, product, or action that is original to the person who produces it." According to this definition, the child who makes a sandcastle is being creative, even though a million other children have made sandcastles. The child who copies another person's sandcastle is not being creative.

In music, there are two types of creative experience: *composing* and *improvising*. The difference between these words is the amount of thought and planning that goes into the creative effort. Composing implies careful, thoughtful preparation of music. Such preparation means either writing the music down on paper or preserving the composition on tape. A person who improvises, on the other hand, makes up music extemporaneously without prior planning. The performance setting is likely to be casual, with no attempt to preserve the musical result. Improvising is usually based on pre-existing guidelines for the type of music being performed, so the performer/improvisor does not make up music out of thin air. Both composing and improvising are important in the world of music, and can be incorporated in a rudimentary form into the elementary classroom.

The Value of Creativity in the Curriculum

There is little disagreement about the value of the creative efforts of people like Ludwig van Beethoven, Thomas Edison, and Leonardo da Vinci. The human race has been bettered by their accomplishments. But what about the value of the creative efforts of most people, especially those of youngsters? Is a child struggling with bells in some way to be compared with the great Beethoven? Are the painted paper plates that children bring home from school as valuable as paintings by Rembrandt or Cezanne?

From the standpoint of inherent artistic worth, the phrases on the bells and the painted paper plates are of virtually no value. However, creative activities are included in music instruction not for the artistic product that may result, but for the benefits that accrue to the child through the act of creating.

One value of creative effort in music is that it encourages individuals to express their own musical thoughts. When trying to create music, people are drawing on their own ideas and manipulating an art form in a personal way. This is an enriching experience in life. Music involves learning not only to reproduce or listen to what others have created, but also to organize sounds for one's own satisfaction. Children should have opportunities to try out their musical ideas.

A second reason for creative activity is the fact that what a child makes seems more valuable to him or her. The paper that third-grader Amy writes on "What I Did Last Summer" is more meaningful to her than what someone else wrote on the topic. By creating something that is uniquely hers, she has contributed to her self-image as a productive and competent person.

A third value of creative effort is the contribution that it makes to the learning of music. When a person is creating music, whether it be a one-measure ostinato with two pitches or an entire cantata, the mind is engaged in much trial and error in considering sounds and how they can best be organized to express what the person has in mind. In short, when people are trying to create music, they are thinking intently about sounds and their organization, which is the essence of music. They are doing such thinking to a greater degree than they usually do when studying what someone else has composed or performed.

For these reasons, then, opportunities to create music should be a part of each child's education.

Adding Creative Elements to Existing Music

The idea of asking children to create music may seem like an unrealistic hope. How can children write music when they don't know how to read notation and can hardly sing an entire song accurately? The answer is: They should not be asked to do so, unless the creative effort is structured and unless the teacher provides much help. Asking children to compose an entire song is one thing; asking them to manipulate a few sounds is quite another. So the basic principle for guiding creative activities in music is this: *Start with short, simple tasks in which the children have a limited number of options.* When they succeed in simple creative efforts, they can move on to more complicated tasks and eventually to complete songs.

One way to introduce creativity into music instruction is to add original ideas to songs the children already know. A song like "Jump Down, Turn Around" (p. 124) is good for adaptation. Because it is short and simple, more children will be able to try out their ideas within the limited time available.

JUMP DOWN, TURN AROUND

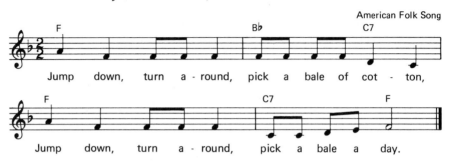

American Folk Song

Four distinct ways of varying the song coincide with the elements of music: rhythm, timbre, pitch, or dynamic level can be altered, either singly or in combination. Here is an example of how such changes might be introduced:

"For several days now, we've been singing 'Jump Down, Turn Around.' Now I'm going to sing the song for you with some changes in it. Some of the notes will be higher or lower than we've been singing them. It won't be a mistake, because I'm making the change on purpose. Listen and tell me where I made the change." [The teacher sings the two notes on "cotton" one octave higher.]

[The children identify the word on which the changed notes appeared, and all sing the revised version.]

"Now see what *you* can do to make some changes in the song. The important thing about these changes is that they will be *your* ideas; they will come from inside your heads. Remember that you're going to change only how high or low *some* of the notes are. Change just a couple of notes and keep everything else the same, the way I did."

"I'll give you a minute or two to think through silently to yourself *one* change in the pitches of 'Jump Down, Turn Around' that you would like to try. When you have your change in mind, you can sing it to us and we'll all do it together. Okay, think of your change for a minute." . . . "Jeremy, what change did you think up?" [Jeremy sings "pick a bale of cotton" with all notes on the same pitch.]

The teacher should show enthusiasm for Jeremy's suggestion and confirm it by replaying the phrase on the bells or piano to make sure that everyone understands what is wanted. If the children can follow notation, the new version can be written on the chalkboard. After hearing the changed version once or twice, the children can try to sing it with the alterations.

The rhythm of "Jump Down, Turn Around" seems especially suitable for a repeated pattern. Clapping the rhythm pattern of the notes will probably suggest to the children a simple figure that they can clap or play on instruments. A possible two-measure ostinato is:

The song can be repeated a sufficient number of times to accommodate the children's ideas for variations in loudness. Perhaps they will want a gradual increase or decrease in the dynamic level, or a sudden change in this aspect of the music. They can be encouraged to experiment with instruments as a means of altering the timbre.

The teacher should be prepared for a variety of responses when children are asked to alter a song. Any response made in good faith should be accepted, because participation is more important than adherence to a compositional plan. For example, a child may suggest sweeping changes that are unrelated to the original. In such a case, the teacher can point out the different character of the new version, and briefly discuss its merits with the class. Sometimes changes in rhythm and pitch are proposed, when only a change in pitch has been requested. The teacher can help the class discover that the changes are more extensive than the recommendation. Even though the changes exceed or stray from what was requested, they should be treated as genuine efforts, because in no way does a teacher want to discourage creative ideas.

In addition to altering an element in the music, the class can also vary the words. Children in the primary grades enjoy doing this, especially if humorous words are encouraged, and they are surprisingly good at it. One or two words may be changed, or an entire new set of words can be created. Here a teacher is trying to stimulate interest in the song by substituting humorous words.

"There are songs that have silly words, songs that people sing just for the fun of it. 'Jump Down, Turn Around' is an enjoyable song that isn't serious, but it isn't funny either. Let's change the words at the end of the first line, 'pick a bale of cotton,' to something else—maybe something silly. Remember, the new words that you choose need to have six parts or syllables, just as 'pick a bale of cotton' does. I'll give you a minute to think of a new set of words that fit where 'pick a bale of cotton' is now. . . . Trevor, what's your idea for new words?"

"How about 'pet a noisy donkey'?"

"All right, here's how the new words go: 'Jump down, turn around, pet a noisy donkey.' Let's sing them in the song to see if they work." [The class sings the song with the new words.]

"Now we need to replace the last group of words: 'pick a bale a day.'
We need five syllables. Take another minute now and think of a good
ending for your song. . . . Bonnie, what are your new words?"
"Pet it carefully." [The class sings the song with Bonnie's words.]

In addition to changing the words and altering the various musical
elements, the children can think up short introductions, conclusions, and
ostinatos (short repeated patterns). Actually, a one- or two-measure ostinato
figure can be extended to serve as an introduction or coda to the song.

Integrating Creative Activities with Other Arts

One way to stimulate creativity is to paint or draw to music. The point
of this activity is to encourage the children to respond to what they hear by
expressing their feelings visually—not necessarily in concrete images but
in the liberal use of color, space, and motion. The teacher in this lesson has
given each child two sheets of manila paper, and has provided a variety of
colored chalk. The children are invited to sit on the floor to draw, or to use
one of the available tables.

"Today we're going to listen to two different pieces of music and just let
our minds wander. Think how the music 'looks' to you. Don't begin
using the chalk until after you've heard some of the music. When you're
ready to put your thoughts and feelings on paper, just start drawing.
You don't need to make a picture of anything, although you may do that
if you want to. Just try to show the feeling of the music you're hearing."

Two appropriate musical selections for this activity are the "Waltz"
from *Swan Lake* by Tchaikovsky, and the "Hoe Down" from *Rodeo* by
Copland. The two sets of drawings can be compared and discussed in terms
of how they differ in style according to the qualities of the music they are
expressing.

A second activity, explained more fully in Chapter 6, consists of adding sound effects to stories or poems.

Another way to encourage creativity is to have the children engage in
interpretive movement or dancing. The children try to express with their
bodies what they think the music is "saying." This activity is more than just
marching or keeping time with the music. Rather, after careful listening, the
children make motions and adopt physical attitudes that to them reflect the
music. Such bodily expression is an individual matter, not subject to a group
decision-making process. Because younger children are usually less inhib-
ited about such activities, the idea seems to work better with kindergart-
ners and first graders than with fourth or fifth graders.

Free rhythmic movement is generally more successful in a small group
in which the teacher can observe the children easily. Large group efforts are

sometimes dominated by one or two of the more aggressive or able children, and such a situation should be discouraged. Also, care must be taken so that the activity does not turn into a free-for-all with children bumping and pushing one another. The available space must be estimated realistically. Where floor space is limited, one solution is to have only a few children engage in free activity while the others sing, chant words, or clap. Another aid is to give the children "space-saving" ideas such as walking in place instead of moving around the room. They can even act out the motions of dancers with their hands on desktops.

Here is how a free movement activity might be introduced:

> "Today we're going to move freely to music. So let's stand and spread out so that you have some distance between yourself and the person closest to you. Now, while you're standing quietly and listening to the music, think how you can show the idea of the music with *just your arms*. If the music seems fast and jumpy, then move your arms that way. If the music seems big and fluffy like a cloud, then move your arms like that and show us a cloud. Ready? Listen carefully. When you feel you have the motions in mind, show me with your arms." [The teacher plays a recording of *Pavane for a Dead Princess* by Ravel. The music is slow and flowing, suggesting movements that are expansive and graceful.]

Experience with expressive movement can be extended by involving more parts of the body than just the arms, by letting the children move about the room, and by providing music of a contrasting character. Children also enjoy impersonating animals and their actions. A direction such as "Gallop like a happy horse" or "Walk like a tired elephant" allows children to express a more specific idea in movement.

Creating Original Music

Spontaneous singing

Many children, even before entering school, engage in spontaneous singing. A child playing alone may sometimes be heard humming or singing quietly. This improvised singing is a natural creative act and should be encouraged. Here is how this might be done.

> "Kyu, I heard you singing about the rain that we're having today. It's a good idea to sing about things. Do you suppose you could sing your song about the rain for the whole class to hear?" [Kyu agrees, but does not sing the same tune that the teacher heard. He does repeat the words sung before: "Wet rain, go away, I want to play."]
>
> "That was a nice song, Kyu. Does anyone else have a song about the rainy day we're having?"

The fact that Kyu did not repeat his previous tune is typical. The previous singing was a fleeting musical expression that he didn't try to remember. But by asking him to sing it for the class, the teacher encouraged Kyu and indicated to the other members of the class that creativity is valued.

Sound exploration

Children have a natural curiosity about their environment, including sounds. They should be encouraged to explore the classroom for the sound-making possibilities it offers. The children can devise games in which they identify what they hear without seeing it. They can rap pencils against flower pots, chair legs, and ventilator grillwork; they can crinkle paper, turn a noisy doorknob, hit chalk erasers together and the like. They should not overlook the possibilities for making sounds with their bodies—clapping hands, stomping feet, snapping fingers, clucking tongues on the roof of the mouth, hissing, whistling, slapping thighs, rapping knuckles on the elbow, and so on. Here is how such an exploration might be organized.

> "There are all sorts of ways to make sounds right here in our room. I'll give you a couple of minutes to go around the room on your own and find three different ways to make sounds. Remember what your three ways are, then come back to your seats and we'll make a list of all those ways." [The children move about the room testing different ways of making sounds.]
>
> "All right, now let's make that list of sounds. I'll ask each of you for one way to make sounds, then I'll go around again to find out your other sounds. Delia, what was the first way that you found?" [Delia suggests tapping on the table with a pencil, and the list grows, but none of the ideas involves making sounds with the body.]
>
> "That's quite a list. But you know what? You forgot some ways of making sounds, maybe because they're as close as the nose on your face. Who can think of more ways that are here in this room right now?" [Eventually Jeffrey remembers that he can make sounds by clapping and snapping his fingers, and this unleashes a spate of body-sound suggestions from the class.]

Random sounds are not music, of course. To become music, they need to be organized. The distinction might be stressed to children in this way.

> "Even though we have a good list of sounds, we still don't have music. If we're going to make them into music, we have to decide first which sounds we're going to use. They should be sounds that all of us can produce at our seats. Pick out your favorite. Betsy?"
>
> "Slapping your leg."
>
> "Okay. Gary, what's your favorite?"
>
> "Stomping my foot on the floor."

"Mark, how about you?"

"Hitting knuckles on the table."

"Good. Let's review the three sounds. First, all of you slap your leg, then stomp your foot, and hit your knuckles on the table.

"Now, how do you want to arrange the sounds? Keep it simple at first, to be sure we can all stay together on our three-sound composition." [Susan suggests performing the sounds, one after another, in an even rhythm.]

"All right, let's do Susan's pattern three times, ending with the first sound to finish off the piece. It will go "*One* two three, *one* two three, *one* two three, *one*.' Got that? All together now, rea-dy go."

On subsequent days the three-sound composition may be expanded, as shown in this example.

"Do you remember the three sounds that you thought up yesterday? Today we'll try the sounds that some of the rest of you have in mind, but this time we'll try to make our piece a little fancier. What three sounds do you want?" [The children suggest a cluck of the tongue, a clap, and a hiss.]

"Three good sounds. Now think for a minute what we can do with them. We can make them more than once; we can make one of the sounds loud and others soft; we can make one sound longer than the others—yes, the hiss is the only sound we can lengthen—or we can make two of the sounds together, except a person can't do the cluck and the hiss at the same time. But we can do *almost* anything we want to with the sounds."

[The class decides to produce this familiar rhythm with the sounds indicated:]

As the children progress in their ability to organize simple sounds, they can begin to evaluate their pieces and to decide what can be done to make them better. The teacher can introduce certain compositional concepts, although the terms for the concepts need not be introduced in the primary grades.

[Leon's piece includes whistling, finger snapping, and a foot sliding on the floor. At his suggestion, each sound has been produced twice in succession.]

"What could we do to make Leon's piece more interesting? Katie?"

"We could make each sound three times."

"All right, let's do each sound three times in a row. Here's the speed." [The teacher gives the tempo through three preparation beats, and the class performs the modified version of Leon's piece.]

"Did we make the piece more interesting by adding an extra sound each time?" [The class responds that the change didn't make a lot of difference.]

"That's true; we didn't change it very much by repeating the same sound more often. Maybe we need to mix up the order of the sounds. This will make some variety, or surprise, for the listener. Who can think of a way to do this?" [Leon volunteers to amend his original piece by proceeding "whistle-snap-slide-snap-whistle."]

"That's a good idea, Leon. It makes a balanced design that the listener can follow. Let's do the piece this new way, then describe the design that it makes." [The class performs the revised version, which the children describe as "going frontways and then turning around," and "going back and forth on a swing."]

"Good! Now let's work the opposite way. I'll describe a design first, then you figure out how to arrange the same three sounds to make that design. Are you ready? Okay: Make a *sandwich* piece of nine sounds—three for the bread, three for the peanut butter, and three for the bread again. The first three sounds and the last three sounds should match, because the slices of bread are just the same."

[The children offer various "sandwich" arrangements such as "whistle-snap-whistle, slide-slide-slide, whistle-snap-whistle."]

The same process can be followed to construct pieces of more complexity. The class can advance to more sounds, longer sections, more complex forms, and varied rhythms. With increased experience, children can devise rather sophisticated and interesting sound pieces.

Improvising

Another way to encourage creativity in music is to ask the children to improvise measures or short phrases in response to musical statements provided by the teacher or another child. Initially these efforts involve only rhythm, and the response is clapped or tapped. In this way the technical problems of performing are reduced to a minimum. The opening musical statement sets the tempo and style for the response. If asked to improvise without any idea of what is expected, a child is likely to feel bewildered. The process of improvising from musical statements can proceed in this way:

"I'll clap a short pattern. You 'answer' my pattern by clapping a pattern of your own, but do *not* clap my pattern over again. For example, I might clap

and you might answer

"See how it goes? The nice thing about this is that there aren't any wrong answers! So don't be afraid to clap whatever comes into your head. Try to make your answer last as long as the statement that I clap for you.

"Let's start with you, Caroline. Here's the statement. I'll clap it for you twice. The second time you join in right after the statement is finished, so that your answer is connected to what I clap. Ready? Here we go."

[The teacher commends Caroline and lets other children improvise clapping "answers" to different statements.]

As the children become more proficient at improvising, they can work in pairs, with one child thinking up a statement and the other improvising an answer. The material can gradually be increased in length, and extended to include meters other than three or four beats to the measure. The activity can also be expanded into a game: A rhythmic statement is agreed on by the class. The first, third, and other odd-numbered members of the class clap it alone when their turn comes, while the second, fourth, and other even-numbered members of the class individually improvise responses. The object of the game is to keep the rhythm going without a break until everyone in the class has participated. The game can be made more complex, if the class is ready for it, by adding the stipulation that each improvised phrase must be different from any previously clapped. This is a particular challenge to the child who improvises last.

Rhythm compositions can also be created in which two or three parts occur at the same time. Again, the initial efforts should be simple, perhaps like this:

As the children demonstrate that they are able to perform easy pieces, they can create more difficult compositions with simultaneously sounding parts, such as this example in $\frac{3}{4}$ meter:

Other types of sounds can of course be substituted for the clapping.

The technique of providing the child with a musical statement can also be employed with melodic phrases. A musical statement like the following can be played or sung, and the child responds by singing or by playing on an instrument.

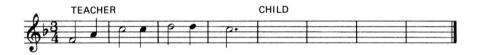

Orff-*Schulwerk* techniques

Many American music specialists have adopted various practices from the Orff-*Schulwerk*, a method of music instruction that was developed under the direction of the twentieth-century German composer Carl Orff and Gunild Keetman.[1] One aspect of the *Schulwerk* involves clapping, chanting, and other means of producing rhythm patterns. The *Schulwerk* also encourages children to improvise and create music. In effect, the method does what has been suggested earlier in this chapter: It permits the child a limited number of options in a highly structured situation. The structure is given in terms of meter, tempo, length of phrase, and a limited number of pitches. The initial efforts at making up a melody are sometimes restricted to only two pitches.

As the children demonstrate increasing competence, the number of available pitches is increased to three and then to the five tones of the pentatonic scale, which sound good in any order.

To make the initial efforts at improvisation even more foolproof, the Orff method utilizes instruments, such as the metallophone, that have removable bars. With the unwanted bars removed, the child cannot hit an "off limits" pitch. Music in two or more parts is encountered early in the *Schulwerk*, and ostinatos are featured prominently.

The use of Orff ideas for creating music requires teacher direction, because the efforts of several children must be coordinated if the composition is to be successful. Here is an example of how the improvisation might be introduced.

Pentatonic Scales

A *pentatonic scale* contains only five different pitches within an octave. In the most common pentatonic scale there are no half steps, because each tone is either one or one-and-a-half steps from its neighbor. The tonal pattern can be easily seen and heard by playing only the black keys on the piano. A pentatonic scale can start on any note, white or black, as long as the essential pattern of steps is preserved.

A pentatonic scale is well suited to the improvisations of children because it lacks the strong feeling of key center inherent in an eight-tone scale. The lack of a well defined tonal center means that any note series will sound good; none will seem more "correct" than another.

"The Riddle Song" (p. 163) is a pentatonic melody based on the scale D E G A B. There are no half steps in the melody itself, but they are implied in the accompanying chords.

The pentatonic scale is found in the folk music of many cultures. The ambiguity of not knowing where the melody will finally "settle down" is one of the charms of pentatonic music.

"Lisa, here's an alto xylophone. As you can see, all the bars have been removed except for two. With those two tones, think up a part that is four beats long. When our composition is played, your part will be repeated over and over throughout the piece. Why don't you go to that end of the room and quietly work out a part."

"Sarah, here's a soprano glockenspiel with all the bars taken off except for two. You can make up the melody for our piece. Think of a tune that's two measures long—it should last for eight beats. You can take the instrument to that side of the room and work for a couple of minutes.

"We need one more part, not for another melody, but just for the interesting rhythm it can make. Let's use this hand drum. Enrique, why don't you take it to that corner and quietly work out a part that lasts for eight beats."

Before trying to put the three parts together, the teacher should hear each one alone to make sure that it fits the pattern by having the correct number of measures and beats. (The pitches are sure to blend if the teacher made a careful selection before giving them to the children.) These limitations of rhythm and pitch are in no sense confining to the children's imaginations, because so many options are available even in the highly structured situation described in the example. One possibility is:

To the example above could be added a coda and contrasting sections of two measures each. The music can be made more complex by adding more instrumental parts, longer phrases, more pitches, and so on. But for most children, the more advanced improvisation can wait until fourth grade or later.

Creating melodies for texts

Another way to help children create music is to give them a short rhyme and ask them to set it to music. The pattern of the words provides a rhythmic structure, and the messge of the text suggests a mood. Here is a stanza from a poem by Christina Rossetti:

> The wind has such a rainy sound
> Moaning through the town,
> The sea has such a windy sound—
> Will the ships go down?

The teacher can focus the children's attention on the text by first asking them to add sound effects, a technique that was suggested earlier.

To stimulate the children's musical ideas as the class is looking at the words, the teacher can play pentatonic tunes on the bells, on the notes C D E G A, for example. The experimentation should suggest a flowing, relaxed rhythm, with a slight emphasis on the more important words of the poem. The pitch combinations can be extremely flexible. After improvising two or three versions of the same poem, the teacher can invite individual children to try.

"Who'd like to try it? Lefanchia, here's the mallet. Experiment by playing the notes in any order you want. Sing or say the words along with your notes. When you find a tune you like for those words, we'll all sing your song."

When trying to motivate the class to compose, the teacher should not just write music on the board, perform it, and then ask, "Boys and girls, do you like that?" If they agree—and they usually do, because it is the teacher's suggested melody—the song is sometimes said to have been composed by the class, which of course is not an accurate description of what took place. The value of creative activity lies in the development and evaluation of music produced through the imagination of the children themselves.

Although creative efforts can occur in a class setting, each new idea is the product of an individual mind; music is not created by committee. Other people may react to and comment on what an individual creates, but the act of creating is the achievement of one person. That is its greatest value in the music education of children. Creating music is a learning experience as well as an enriching activity. For this reason, creative activities need to be included in the education of every child.

NOTES

1. Beth Landis and Polly Carder, *The Eclectic Curriculum in American Music Education: Contributions of Dalcroze, Kodály, and Orff* (Reston, Va.: Music Educators National Conference, 1972), pp. 69–107.

Review Questions

1. What is the difference between composing and improvising?
2. Give three reasons for including creative activities in the music education of children.
3. What principles should teachers follow in helping students to create music?
4. Cite at least five ways to add creative aspects to a song that the children know.
5. a. Describe one way in which creative activity in art can be combined with music.
   b. Describe one way in which creative movement or dance can be combined with music.
6. Describe how a teacher can guide children to organize simple pieces of music composed of sounds available in the classroom.
7. In what ways does the Orff-*Schulwerk* method establish a structure for a child's initial effort at improvising?
8. What procedure might a teacher use in guiding children to create a short piece for glockenspiel, alto metallophone, and triangle?

Activities

1. From one of the music series books for the primary grades, select a song to which you and other members of the methods class will add creative ideas.
   a. Make two or three changes in the pitches.
   b. Make two or three changes in the rhythm.
   c. Add a simple part for an instrument, one that contributes an appropriate rhythm pattern or tonal effect.
   d. Write a new set of words.
2. In class or elsewhere, make two drawings while listening to two contrasting pieces of music.
3. In class or elsewhere, develop a pattern of body movements expressing a piece of music. Demonstrate the movements to the class.
4. Discover six sound-making possibilities in the classroom. Then organize the six sounds into a composition. Determine the order of sounds, the rhythm, the dynamic level, and the manner in which two or more sounds will be handled if they occur simultaneously.
5. a. Develop two clapped rhythm patterns to which another class member can respond.
   b. Develop two melodic statements to which another class member can respond.

Skill Exercises

1. Create two short pentatonic melodies using only the five adjacent black keys of the piano, or the melody bells C♯ D♯ F♯ G♯ A♯.
2. Notate the two melodies you created for Skill Exercise 1.

C H A P T E R

10

Moving to Music

Because movement is a natural human response to music, children should be encouraged to move to the musical sounds they hear. A teacher can often help youngsters to move expressively simply by suggesting, "Show us what the music tells you to do."

Experience with movement provides a change of activity in the music lesson and this variety is often beneficial to the learning process. Furthermore, because motion is overt, the teacher can easily tell by the youngsters' actions whether they are engaged with the music.

The movement activities suggested in this chapter are intended not as an end in themselves, but as a means to increase the children's understanding of music. The children should encounter the music first, then devise motions that express what they hear.

Fingerplays

A fingerplay is a series of finger, hand, or arm motions performed rhythmically to depict the images suggested by a song or rhyme. Most youngsters have sufficient manual dexterity to perform fingerplays competently, and children enjoy the muscle manipulation required to act out a story with the hands.

The significance of this process was noted many years ago by Friedrich Froebel, the German educator who established the kindergarten/nursery school movement early in the nineteenth century. He believed that children begin to understand the things they imitate. His idea that children learn through play was reinforced as he went about the countryside observing peasant mothers and their young children. He collected their fingerplays and games and used them in his own teaching.

The following fingerplays are known to most teachers and children: "The Eency Weency Spider" (p. 44), "This Old Man," "Here Is the Beehive," "Ten Little Indians," and "Where Is Thumbkin?" The motions are varied and each is sung to a standard tune rather than merely recited. Young children seem not to tire of these and similar songs.

Guiding Early Movement Activities

To be expressive, every movement needs direction and a focus of attention. A teacher can demonstrate purposeful motion by showing the children a few moments of aimless wandering or random motions, then asking the youngsters how they would draw the motions on paper—would the marks look like scribbles or a definite design? Volunteers can be invited to present other examples, while the class decides whether the actions are jumbled or clearly patterned.

A motion seems to be more expressive when it is preceded by a preparatory movement in the opposite direction. Children are generally able to understand the principle if it is related to their experience. They can experiment to see for themselves that they can't jump *up* unless they first bend their knees and *lower* their bodies a bit, nor can they snap a rubber band without first stretching it in the opposite direction. Other movements are prepared in the same manner.

The role of imitation

As with fingerplays, the children's first experiences with moving the whole body to music can be imitative. Following the motions of a leader helps to stimulate the youngsters' own ideas. By thinking aloud, "What can we do here?" and then quickly showing appropriate motions while encouraging the children to do the same, the teacher helps them learn that movement can be spontaneous and that many different motions are possible. This provides a valid basis for their own creativity.

Imitative movement need not occur simultaneously with the teacher's motions. Instead, the children can follow the teacher's movements in echo fashion. Youngsters will understand the procedure if told that the class is "taking turns" with the teacher.

The song "Are You Sleeping?" (p. 40) is ideal for echo-type motions because each of the four different phrases is repeated before the next one occurs. Echo-clapping is a good introduction to the procedure because only one type of motion is involved. The teacher can sing through the song, clapping with the words in measures 1, 3, 5, and 7 and signaling for the class to clap in the same way at measures 2, 4, 6, and 8.

As the children become more adept at waiting for their turn and repeating a phrase accurately, the teacher can change motions for each new phrase and then change within a single phrase. If desired, the song text can be replaced with specific directions, as in this version of "Are You Sleeping?," to be sung and performed in place from a standing position:

Step the beat now,	(children imitate)
Turn a-round,	(imitate)
Clap your hands to-geth-er,	(imitate)
Step once more.	(imitate)

After seeing the teacher lead the group with different motions, a child may be invited to lead with other ideas. The youngster's movements may in fact be exactly like the teacher's previous actions, but the child will be pleased to be named "leader," and enjoyment is the initial goal of the activity.

Moving in a structured situation

When children first attempt to move freely in a large area, they need to know that their actions are influenced by rules and limits. They must find their own space and respect the space of others. They should not touch other people unless the teacher suggests that they do. Their attention needs to be on the music so that their motions reflect what they hear. As they gain experience in self-direction and attentive listening, they are becoming better prepared to work with partners and participate in large-group endeavors.

Limits and boundaries also help to focus the children's attention on what they are doing. They respond well to requests that are phrased like a challenge: "How far can you reach with your elbow?" "In how many ways can you move your foot?" "Can you touch your nose to your shoulder?" Such suggestions may appear to be confining, but they actually encourage imaginative movement.

The teacher should be aware of the limitations inherent in the physical setting, and plan accordingly. Actions that require a child to move from one place to another—*locomotor* activity as opposed to the "in place" nature of *axial* or *nonlocomotor* activity—must occur in a safe environment. Children in stocking feet can slip on tile floors, but rubber-soled shoes, especially on a carpet, make skipping and certain other movements difficult to perform. If space is severely limited, some children can be assigned to provide the music while others move; then the groups can trade roles.

Action Songs

Action songs differ from fingerplays by involving more parts of the body. In contrast to fingerplays, which appeal primarily to the very young, action songs are enjoyed by older children as well as younger ones. The motions should be decisive and energetic, unless the music is gentle in character. When children move with vigor and precision, they feel more confident and tend to duplicate the rhythm more accurately—two outcomes that increase their enjoyment of the activity.

"Johnny Works with One Hammer" is strongly rhythmic and ends with movement of the entire body. The children's names can be substituted for "Johnny" to involve them more completely in the music. The singers pound with one fist for "one hammer" and with two fists for "two hammers." Unless the children are able to move confidently from a standing position, they should remain seated as they do this song, because the "three hammers" verse requires balancing on one foot and tapping with the other, "four hammers" requires jumping (to tap with both feet), and "five hammers" requires jumping plus nodding the head in a way that may cause dizziness if attempted too vigorously.

JOHNNY WORKS WITH ONE HAMMER

American Folk Song

John - ny works with one ham - mer, one ham - mer, one ham - mer.

John - ny works with one ham - mer, Now he works with two.

2. Johnny works with two hammers (etc.) . . . Now he works with three."

3. Johnny works with three hammers (etc.) . . . Now he works with four."

4. Johnny works with four hammers (etc.) . . . Now he works with five."

5. Johnny works with five hammers (etc.) . . . Now he takes a rest."

The following suggestions can be adapted to children of any age who are engaged in action songs:

1. Insist that the children stop moving when the music stops. Because an abrupt ending to the music may catch them off balance, alert them to the approaching end by exaggerating the motions, offering verbal cues, or slowing the tempo slightly. Precision is as important at the end of a song as it is at the beginning.

2. Help the children develop lateral balance by encouraging them to use both sides of their bodies for foot-tapping, finger-snapping, waving, winking, and so on. Transferring a motion occasionally to the other side of the body is not likely to upset a child's sense of handedness, and it is beneficial because it engages more body parts in the activity and sustains interest during review of the music. A song such as "Hokey Pokey," with its references to "right" and "left," is a good choice to reinforce the concept of equal body sides.

3. Promote spatial orientation by helping the children to produce sounds through body movement at different levels: a foot tap at floor level, a thigh slap called a "pat" or "*Patsch*" (a German word for which the plural is "*Patschen*"), a clap at waist level, and a finger snap at shoulder level (achieved by slanting the forearms upward so that the hands are above the elbows). If some children cannot snap, a hand bounce is a good substitute. Let the children make up rhythm patterns of these four motions and apply them as accompaniments to songs. The levels can be notated on a partial staff:

4. To encourage buoyancy in skipping, choose music (or provide a drum beat) in compound meter that starts with a pickup:

This suggests a lift, in contrast to a long first note that is too static to encourage forward movement.

5. Solicit ideas from the children for altering a song text or adding extra verses, to provide further actions. Be prepared to offer an idea or two of your own if the children do not suggest something within a few moments.

6. Prepare a repertoire of animal motions to propose for songs that mention animals.

Elephant—lean forward from the waist, clasp hands together by the knees, and swing arms sideways with stiff elbows

Pony—prance by stepping in place, lifting each knee high with toe pointed down

Horse—gallop forward while slapping one hip

Bear—keep knees slightly bent and walk with legs apart, shifting weight from side to side and holding limp wrists against chest

Frog—squat with hands touching floor between legs and jump forward

Duck—squat with feet apart and bottom almost touching floor; waddle forward by shifting weight onto alternate legs, and bend arms so that limp wrists are shoulder high, with hands pointing outward

Butterfly—cross wrists and wave hands gently

Penguin—walk stiffly with knees straight, toes out, and arms held stiffly against sides

7. Do not impose a concrete story onto the music if the composer did not do so. The children can still move expressively to the music, whether it implies specific images or not.

8. Remember that props such as scarves to wave and balls to bounce are not necessary for experiencing movement. They may in fact distract the children's attention from the fine bond between the music and their response to it.

"Stretching Song" (p. 300) is a good choice for young children. The words clearly describe the recommended actions, and the actions correlate well with the pitch levels in the melody. Besides, the bending and stretching is fun!

Moving to Show Recognition of Musical Elements

Actions have another value in music: they can indicate whether the children are aware of particular features of the music itself. To help the children notice what they hear, the teacher can first help them to distinguish between opposites, and then ask them to show their understanding by a simple action response. The initial procedure can be as basic as, "Move like this when the music moves, and stop when the music stops." This is the premise of stop-and-go games like "Musical Chairs" and "Statues." After experiencing the difference between "stop" and "go," the children can be invited to think up more pairs of opposites that relate to music or movement—high/low, up/down, loud/soft, heavy/light, fast/slow, right/left, forward/backward, in/out, over/under, and so on—and then to act them out for the class.

As children gain experience in listening and responding nonverbally to what they hear, they can begin to use movement to illustrate their recognition of musical concepts. At this more advanced level they are listening not merely to identify opposites or extremes, but to evaluate subtle differences. They are learning to keep track of one aspect of music as it progresses from moment to moment, and this skill helps them to remember longer segments of music and to compare new sections with those heard earlier.

By asking the children to change motions when they hear particular details in the music, the teacher can assess their understanding of musical concepts such as beat, tempo, meter, pitch, duration, dynamic level, timbre, and form.

Singing Games

Unlike action songs, which are characterized by individual efforts undertaken in relative isolation, singing games require cooperation and similar motions from the participants. Singing games are more structured and take place in a particular formation, often a circle. The teacher should consider the following factors when planning and directing singing games:

1. If partners are required, the selection process should do no harm to any child's self-image. Singing games should help all the children to feel good about themselves and the music experience.

2. If the children must move sideways in a circle while touching, they may rest their hands on their neighbors' shoulders or place one hand at each neighbor's elbow. Youngsters are apt to stretch the circle and pull at other people if they are holding hands, and if they link elbows they are pulled too close to move freely.

3. The purpose of a singing game in music class is to help the children move to music in cooperation with others. This may be a new idea for a youngster who regards a singing game as a contest to see who can sing loudest, move fastest, or "win" in some aspect of the endeavor. By referring frequently to the music, the teacher can help the children understand the purpose of the activity.

Folk and Social Dancing

Movement in dancing is organized even more strictly than in singing games. A dance involves well-defined stepping movements and characteristic body gestures. To give the children a repertoire of dance music, the teacher can play recordings of folk songs appropriate for dancing, or have the class sing songs like those on page 145, which are typical of square dance tunes and are known to most children in the upper elementary grades.

The most direct way to introduce dance steps is simply to go through them while everyone is standing in a circle. The teacher can guide the activity by describing the steps and demonstrating them as in the following examples.

POLKA: "Here's an easy dance pattern. Watch me do it first in slow motion: step to the right, put the left foot close to it, step to the right again, and hold. Got it? Do it with me, a little faster. *Right* step *right* hold, *left* step *left* hold, *one* and *two* hold, *pol*-ka step—, *pol*-ka step—, *now*-we'll -*stop*. You're off to a good start!"

SCHOTTISCHE: "Now hop instead of hold. Start with your right foot. *Right* step *right* hop, *left* step *left* hop, *one* and *two* and, *stop*- and-*rest*. That was a *schottische*. Try it again while we sing 'Little Brown Jug.'"

On another day the teacher might review the dance movements presented to the class earlier, and then introduce additional easy steps:

WALTZ: "Let's do a dance in three-beat meter today. We need to make each step even, like this: *right* slide right, *left* slide left, *one* two three,

$\frac{2}{4}$ Meter

Arkansas Traveler	O Susanna
Bingo	Pawpaw Patch (Ten Little Indians)
Dixie	Polly Wolly Doodle
Down by the Riverside	Sandy Land
Go Tell Aunt Rhody	Shoo Fly
Go Tell It on the Mountain	Skip to My Lou
Little Brown Jug	Turkey in the Straw
Marching to Pretoria	Yankee Doodle
Muffin Man	When the Saints Go Marching In

Fast $\frac{3}{4}$ Meter

Goodbye, Old Paint
How D'You Do, My Partner?
My Bonnie Lies over the Ocean
O My Darling Clementine
Skaters' Waltz
The More We Get Together

$\frac{6}{8}$ Meter

A-Hunting We Will Go
Here We Go 'Round the Mulberry Bush
Rig-a-Jig-Jig
Pop! Goes the Weasel

one two three, *fast*-er now, *one* two three, *one* two three, *now*-you-are-*waltz*-ing!-Get-*rea*-dy-to-*stop*. That's the way, class! This is a good dance with 'O My Darling Clementine.' We'll sing it as we waltz around again." [The class waltzes and sings.]

For many dance movements the class members should be in partner formations. To expedite the choosing of partners and avoid the need for boy/girl pairings, the teacher can ask the children to count off by twos, with one group being the Blues, for example, and the other being the Golds. If the children wear identifying patches of color, prepared in advance by the teacher, they will find it easier to keep their places and the dances will proceed more smoothly.

Most children are intrigued by basic square dance movements and learn them easily. In this example the teacher is demonstrating the do-si-do.

"For the do-si-do, you need to form two lines that face each other. Leave a little more room between neighbors . . . that's the way. Now hold your forearms crossed together in front of you, then skip forward so that opposite people meet in the center. Go around each other with right shoulders close, always facing forward, then move backward with left shoulders close, still skipping, and return to your places. Keep your arms folded through all of this. We'll try it to a good skipping song like 'Here We Go 'Round the Mulberry Bush.'"

The children need to realize that dancing involves more of the body than just the feet and legs. The teacher can demonstrate various ways in which to position the arms, in addition to the folded arms that the children have already experienced. Partners may want to try these possibilities: clap own or partner's hands, raise joined hands while walking into a circle and lower them while backing out, face in opposite directions and link elbows, join crossed hands in the *skaters' position*, join both hands and turn back to back to "*wring the dishrag*," make arches for people to go under, create a *star* formation with joined right hands of other dancers, and proceed around a circle in a "shake hands" manner to form a *grand chain* or *grand right and left*. These and other common dance terms are described in Appendix B.

The following square dance is especially appropriate for beginners because it is sung to a familiar tune—"Turkey in the Straw"—and the dance movements are described in the words of the song itself. Slurs should be inserted as needed to make the italicized syllables occur on the strong beats.

> Verse 1: Now *stand* up *tall* as you *make* a *square*;
> Turn and *face* your *part*-ner *stand*-ing *there*.
> Then *back* to *back* in a *do*-si-*do*,
> Now *swing* your *part*-ner, *here* we *go*!
> Chorus: *Step* to the *cen*-ter, *raise* your hands *high*,
> *Back* to your *pla*-ces, *give* it a *try*.
> Now *stamp* three *times* and *clap* your *hands*.
> Turn a-*round* in *sev*-en steps where *each* one *stands*.

(For verse 2, change "partner" to "corner" and repeat action with the other neighbor.)

Older children may enjoy creating square dances to familiar tunes like those listed on page 145. The choreographers will need to consider the meter and the length of the musical phrases so that strong motions will occur on accented beats and movement patterns will change when the phrases change.

Dramatizations

Dramatization means acting out a story through movement. It implies at least a rudimentary plot and a degree of character development. Mime is a good example of the drama that can be conveyed by movement alone.

Most elementary music series books include stories to be acted out to music. The dramatizations range from simple children's tales for young groups to scenes from operas and musicals that can be enacted by older children.

Meaningful experiences with movement require attention to its four components: *time*—the sense of orderly progression through past, present, and future; *space*—the realm of line, direction, and distance; *weight*—the feeling conveyed by varying degrees of emphasis; and *idea*—the concept or object being described by the movement.

The teacher's goal in providing experiences with movement is to lead the children to hear the essence of the music and respond to it with pleasure, intellectual recognition, and physical ease.

Review Questions

1. What is the purpose of providing movement activities in a children's music class?
2. What is the role of imitation in preparing children to move creatively?
3. What is the difference between locomotor and nonlocomotor activity?
4. To what extent, if any, is a concrete image necessary when children move to music?
5. Name and describe four components of descriptive movement.

Activities

1. To the tune "Are You Sleeping?" write new words to provide the children with four suggestions for simple movements that they can do while they sing in echo fashion with the teacher.
2. To the rhythm of "Are You Sleeping?" prepare a version that makes use of the four-level "tap, pat, clap, snap" motions, and teach your rhythm composition to the class.
3. Look through a music series book and select two songs in $\frac{6}{8}$ meter that would be appropriate in both tempo and song text to accompany a skipping activity.
4. Demonstrate motions to depict the movements of two animals not included in the list on page 142.
5. Choose one basic music concept and prepare a lesson segment in which the children show their recognition of that concept through a movement response.
6. Create a simple four-phrase square dance to a song selected from the list on page 145.

P A R T

III

Teaching Music in the Upper Elementary Grades

Although this book discusses music teaching in only two broad categories—primary and upper elementary grades—there is no clear line distinguishing the musical development of children at either level. The changes that occur as students progress through school are gradual and individual, and they are affected in large part by the child's previous experience and education in the subject.

Much of what students do in music in the upper grades is a refinement of skills and information started at the primary level. The main difference, especially in skills such as singing and reading music, is that older children can perform more accurately and easily than they could in the earlier grades. They can relate to pieces of music that are longer and more complex, and they can perform them more impressively.

Playing the recorder is one example of a music skill that seems to develop more quickly when introduced in the upper grades. Topics such as form and harmony, which are rather abstract in nature, are also best emphasized in the upper grades because of the conceptualization required in these areas.

C H A P T E R

11

More Complex Rhythms

The musical education of children in the primary grades is important because it forms the foundation on which subsequent learning is built. This fact is especially true of rhythm. Few of the aspects of rhythm described in this chapter will be understood by upper elementary level children unless they have a prior understanding of the topics presented in Chapter 4. For expanding on those ideas with older students, however, the order in which the concepts are developed is not significant. No pedagogical sequence is implied, therefore, by the order in which topics are presented in this chapter.

The difference between rhythm instruction in the primary grades and in the upper grades is revealed in the greater complexity of the music studied at the upper levels, and in the increased role of notation. Older children do not outgrow their need for physical experiences with rhythm, however. Trying to learn notation without a sense of what the symbols mean in terms of actual sound and physical sensations—like clapping—is largely a wasted effort.

Sixteenth Notes

Children can usually perform sixteenth notes with ease, especially after experiencing the 2:1 ratio of the more common note and rest values. If the children can sense the division of one note into two even sounds, they can sense sixteenth notes as subdivisions of eighth notes.

The machine-like connotations of "Clear the Tracks" (p. 154) encourage evenness and precision in performing the sixteenth-note patterns.

Here is how a teacher might approach the teaching of sixteenth notes:

"If you look at 'Clear the Tracks' in your books, you'll see some notes that we haven't talked about before, even though you've sung them in songs already. Chad, what do the new notes look like?"

"I don't know, but I've got a different question," says Chad. "What's a 'bullgine'?"

"It's a short way of saying 'bull engine,'" answers the teacher. "It's the engine of a steam locomotive. Now, back to our unfinished business, Chad, what do the new notes look like in this song?"

"Um . . . they have two bars over them?" Chad guesses.

Sixteenth Notes, Ties, and Dotted Notes

The relationship of sixteenth notes to other note values is evident in the chart on page 39.

The following exercise may help to convey the difference between quarter, eighth, and sixteenth notes. It may be performed several times in succession while the performer claps or taps an even beat and says rhythm syllables aloud. The pattern of four sixteenth notes can be spoken as "ti-ki-ti-ki" or "ti-ri-ti-ri"; in either case the "ti" syllables coincide with the eighth note background to clarify the relationship between eighth and sixteenth notes.

1	2	1	and	2	and	1 -	ee-and-a	2 -	ee-and-a	1	and	2	and	1	2
ta	ta	ti	ti	ti	ti	ti-ki	ti-ki	ti-ki	ti-ki	ti	ti	ti	ti	ta	ta
ta	ta	ti	ti	ti	ti	ti-ri	ti-ri	ti-ri	ti-ri	ti	ti	ti	ti	ta	ta

Sometimes the desired length of a sound lies somewhere between the durations of the basic note values. To accommodate this situation, it is possible to combine two or more notes *of the same pitch* into one continuous sound. This is called a *tie*, and is indicated in notation by a curved line extending from one note head to the next. In the example below, the combined duration of each tied group is figured on the basis of a quarter-note beat.

A 1½-beat sound   A 3-beat sound   A 1¾-beat sound

When the second note of a tie is exactly half the duration of the first one, as in the examples above, the second note can be replaced by a dot. *A dot to the right of a note extends its duration by 50 percent.* The value of a dot changes, therefore, depending on the value of the note with which it appears. If a quarter note lasts for one beat, the length of each dotted note here is:

$$♩. = ♩ + ♪ \quad = 1 + \tfrac{1}{2} = 1\tfrac{1}{2} \text{ beats}$$

$$\textit{d}. = \textit{d} + ♩ \quad = 2 + 1 = 3 \text{ beats}$$

Dotted notes are related to one another in the same way that non-dotted notes are related: both reveal a 2:1 ratio. This relationship can be seen in the example below, and in the chart on page 39.

Although the foregoing examples of ties and dotted notes have each illustrated a 50 percent increase in duration, a tie is not confined to that proportion of note values. In the following examples, a tie is the only appropriate notational device; it cannot be replaced by a dot.

A tie is also useful in extending a note duration from one measure into the next, so that each measure can retain the correct number of beats:

A tie should not be confused with a *slur*, which is also represented by a curved line. In a slur, the curve forms a single arch spanning two or more notes of *different pitch*. A slur indicates not lengthened note values, but smoothness in performance style. It is a symbol of interpretation rather than rhythm.

CLEAR THE TRACKS

For autoharp, transpose to D minor

Traditional

1. Oh,   the   smart-est   clip-per   you   can   find,
2. We'll   be   on   our   way when the wind   doth   blow } Ah-hee, oh-ho, are
3. When   the   time comes round   to   say   fare-well

you   most   done? { Is   the   Marg-'ret   Ev-ans   of   the   Black   X__ Line,
Just__ one   big   blast__ and   a-way   we'll__ go. } So
We'll__ say   good-bye__ and__ wish   them__ well.

clear a-way the track, let the bull-gine run.   To my hey rig-a-jig in a

low back car, Ah-hee, ah-ho, are you most done? With   Li-za Lee all

on   my__ knee, So   clear   a-way   the   track, let   the   bull-gine   run.____

"That's right. We call them 'beams.' Do you know what those two-beam notes are called, Tina?" [Tina shakes her head.]

"Does anyone know? Samantha?"

"Well, in piano they're 'sixteenth notes,'" Samantha answers.

"Yes, and they're sixteenth notes in singing, too. They're so short that it takes two of them to last as long as an eighth note. Look at the second measure of the second line of 'Clear the Tracks.' Here's how the pattern should sound." [The teacher claps the beat while articulating the rhythm on a neutral syllable. The children imitate.]

"Clap the beat with me at this tempo, class, then say the words of the song when I cue you." [All clap together at a moderate tempo, then the teacher says, "Rea-dy, go" in the rhythm of two eighths and a quarter note, and the class recites the words in rhythm.]

After several experiences with a pattern, most children will be able to figure it out when they see it in notation, and not rely on imitation. Again, experience must precede symbolization.

Dotted Notes

A simple approach for teaching children to read dotted notes is to consider the dot as an abbreviation for an additional note value that is half as long as the printed note. Singing the round "Come, Follow Me" is an appropriate introduction to the concept because a dotted quarter note appears in the same rhythm and with the same words in three consecutive measures.

COME, FOLLOW ME

1. Come, fol - low, fol - low, fol - low, Fol - low, fol - low,

fol - low me! Whith-er shall I fol - low, fol - low, fol - low,

Whith-er shall I fol - low, fol - low thee? To the green - wood,

to the green - wood, To the green - wood, green - wood tree.

Here is one way a teacher might introduce dotted notes.

"All of us come across shortened words every day in what we read. We see S T for 'street' and M R for 'mister.' We have shortcuts in written music, too. You all know the round 'Come, Follow Me.' Think of the last part that goes 'To the greenwood' three times. As you can see in your books, each word 'to' is a quarter note with a dot after it. The dotted quarter note could also be written as two tied notes, like this."

[The teacher draws on the chalkboard.]

Instead, the eighth note is abbreviated into a dot. This particular dot adds half of a beat to the quarter, just as the tied eighth note added that amount.

"The thing to remember is that the dot *to the right* of a note always adds half again as much duration as the note has by itself. Here's another problem for you to figure out." [The teacher writes a dotted half note on the chalkboard.] "Assume that the half note gets two beats, which it usually does. How much does the dot add to it? Jenny?"

"Half a beat," Jenny answers quickly but incorrectly.

"Jenny, you're still thinking of the dot that's beside a quarter note. The value of a dot changes, remember, depending on the note beside it. This one's next to a two-beat note. Half of two beats is . . ."

"One beat," Jenny responds correctly, then whispers "I goofed" to her neighbor.

A few students may be willing to make posters illustrating the effect of a dot on various note values, and these can be displayed in the room as a reminder of the "shorthand dot."

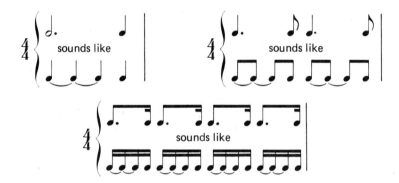

Compound Meter

"Git, Along, Little Dogies" is a song in which each beat divides into threes. When the children can sing it fluently, the teacher can direct their attention to the way in which the rhythm is notated.

The children may need help in perceiving that in compound meter the beat is represented by a dotted note.

[The teacher writes two sets of three-beamed eighth notes on the board.] "This is the basic rhythm of our song. Clap the beat with me as I point to the first eighth note in each group, and say 'One-la-lee, two-la-lee' for the eighths. *Rea*-dy-now, *here*-we-go." [The class performs the rhythm several times.]

"That's the way. Now, what note value should we assign to the beat? It can't be a quarter note, because that divides into only two eighth notes. The beat can't be a half note, either, because that divides into

GIT ALONG, LITTLE DOGIES

American Cowboy Song

1. As I was a-walk-ing one morn-ing for pleas-ure,
2. Now ear-ly in spring-time we round up the do-gies,
3. It's whoop-ing and yell-ing and driv-ing the do-gies,

I spied a cow-punch-er a-rid-ing a-long;
We mark them and brand them and bob off their tails;
Oh, how I wish you____ would go right a-long;

His hat was thrown back and his spurs were a-jing-lin',
We drive up our hors-es and load the chuck wag-on,
It's whoop-ing and punch-ing, git on, lit-tle do-gies,

And as he ap-proached he was sing-ing this song.
Then throw____ the do-gies out on-to the trail.
You know that Wy-o-ming will be your new home.

Refrain

Whoop-ee ti-yi-yo, git a-long, lit-tle do-gies.

It's your mis-for-tune and none of my own;

Whoop-ee ti-yi-yo, git a-long, lit-tle do-gies,

You know that Wy-o-ming will be your new home.

four eighths. So the beat will have to be the note value that's between a quarter and a half note in duration. What note is that?"

[The room is silent. The teacher finally gives a hint by suggesting that a dotted note can represent a beat.]

"Oh, I know!" Nathan suddenly calls out, beaming broadly. "A dotted quarter note!"

Compound Meter

In *simple* meter the beat subdivides into two background pulses; in *compound* meter the beat subdivides into three background pulses. The song "Git Along, Little Dogies" (p. 157) is in compound meter, and it reflects the triple subdivision by showing the eighth notes beamed into groupings of three when possible, as at the words "a-walking one morning for pleasure" in the first line.

Although the 8 in the meter signature suggests that an eighth note lasts for one beat, it is clear that the eighth note in this song moves too quickly to represent the beat. The beat is felt only on the first of every three eighth notes, so what note does represent the beat? The beat cannot be a quarter note, because that divides into only two eighth notes. It cannot be a half note, because that divides into four eighth notes. The only note value that divides into three eighth notes is a dotted quarter note, and that is the beat value in this song.

$$ \text{♩.} = \text{♩} + \text{♪} = \text{♪♪♪} $$

The difference between compound and simple meter is shown in this chart:

Simple meter	Compound meter
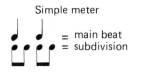	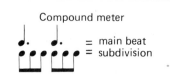
The main beat is divided into twos, making a 2:1 ratio between beat value and subdivision.	The main beat is divided into threes, making a 3:1 ratio between beat value and subdivision.

"Good, Nathan! Are there any dotted quarter notes in this song, Melinda?"

"I can't find any," Melinda answers after a moment.

"You're right; there don't happen to be any. It's interesting that we know all about the beat note by hearing this piece and seeing the notation, but it never once occurs in the song."

There are several ways to count the rhythms in compound meter. The syllables *"One* la lee, *two* la lee" are useful. Because the tempo of the music affects one's perception of the meter, it is also possible to count the subdivisions with consecutive numbers, and to let the feel of the music determine whether those shorter note values are the beats or the subdivisions of the beat:

In compound meter signatures the bottom number indicates not the value of the beat note itself, but rather the value of the beat *subdivision*. The top number tells how many of those subdivisions occur in a measure.

The top number of a compound meter signature can be divided by three, so any signature with 6, 9, or 12 as the top number is compound. (Numbers larger than 12 are rare.) When the top number is 3, the tempo and character of the music determine whether the meter is simple or compound. All other top numbers indicate simple meter.

Music in compound meter has a "swing" that makes it an appropriate accompaniment for galloping and skipping activities, which are by nature a bit lopsided. The more symmetrical subdivisions found in simple meters suggest marching and other balanced movements involving an even "right-left" or "up-down" motion. The difference in rhythmic feel is especially evident in the few pieces, such as "Wassail Song" on page 160, that contain both types of meter.

"Git Along, Little Dogies" contains several of the patterns that typically occur within a beat in $\frac{6}{8}$ meter:

These can be written on the board and read rhythmically by the class, while a steady beat is maintained and the teacher points to the patterns in random order.

The familiar "Wassail Song" contains both compound and simple meters. The music retains the feel of two-beats-per-measure throughout, but there is a distinct difference in mood between the waltz-like $\frac{6}{8}$ and the march-like $\frac{2}{2}$ sections.

WASSAIL SONG

Traditional English

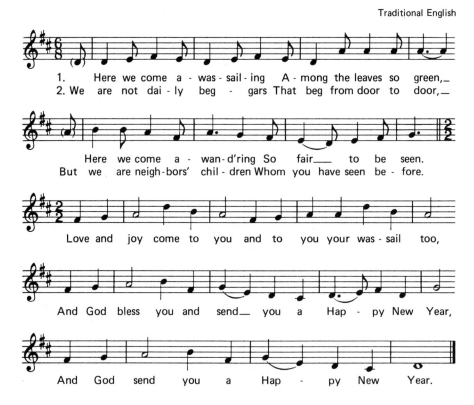

[To illustrate the difference in feel between the two meters in "Wassail Song," the teacher writes the following basic note values and syllables on the board.]

"Jon, would you come up and point to beats 'one' and 'two' as the rest of the class says the subdivisions? Give a good poke to each number to help us keep together. Everyone, watch my cue to know when we're going to change meter. When I hold up three fingers, we'll all say the compound pattern. Two fingers means the simple pattern."

[As Jon comes to the board, the teacher demonstrates by holding up three fingers and saying "*One* la lee, *two* la lee," then holding up two fingers and saying at the same beat speed, "*One* and, *two* and."]

"Okay, class, count with me. *One* la lee, *rea*-dy-now." [The class performs the exercise while Jon points according to the teacher's finger signals.]

"Thanks, Jon. Now let's have someone else come up and point . . . Okay, Abigail. This time half of the class will sing the 'Wassail Song' and the other half will count. Be prepared for the measure where the meter changes right in the middle. It'll go '*One* la lee, *two* and.' Abigail, you'll need to jump with your pointing from the extreme left of the chart to the extreme right, all in one measure. I'll give you a good cue. Everyone ready? Counting people, give us a measure of preparation: *One* la lee, *two* la lee."

[The class performs the song in the manner suggested.]

Borrowed Notes

Although most songs maintain standard note proportions, a few pieces of music exhibit rhythmic features that depart from the norm. They are called "borrowed" notes. A common borrowed pattern occurs when a three-note figure is inserted into a beat where a two-note background is expected. This pattern carries the logical name *triplet*. To indicate that three equal notes are being inserted into a time span that would normally contain only two, the music must include the number 3 written over or under the triplet, to indicate the unusual division of the beat. The round "Ev'rybody Loves Saturday Night" (p. 162) contains two triplet figures.

Other borrowed patterns are encountered occasionally in the repertoire of elementary school music classes. Two notes may occur where three are expected, or five may replace four; any alteration is possible. A borrowed figure may consume more than one beat or less than one. But always there should be a notice of the change, in the form of a number appearing above or below the group of notes. Furthermore, the borrowed figure should not distort the steadiness of the beat when the pattern is performed.

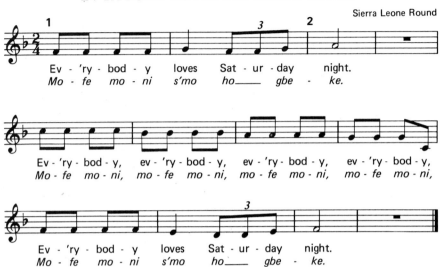

Syncopation

Syncopation is the removal of an expected accent or the addition of an unexpected accent. This rhythmic device occurs in many of the songs sung in elementary school.

In "The Riddle Song," the normal expectation is that the fourth beat of measures 1, 3, 5, and 7 will have a note that starts at the beginning of the beat, not someplace within the beat. Instead, the last syllable of "cherry," "chicken," and similarly placed words is held over so that no new syllable occurs at the start of the last beat, where a new syllable is expected. This creates syncopation. Children can sense it easily, especially if they examine the song by clapping a steady beat and compare it with the unusual accents of the words.

Children enjoy the "alive" quality of syncopated song, and usually have little trouble duplicating its rhythm.

Mixed and Irregular Meters

By the end of their elementary school experience, children should be aware that not all music conforms to a few rhythmic patterns and meters. Much of the music familiar to them is regular in its rhythm, but some interesting types of music are not.

THE RIDDLE SONG

American Folk Song

1. I gave my love a cher - ry that has no stone;
2. How can there be a cher - ry that has no stone?
3. A cher - ry when it's bloom - ing, it has no stone;

I gave my love a chick - en that has no___ bone;
How can there be a chick - en that has no___ bone?
A chick - en when it's pip - ping, it has no___ bone;

I gave my love a ring___ that has no___ end;
How can there be a ring___ that has no___ end?
A ring___ when it's roll - ing it has no___ end;

I gave my love a ba - by, there's no cry - en.
How can there be a ba - by, there's no cry - en?
A ba - by when it's sleep - ing, there's no cry - en.

One piece in *mixed meter* is "Sim Sala Bim" (p. 164), a Danish folk song that changes meter to accommodate the pattern of the text. Aside from the changes of meter, the song is quite conventional.

A teacher might introduce mixed meter in this way:

"Amber, which beat in a measure is usually the strongest?"

"The first?" Amber wonders.

"Okay. Now Amber, if we change the meter at every measure, will the strong beats fall regularly, like once for every two or three beats?"

"Well, no."

"Why not?"

"'Cause the first beat will land at different places, so you'll have different spacings between all the first beats."

SIM SALA BIM

Danish Folk Song

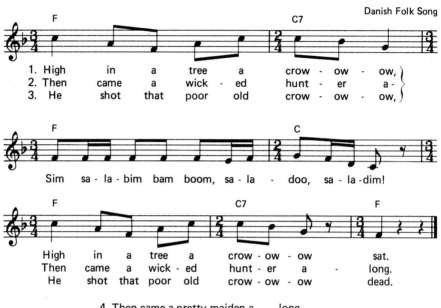

1. High in a tree a crow - ow - ow,
2. Then came a wick - ed hunt - er a -
3. He shot that poor old crow - ow - ow,

Sim sa - la - bim bam boom, sa - la - doo, sa - la -dim!

High in a tree a crow - ow - ow sat.
Then came a wick - ed hunt - er a - long.
He shot that poor old crow - ow - ow dead.

4. Then came a pretty maiden a- . . . long.

5. She took that poor old crow-ow-ow . . . home.

6. Now comes the happy ending: . . . soup!

"That's true. So in 'Sim Sala Bim,' some strong beats will occur closer together than others. Let's read the words of the first verse in rhythm, and give a little emphasis to the first beat of each measure."

Children can generally perform mixed meter songs with ease, and recognizing them in notation is no problem because the extra meter signatures are evident after only a brief scan of the music. Reading music in mixed meters is relatively easy if the beat note remains the same; reading is more difficult if the note value of the beat changes often.

Irregular meters, such as those with five or seven beats in a measure, are unusual in traditional American music. "Friend, Since You Want to Take a Wife" is a Greek folk song. Its meter is asymmetrical, and can perhaps best be felt as having three quarter note beats per measure, with an extra eighth note inserted after the first beat. The pattern is not hard to perform after the children get the feel for it.

Here is how the meter might be presented:

"Today we're going to try a song with an unusual meter. I'm writing across the chalkboard the numbers '1' to '7' equally distant from each other. Now say the numbers *evenly*, over and over, rather fast—at this tempo: 1 2 3 4 5 6 7, here-we-go." [The class says the numbers together several times.]

FRIEND, SINCE YOU WANT TO TAKE A WIFE

M. L. H.   Greek Folk Song

1. Friend, since you want to take a wife, Think how this step will
2. Don't choose a girl with lots of wealth, Rich liv - ing's sure to
3. Don't choose one who is old or young, Too qui - et or too

change your life. I'll ad - vise you, I will tell you
break your health. And of course don't try to take a
quick of tongue. Do not choose a wo - man who is

what to do. Take your time, lis - ten well and think it through.
bride who's poor, or the wolf will be stay - ing at your door.
short or tall. May - be you should not take a wife at all!

"Fine. This time we'll emphasize certain numbers. I'll circle 1, 4, and 6. Say the numbers again at the same speed as before, only this time 'lean' a bit on 1, 4, and 6. Rea-dy, go." [The class says the numbers again, emphasizing 1, 4, and 6.]

"Now you're getting it! Let's emphasize 1, 4, and 6 even more by clapping on 1, 4, and 6 as we say all the numbers. Don't rush, and keep the numbers coming evenly. Rea-dy, go." [The class says the numbers and stresses the beats by clapping on 1, 4, and 6.]

"Can you just *think* the numbers, but still clap on 1, 4, and 6? Those are the beats in this music. Try it." [The class claps on the beat while thinking the numbers.]

"See how you can 'ride' along with the pattern? I know the three beats aren't equal, but who wants every song to be alike? This time I'll play you a recording of a song called "Friend, Since You Want to Take a Wife." As you listen, softly tap just the beats as you think of the seven numbers."

For a similar drill on another occasion, the class can divide so that some of the children tap or count out the seven background notes while others clap or tap the beats. When the class sings the Greek folk song in its complete form, one or two students can continue to sound the seven background counts on an instrument.

Many works written in the twentieth century feature mixed meters. One of these is Aaron Copland's *El Salón México*, which is a musical impression of a dance hall in Mexico City. In addition to several Mexican folk tunes and much syncopation, the music contains mixed meters alternating between $\frac{6}{8}$, $\frac{3}{4}$, and $\frac{4}{4}$. It begins with this theme, in which the beats have been marked with lines.

The fourth theme is an alternation between $\frac{6}{8}$ and $\frac{3}{4}$ meter.

El Salón México is a type of music that captures the imagination of ten- and eleven-year-olds.

Reading Rhythm in Notation

Most of the discussion of rhythm has involved developing an association between what the children hear in the rhythm pattern and what they see in notation. Additional efforts may be necessary to clarify this association.

A visual technique unrelated to the viewing of notation may help children understand the proportionate nature of the note durations that are basic to our rhythm system. This procedure is useful:

1. Cut 2″ strips of heavy cardboard into sixteen 16″ lengths.
2. Set two of the strips aside and cut the remaining 14 strips into lengths as specified on this chart; two will be dotted half notes, two will be half notes, and so on:

Whole note	16 inches
Dotted half note	12 inches
Half note	8 inches
Dotted quarter note	6 inches
Quarter note	4 inches
Dotted eighth note	3 inches
Eighth note	2 inches
Sixteenth note	1 inch

3. Save the discarded ends of the strips to convert into a reserve supply of smaller note values.

4. Arrange all strips into two identical piles—one set for note values and one set for rests.

5. Make each strip a different color but maintain the same color for the notes and rests that are of equal value.

6. Draw the particular note or rest on each strip, to reinforce what the class is learning.

7. Attach loops of masking tape along the back of each strip, for mounting horizontally onto a chalkboard or large piece of blank cardboard.

The rhythm strips can be used in several ways. Patterns can be displayed for the children to clap or tap at sight, perhaps before attempting to sing them in a song. The advance preparation improves the accuracy with which children sing the song and gives them practice in reading notation in a simplified setting.

Another technique is to display a few measures of rhythmic patterns that include an occasional error for the class to find and identify. A variation of this procedure is to present measures that are not complete, then ask individuals to add the one note or rest that will properly complete the measure.

Finally, the rhythm strips are helpful in illustrating the need for rhythmic accuracy. In the following example, the class has just sung "Clear the Tracks" (p. 154).

"That first rhythm figure of a dotted eighth note and a sixteenth needs to be snappier; it sounds too lazy. We'd better find out how to fix it.

"First of all, the pattern lasts for exactly one beat. What note lasts for one beat in this piece, Justin?" [Justin says it's a quarter note.] "Okay, you put up the rhythm strip for a quarter note, please.

"Eli, would you put up right under it the rhythm strips for the dotted eighth note and the sixteenth note?" [The class observes that the two lines are identical in length.]

"Now, class, if you think sixteenth notes in your head, how many of them should go by before you let go of this dotted eighth note?"

[No answers are forthcoming, so the teacher asks Laura to put four sixteenth-note strips side by side under the two lines already posted, and to compare the durations of the three lines.]

"Laura says they're all the same length. Is she right, class?" [They agree that she is right.] "Okay, now count the four sixteenths rather fast, like this: *1* 2 3 4 *1* 2 3 4 *1* 2 3 4. Rea-dy, count." [The class counts out the four numbers several times. The process is repeated, each time at a faster speed, until the class reaches the tempo of the song "Clear the Tracks."]

"Fine. This time leave out the counts 2 and 3 so that you say only

1 . . 4 1 . . 4 1, and so on. Rea-dy, count." [The class counts, leaving out 2 and 3.]

"Now hold the '1' through the rests; don't make a break before '4.'" [The class says the pattern, holding "1" for three-fourths of a beat.] "Good! That's all there is to it. You're getting the dotted eighth and sixteenth pattern exactly right. Just keep that same accuracy for the first two notes of 'Clear the Tracks.' Sing the whole song now, and pay special attention to the rhythm at the beginning."

There is little consensus among teachers regarding the role of rhythm syllables in the upper grades. If the children learned them in the primary grades and still find them helpful, they can be continued. For most older students, however, they become less useful. In fact, complicated patterns are learned more easily without rhythm syllables.

Some teachers insist that their students learn to count out rhythms by assigning the proper beat number and particular syllables to every pattern. Others believe that counting systems are not as important as many other aspects of music instruction in elementary school. If the children respond to rhythm energetically, produce it accurately, and create it with enjoyment, they are learning this basis element of music.

Review Questions

1. What are the similarities and differences between rhythm instruction in the primary grades and in the upper grades?
2. What underlying idea should the students understand about the relationship of sixteenth notes to other note values?
3. What are some procedures for guiding students in their understanding of dotted notes?
4. What is the fundamental difference between compound meters and simple meters? What are some methods for making children aware of this difference?
5. Sometimes $\frac{6}{8}$ meter is performed with two beats per measure, and sometimes it is performed with six beats per measure. What determines the number of beats that should be felt when performing in $\frac{6}{8}$ meter?
6. How can a performer recognize a borrowed pattern in the notation of a song?
7. In addition to a verbal definition of syncopation, what teaching procedures might help children to become more aware of syncopation in music they hear or perform?
8. What visual material can aid children in their understanding of note and rest values?
9. To what extent are rhythm syllables useful in reading rhythms in the upper grades?

Activities

1. Find a song that contains one or more sixteenth note patterns. Teach yourself to sing or play the song. Then decide how you would teach children in the upper grades to sing the patterns correctly. Write down the procedures you would follow.

2. Prepare for display a set of rhythm strips with lengths varied in proportion to the note and rest values each represents. Arrange them in various combinations to create two measures in $\frac{4}{4}$ meter, two measures in $\frac{6}{8}$ meter, and two measures in $\frac{5}{4}$ meter.

Skill Exercises

1. Say the following rhythm patterns with a neutral syllable or with rhythm syllables. Then clap or tap the pattern.

2. Say the following patterns with a neutral syllable or with rhythm syllables. Then clap or tap the pattern.

C H A P T E R

12

Features of Melody

The process of making children more knowledgeable about melody should start in the primary grades. Through their singing of songs at that level they experience the concept of melody, learn the difference between steps and leaps, and begin to notice phrases. In the upper grades they examine more aspects of melody, learn how melodies function in different pieces of music, and continue to improve in their ability to sing and listen.

Whole and Half Steps

In the primary grades the children are introduced to the idea that every note in a melody is either a step or a leap from its neighbor (if it is not simply repeated). This concept of interval is further developed in the upper grades as the students learn to distinguish between whole and half steps. Because adjacent lines and spaces on the staff do not in themselves provide this information, the children will need practice to determine whether notes on adjacent lines and spaces are a whole or a half step apart.

A piano or xylophone-like instrument is useful in interval practice not only because it presents consecutive pitches visually, but also because the students' playing of intervals provides physical reinforcement of the distances they see and hear.

The teacher can ask a child to play two pitches either a half step or a whole step apart so that the class can determine, from listening, which was played. To engage an additional student in the interval identification activity, the teacher may display a representation of a keyboard and invite a child to point out the half and whole steps as they are played by a classmate. The teacher can say "Start on G," the instrumentalist plays that note plus one other, and the "pointing" person must decide whether the sound went up or down, and how far it went from the initial G. For variety, the process can be reversed so that the pointer indicates a note on the simulated keyboard and directs the player to "go up a whole step" or to "go down a half step"; the class decides whether the directive was carried out properly. The first note need not be named in this procedure, because everyone, including the player, can identify it visually according to its placement on the posted keyboard. When *sounds* are to be identified, however, and either placed into notation or pointed out on a displayed keyboard, the listeners must be told the letter name of at least the first sound. A few persons can name any random pitch they hear, without reference to other information, but this ability is rare even among the adult population and should not be expected of elementary school children.

Scales

Some songs are especially suitable for conveying the idea of scales. "The Singing School" round is unusual in the fact that it features both a complete ascending and a complete descending scale.

THE SINGING SCHOOL

Traditional Round

From *101 Rounds for Singing*, published by World Around Songs, Burnsville, North Carolina, 1965.

Here is how a teacher might present "The Singing School" to introduce the concept of scales:

> "Now that we've sung this song, did you hear anything different about the pitches? If you don't remember from the sound, look over the music carefully to see what's different about it. The rhythms are easy, but what about the order of the notes? I'll give you a minute to study the notation by yourselves. . . . All right, who's found something unusual in this song? Javier?"
>
> "Well, in the fifth line the notes don't jump around very much. They just go straight up for a while."
>
> "That's right! It's a scale beginning on C. Sing the notes with me, class, with their letter names: C D E F G A B C." [The class sings the scale.] "Does a scale appear anywhere else in the song?"
>
> After a pause, Elizabeth volunteers, "Yeah, in the first line. The notes go down, but a couple of them stop and repeat along the way."
>
> "Good, Elizabeth. Why don't you and Javier go to the bells and play the scales you discovered. Javier, play yours first. Class, sing the letter names along with him." [The scale is sung by the class.] "Elizabeth, you don't need to repeat notes at those two places in your scale. Just play them once in order; class, sing." [The scale is sung in descending order.]
>
> "Now let's do the song again. Notice how the notes all seem to be related to the sound of the scales."

Major and Minor Keys

Songs in both major and minor keys are sung with ease by children in the early grades. By the upper elementary grades, students can be made familiar with the distinctive features of each tonality.

An easy first step in learning to compare the difference in sound between major and minor keys is to sing "Go Tell Aunt Rhody" in both tonalities. The conventional version, which is in major, is shown here.

GO TELL AUNT RHODY

Pennsylvania Dutch Song

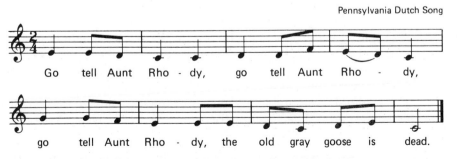

Minor Scales and Key Signatures

A *minor scale* is formed when the third step above the keynote is lowered. Other notes in a minor scale may also be lowered, but the lowered third step is the essential feature of minor keys. The basic pattern of whole and half steps is:

In the basic minor scale, called *natural* minor, steps 3, 6, and 7 are lowered a half step from their position in the corresponding major scale. The dotted lines in the diagram below show where steps 3, 6, and 7 would be if the scale were major.

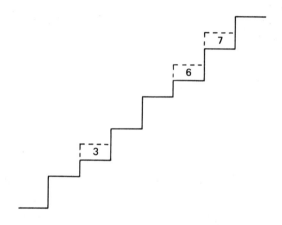

Two other forms of minor scale are sometimes encountered in music. In *harmonic minor*, scale step 7 is raised so that it is only a half step below the upper keynote, step 8. This alteration provides a strong lead-in to the upper keynote, but it creates a wide interval of one and a half steps between the lowered step 6 and the raised step 7. The problem is resolved in *melodic minor* by raising both steps 6 and 7 when the melodic line ascends and lowering them (to duplicate the sound of natural minor) when the melodic line descends. This compromise preserves the "leading tone" quality of step 7 moving up to the nearby step 8, and it also eliminates the awkwardly wide interval found in the harmonic minor scale.

Minor scales, in whatever form, have a characteristic sound that is sometimes called "sad" or "dark," although no words can adequately describe a musical quality. The melancholy aspect of music in minor keys may be due in part to the consistently lowered step 3, which distinguishes such music from the sound of the more frequently heard major keys.

Minor key signatures conform to the pattern of the natural minor scale. Here are the signatures for all minor keys:

When this chart is compared with the one for major key signatures on page 118, it will be noticed that each minor key has three more flats (or three fewer sharps) than the major key built on the same note. These lowered notes represent the lowered steps 3, 6, and 7 of the natural minor scale.

A key signature must account for every sharp or flat in the key, even though a few pitches may not be present in the melody. A complete key signature gives information about the music, and the harmonizing chords are likely to involve any pitches not included in the melody.

Every key signature does double duty, because it can serve for either a major or a minor key. Major and minor keys that share the same signature are called *relative* keys. To find out whether the major or the minor key is intended by a particular signature, one can look at the notation of the song to see what pitch seems to be most prominent, especially at the beginning and end of the piece. If the note is a half step above the last sharp, or a fourth below the last flat, it is the keynote for a major key. But if the important note is three half steps below what would be the major key center, the piece is in a minor key and the predominant note is the key center.

The teacher can write the music on the board (and the words, if they are unfamiliar to the class) and proceed as follows:

"Here's a song in a major key. It looks like simple stuff, but don't worry—I'll take care of that. Sing it through with me." [The class sings all verses.]

"That's the way! You either have good memories from singing this song in the primary grades, or you're turning into good sight-singers. Now that you've performed this piece in its traditional major setting, you're ready to transpose the music into the corresponding minor key.

"You do this simply by lowering the *third step* of the scale from E to E♭ whenever you come to it in the song. Seth, would you come to the board and write downward-pointing arrows over every E as a reminder to the class. The arrow will mean two things: 'This is the note!' and 'Sing it lower!'"

[Seth finds every E, with some coaching from the class, and draws an arrow over each one. As he works, the teacher explains further to the class.]

"E is what step number in this key?" [A few people recall that it is step 3.] "If E is step 3, what note is step 1, where we would start the scale for this song?"

[The class is silent, so the teacher offers help.] "From E, which is step 3, count downward '3 2 1.' Or go backward in the alphabet E D C. C is the keynote."

"Seth has our music ready now. Here's how it will sound." [The teacher sings the first verse in minor.]

"Sing the song with me this time. Here's our E♭ starting note." [The class sings all verses in minor.]

"Do you notice a difference in sound between this minor version and the original major version? We'll do it again, just for fun. But first, Roberto, would you come up and put a flat sign in front of every E? That's how the note E♭ should really look."

[Roberto hesitates to leave his seat, but after a friend traces a flat in the air, Roberto goes to the board and draws that symbol satisfactorily.]

"Thanks, Roberto. This time, class, notice the words and make the music sad! Make me cry with your singing!" [The class laughs and sings the song.]

The students' feeling for key, whether major or minor, should be reinforced frequently. They should be given opportunities to sing a scale, recognize aurally and visually whether a phrase stops on the keynote or not, and sing the nearest keynote from any scale step in a song.

Contour

Students in the upper grades should become increasingly aware of the shape or *contour* of melodies. This aspect of music considers the pitches of a melody not as they relate to a key center, but as they relate to one another in the flow of melody. Contour is determined by two factors: direction (does the pitch move up or down or stay the same?) and interval (does the pitch move by step or by leap?) When students notice the contour of a melody, they are scanning a line of music in a way that will help in reading music and in analyzing form.

The Russian folk song "Minka" has a rather even contour with many repeated notes, except for two measures. Here is how a teacher might lead a class to notice the melodic features of "Minka" (p. 178).

> "I'm drawing eight blank measures on the board; here are the bar lines. I'm going to make a dot for every pitch in 'Minka,' then one of you can come up and 'connect the dots' to show us the shape or contour of the melody. Sing 'Minka' with me now, on 'la.'"
>
> [The class sings as the teacher draws a dot for every note, in time with the music. By the end of the song, the board reveals this pattern of dots:]

> "Who wants to come up now and connect the dots so we can check the contour of the song? Okay, Torisha." [Torisha draws the lines.] "That's good. Thanks.
>
> "Ellen, how would you describe the contour for the first eight measures of 'Minka'? Is it rather even? Jagged?"
>
> "Well, it doesn't move a whole lot. I'd say it's pretty even," Ellen decides.
>
> "Okay, Ellen. Now Christopher, why do you suppose measure 7 has a different contour from the other seven measures?"
>
> Christopher shrugs and speculates, "Maybe if people aren't paying attention, they'll all of a sudden notice what's going on when the music gets to that place."
>
> "Could be," the teacher agrees. "If the music didn't move around, the song probably wouldn't be as interesting. To test your theory, Christopher, we'll all sing the first eight measures, but this time in measure 7 we'll repeat the first note four times while singing 'Min-ka, Min-ka.'"

The class can compare the contours of various songs. "Minka" and "Tum-Balalaika" (p. 180) present two very different contours. When the children have learned the latter song, the teacher can solicit their ideas as to how its melodic contour compares with that of "Minka," and what features in the music might account for the difference.

> "Then the consensus of the class is that 'Minka' has a smoother contour and generally smaller intervals than 'Tum-Balalaika.' You say the melody's easier in 'Minka.' Is there any reason for this, do you think? Tyler?"

MINKA

English words by W. S. Haynie   Russian Folk Song

"Uh, well . . . maybe this guy's serenading to Minka on a guitar and he doesn't know how to play very well, so he has to make up an easy song." [The class considers this a likely reason and regards Tyler approvingly.]

Alterations and Decorations

A composer or performer can change a melody simply by adding ornamental or decorative notes. If the ornamentation is the idea of the composer, the added notes are written into the notation. Sometimes, how-

See the full moon shin - ing,
win - ter snow is fall - ing,

full moon shin - ing, Then I will for thee be pin - ing,
snow is fall - ing, I must go for love is call - ing,

(Melody)

Min - ka, Min - ka, fair - est maid - en, Min - ka, Min - ka mine.
Call - ing me to be with Min - ka, Fair - est Min - ka mine.

Min - ka, Min - ka, fair - est maid - en, Min - ka mine.
Call - ing me to be with Min - ka, Min - ka mine.

From E. Boardman et al., *Exploring Music*, Book 6. Words copyright © 1975 by Holt, Rinehart & Winston, Publishers.

ever, the singer or instrumental soloist adds them extemporaneously. This is done particularly by singers in the folk and popular idiom.

"I'm on My Way" (p. 181) is an expressive and folk-like melody that contains *grace notes*. In appearance, a grace note is about half the size of a regular note, and it has a slash running diagonally through the stem and flag. Theoretically a grace note has no rhythmic value, although in fact it must consume a small amount of time. To sing a grace note, the performer must "flick off" the note quickly, so that it sounds like a catch in the voice.

Decorative notes are more common in instrumental than in vocal music. Phrases that are conceived instrumentally are usually hard to sing, but the class should hear and study at least a few examples of instrumental music to observe how melodies are enhanced through ornamentation. Here is how a teacher might introduce Chopin's *Fantasie-Impromptu*, Op. 66:

"As we sing 'I'm on My Way' again, notice those two short, quick notes that are called 'grace notes.'" [The class sings the song.] "The same kind of ornamentation also occurs in instrumental music. Here's a work for piano by a composer named Chopin. His name is spelled this way." [The teacher writes the name on the board.] "But it's pronounced 'Show-pan.'

"This piano piece is in three rather long sections. There are a lot of fast notes in the first section. The music is supposed to sound made up.

TUM-BALALAIKA

Jewish Folk Song
Arranged by Mary Val Marsh

From Mary Val Marsh et al., *The Spectrum of Music* 1975, Macmillan Publishing Co., Inc. Used by permission.

I'M ON MY WAY

Words Adapted by Venoris Cates

Afro-American Spiritual

1. I'm on my way____ And I won't turn back!____
2. I'm on my way____ to the Free - dom Land!____

I'm on my way____ and I won't turn back!____
I'm on my way____ to the Free - dom Land!____

I'm on my way____ and I won't turn back!____
I'm on my way____ to the Free - dom Land!____

I'm on my way,____ My Lord I'm on my way.____
I'm on my way,____ My Lord I'm on my way.____

3. I asked my brother to come with me.
   I asked my brother to come with me.
   I asked my brother to come with me.
   I asked my brother, My Lord, to come with me.

From Mary Val Marsh et al., *The Spectrum of Music* 1975, Macmillan Publishing Co., Inc. Words used by permission of Venoris M. Cates.

In fact, the title of this piece is '*Fantasie-Impromptu*,' which means 'imagined and made up on the spot.'

"The second section is more singable, and that's the melody to which Chopin adds a lot of decorative notes. The third section returns to the same music that occurred in the first section. Listen carefully to this music now, especially to the decorative notes that Chopin adds to the middle section."

Style of Performance

Sometimes a melody, by its very nature, seems to call for a certain style of performance, regardless of the words set to it. "Greensleeves" is such a melody. It glides along in a smooth and graceful way, partly because of its compound meter, perhaps, and partly because of its tempo. Whatever the reason for the listener's expectation, a choppy, forceful style for this melody would seem to destroy its graceful quality, no matter what the words might be. Actually, other words have been set to this melody, one of the most familiar texts being "What Child Is This?" That text also contributes to the gentle feeling of the melody.

Students can learn more about performance style, or *interpretation*, if the teacher provides opportunities for them to experiment with different types of melodies.

> "You're singing 'Greensleeves' very well, with a smooth, graceful quality. You've done one interpretation; now do a different one. How do you think 'Greensleeves' will sound if you sing it loudly, in a choppy style?" [Rasheed emits an unsolicited "Yecch."] "Rasheed has let us know his feelings, but keep an open mind, Rasheed."
>
> "Let's run a comparison in which we sing two songs in the opposite style from the way in which we first sang them. First we'll sing 'Greensleeves' forcefully, with separation between the notes, then we'll do 'Minka' in a smooth and gentle style."
>
> [The teacher sets a brisk tempo for a strongly accented rendition of "Greensleeves," and slows the customary tempo of "Minka" to allow for an expressive legato quality.]

It may not be easy for the class to sing in an inappropriate style; it requires concentration, especially if one interpretation of the song has become habitual for the singers. Occasional altering of the style, as a classroom exercise, can be beneficial to the students, however. It causes them to think about interpretation, and it helps them to be more flexible in their singing. After each classroom experiment in interpretation, the students should be encouraged to share their impressions of the musical effect. The following exchange of ideas might occur following the singing of "Greensleeves" and "Minka" described earlier.

> "There now. You've sung the two songs with opposite interpretations. What are your impressions?" [A few class members convey their reactions by facial expressions of distaste.]
>
> "Joni, you don't seem too thrilled with the results. Why?"
>
> "I don't know. The 'Greensleeves' sounded like someone ahead of me, jogging, and I kept wanting them to slow down and get serious about the song. I felt like they were running faster than I wanted to go," Joni adds uncertainly.

GREENSLEEVES

For autoharp, transpose to D minor

Old English Folk Song

1. A - las! my love, ___ you do me wrong, ___ To
2. Ah, Green - sleeves, now___ fare - well, a - dieu, ___ To

cast me off___ dis - cour - teous - ly; For I have loved_ you,
God I pray_ to pros - per thee, For I am still___ thy

oh, so long,___ De - light - ing in ___ your com - pa - ny.
sweet - heart true;___ Come once___ a - gain___ to meet ___ me.

Refrain

Green - sleeves_ was all my joy,___ And oh, Green- sleeves_ was my de- light,

Green - sleeves,_my heart of gold,_ And all___ for La - dy Green - sleeves.

"I know the feeling, Joni. Any other comments about the style? Richard?"

"The 'Minka' sort of dragged along and sounded real dull. I like it better fast."

"I do too, Richard. Class, both Joni and Richard have made a good point about interpretation. Did the rest of you notice that we changed several aspects of these songs as we tried to create a different style? Joni and Richard mentioned that we changed the tempo, and that made a difference. What else?"

[With urging, the class remembers the changes they made in the level of loudness. The teacher points out that the accents fall into this category, because an accent is a moment of sudden loudness.]

"So you see, class, a lot of factors go into your interpretation of a song. Your job as a performer is to notice all you can about the style of a song, and then sing or play it in a way that you think will best convey its meaning to the listener."

In all discussions of style, the teacher must be careful not to say that certain interpretations are "right" or "wrong," "correct" or "incorrect." It is better to convey to students the importance of keeping an open mind, especially in matters as subjective as musical expression. A particular interpretation can be evaluated with words like "appropriate" or "inappropriate," and even "I like it that way" or "I don't like it that way." But categorical statements as to rightness are hard to substantiate, even when they are backed by tradition and the consensus of knowledgeable musicians.

Listening to Melodies

To many children, "melody" is synonymous with "song." Older students should begin to understand, however, that a melody can be more than a singable tune. When a melody is conceived as the basis for a long work of music, it is called a *theme*. In instrumental music, the theme need not be songlike; in fact, it may be quite unsingable. It can be remembered by the mind, but if it is intended for instruments, it may be too complex or too angular in contour to be sung.

The second movement of a symphony or concerto usually features melodic writing, and such music, if not too long or complicated, is attractive to children who are learning to listen to melodies in instrumental music. Here is how a teacher might present the second movement of Mendelssohn's Symphony No. 4 ("Italian") to help students learn about melody in symphonic music.

"Here's a portion of a symphony by a man named Felix Mendelssohn, who lived in Germany about 150 years ago. The music has a songlike melody, and to help you remember it, I'll play the first 45 seconds of the music for you twice. Notice that the melody doesn't start right away; there's a short introduction of about 10 seconds. Okay, here we go. Listen carefully and try to remember what you're hearing."

To appreciate Mendelssohn's later treatment of the melody, the listener must be able to remember its original sound, so committing the theme to memory is important. The teacher can aid that process by asking the students to participate in a limited way.

> "I'm going to play those first 45 seconds once more. This time, hum along softly with the orchestra as it plays the melody. That will help you remember it."

The class needs to realize that symphonic music generally involves a broad time span. This means that the listener must notice not just the melody itself, but also the thematic changes and transitional material that may occur between appearances of the melody. The teacher might continue:

> "The first melody in this music by Mendelssohn is basically a song consisting of four two-measure phrases. You've already hummed it, and it's starting to sound familiar to you. This time I'll let the recording play longer. See if you can keep track of the four phrases as the song is repeated three more times. The first two phrases get changed quite a bit, but you'll recognize the end of each appearance of the song because the notes move evenly downward by step." [The teacher plays about the first two minutes of the movement.]

When students work on an activity that requires intensive concentration, as careful listening does, the teacher should limit the amount of time devoted to that activity in a single sitting. On another day the teacher may want to continue working with the second movement of Mendelssohn's Symphony No. 4.

> "I hope you remember the melody that Mendelssohn composed for the second movement of his 'Italian' Symphony, because we're going to study it some more today.
>
> "You'll hear the melody four times. Next, the music takes on what I'll describe as a 'Halloween' feeling, because the instruments sort of quietly sneak around. Then you'll hear something different. At that point, raise your hands. I'll stop the recording and ask you what's different about the music." [The children discover that the contrasting section is in major and has a rich full sound.]

Following the same basic procedure, the teacher can help the class notice other melodic features of this movement. Perhaps most obvious to inexperienced listeners is the fact that the main theme is accompanied by continuous "walking" notes in the low strings each time it occurs. A somewhat harder assignment is for the class to notice that the two-note figure near the end—the one that serves to unify the movement—is derived from the theme.

Skillful manipulation of themes and melodic ideas is prevalent in most of the music heard in concert halls. In fact, it is the basis for *sonata form*, which has long been a favored organizing technique in movements of symphonies, concertos, and chamber works. Sonata form consists of three large segments, the middle one of which is called the *development* section. That section is expressly devised for thematic development, which refers to the manipulation of melodic ideas. Many other types of concert music also feature an imaginative treatment of themes. A melody can be structurally important and can be recast in different contexts by a skillful composer.

Review Questions

1. Suppose that a class does not understand the difference between a half step and a whole step. In addition to providing a verbal explanation, what can a teacher do to help the class understand the difference?
2. (True or false?) Complete ascending or descending scales occur rather frequently in songs.
3. What is the main difference between the pattern of whole and half steps in major scales and the pattern in minor scales?
4. a. The word that refers to the shape or outline of a melody is (scale, tonality, contour, pitch, content).
   b. What are some ways to help a class notice the shape of a melody?
5. Which song has a wider range, "I'm on My Way" (p. 181) or "Greensleeves" (p. 183)?

Activities

1. Select a song from one of the music books designed for the upper elementary grades. Then do the following:
   a. Determine what notes appear at least once.
   b. Put the notes into ascending or descending order.
   c. Determine which is the keynote.
   d. Write down the pattern of whole and half steps of the scale.
   e. Decide if the scale is major or minor.
   f. Draw on a blank piece of paper the contour of each line of the song.
   g. Decide if the melody itself (*not* the words) seems to require a certain style of performance.
2. Referring to the song selected for activity 1, choose two aspects of its melody that you might teach to a class of fifth- or sixth-grade students. Write a plan or strategy for teaching those two aspects.
3. Select a second—or "slow"—movement of a symphony, concerto, string quartet, or piano sonata. (The music series books discuss a few such

works.) Listen to the movement enough times to feel familiar with it. After you have in mind how the composer has treated the melody, decide how you might teach this aspect of the music to a class of upper elementary school students.

Skill Exercise

Play the following minor-key melodies on an instrument, then sing them. The symbols in parentheses are reminders about the key signature.

13

Harmony and Counterpoint

Although primary grade children experience the simultaneous sounding of pitches in the music they hear and in their singing of rounds and accompanied songs, they are generally unaware of its significance. In the upper grades, however, they can begin to study harmony as a basic aspect of music. A knowledge of harmony goes beyond the admirable skills of being able to sing a song in parts or to push the buttons on an autoharp; it implies that the students understand the organization of the simultaneous sounds that are being produced.

Harmony is the effect created when pitches are sounding together at a given moment. In music notation such sounds are aligned vertically on the page, and form an entity known as a *chord*. *Counterpoint*, on the other hand, is the occurrence of two or more melodies at the same time. Because melodies move from left to right in music notation, counterpoint is sometimes described as being linear or horizontal. The sounds of harmony and counterpoint, of course, are neither vertical nor horizontal, because music is an art of time rather than space. The visual association is helpful, however, as a reminder of the way in which harmony and counterpoint each engages the listener's attention.

Counterpoint

Elementary school children are experiencing counterpoint whenever they sing a round. Rounds are a logical introduction to such music because the same melody is sung by everyone, but at different times, of course. Furthermore, a round clearly illustrates a characteristic feature of counterpoint, or *contrapuntal* music: the melodic lines should be perceived as being equally important. When the lines are identical, as in a round, they should receive equal attention.

The next step beyond rounds in terms of complexity is music in which two different melodies occur at the same time. It requires a little more ability to conceptualize two different lines of music performed together than it does to think of the same melody being performed a few beats later. A good way to present the varying lines of counterpoint is to let the class sing *partner songs*, which are two different songs that can be sung at the same time. Here is how partner songs might be introduced:

"Let's check out your singing of a couple of songs that you've known for years. First, 'Three Blind Mice.' Here's the starting note. Rea-dy, sing." [The class sings through the song, beginning on E.]

"Fine. Now another old favorite. Here's the starting pitch for 'Are You Sleeping?' Rea-dy, sing." [The class sings through "Are You Sleeping?" beginning on C.]

"Okay. But I need to check out one more thing. Can you keep each song going if only half the class is singing it with you? We'll see. You people from here to the door sing 'Are You Sleeping?' Rea-dy, go." [Half the class sings the song.] "The rest of you sing 'Three Blind Mice.' Rea-dy, go. [The other half sings "Three Blind Mice."]

"All right, here comes the payoff: Sing the two songs together. Remember, no rushing, and no trying to drown out the other song. 'Mice' people, here's your pitch . . . and 'sleeping' people, here's your pitch. . . . Rea-dy, sing." [The class sings the two songs at the same time.]

"See, it worked! Want to trade songs? This time, sing your new song on 'la' instead of with the regular words, so that you can give your attention to the way the tunes combine. Here are your notes. . . . Rea-dy, 'la.'" [The class sings the songs together again.]

"The tunes sound pretty good together, don't they? When you perform two melodies at the same time, you're producing *counterpoint.*"

Partner songs are more likely to be successful when the class knows both songs well and the teacher gives clear directions as to tempo and starting pitches. A cue sheet is a helpful aid to the teacher:

	Starting Note		**Starting Beat**
Home on the Range	low A	} in the key of D	3 in 3-beat meter
My Home's in Montana	high A		
This Old Man	high C	} in the key of F	1 in 2-beat meter
Skip to My Lou	A		
Ten Little Indians (Pawpaw Patch)	F		
Go Tell Aunt Rhody	F♯	} in the key of D	1 in 2-beat meter
London Bridge	A		
Merrily We Roll Along	F♯		

Counterpoint is not always so obvious as the combining of two known songs. In elementary music series books, counterpoint is usually produced by adding a *descant*—a decorative line performed with a more important melody, generally in a higher pitch range than the basic melody and in contrast to it. The words of a descant are usually similar to those of the melody, but the descant is not just a "shadow" of the melody, even though it is the less familiar of the two parts. A good descant possesses a melodic character of its own. It provides counterpoint because it is an independent line that is attractive in itself.

The arrangement on page 192 of "Joy to the World" is interesting for several reasons. First, the composer of the melody is generally believed to be George Frideric Handel, the same man who composed *Messiah*. The descant is by Lowell Mason, who established music in the public schools of the United States. The melody of "Joy to the World" contains one of the rare appearances of a complete scale within a song.

The teacher may want the class to notice some of the places where the descant differs from the melody.

"All right; you've spotted several phrases in which the descant goes off differently from the melody. Now here's a harder question. What do you notice about the two lines when each one has the words 'And heaven and nature sing'?" [Silence.]

"Then figure it out with me, class. When the melody is singing 'And heaven and nature sing,' what's the descant doing? Melanie?"

"Nothing; they have a rest," reports Melanie.

"Okay. What's the melody doing in the next measure when the descant sings some words? Carla?"

"The melody's holding on the word 'sing' through most of the measure," Carla says.

"Right. Now one more bit of research. Stefan, what happens in the next measure when the melody has words and notes? What's the descant doing?"

"Where? . . . Oh, yeah. The descant has just the word 'sing' and then a rest," Stefan decides.

"Good. So here's that question again. What can you figure out about the melody and the descant? Rebecca."

"Well, it seems like when the melody has activity, the descant holds more still, and when the descant moves, the melody holds still. The parts sort of trade off in how they move around," Rebecca concludes.

"That's it, Rebecca. It's a basic idea that happens often in counterpoint. If both parts are active all the time, the listeners have a hard time telling which part is which, and they lose interest. But if their attention is directed to one part and then another, the lines of melody stand out better and the piece is more appealing."

Intervals

The students can take a "sample" of the intervals in a two-part song such as "Joy to the World" and from that sample draw an important gener-

JOY TO THE WORLD

Words by Isaac Watts (from Psalm 98)

Music Arranged from
George F. Handel by Lowell Mason

alization about music. In the following situation, the teacher has taught the class how to find basic intervals.

"The other day you learned how to tell if an interval is a second, third, fourth, and so on. Today you'll use that knowledge to discover something important about music. We're going to run a survey of every other measure in 'Joy to the World' and find out what intervals occur most often between the melody and the descant. Jason, would you please keep score of the various intervals as they're mentioned by people in the class.

"Casey, what's the first interval in the first measure?"

"Uh . . . both parts have the same note . . . but I don't know if there's a name for that," Casey hesitates. [The teacher informs the class that such an interval is called a *unison*.]

"What's the first interval in the third measure?" asks the teacher, quickly taking the class through the initial intervals of the odd-numbered measures.

"Now we'll ask Jason, our record-keeper, to tell us the results for the first notes of the ten measures we looked at."

"There were five unisons, one third, three sixths, and one eighth," Jason reports. [The teacher reminds him that the name for "eighth" is "octave."]

"Remember, class, that an octave and a unison are practically the same thing, because the notes have the same name and blend together so well."

[Jason proposes that the class should now survey the even-numbered measures—a project for which he volunteers to serve again as reporter.]

Students in the upper elementary grades should have a chance to listen to contrapuntal music. Sometimes this music is like a round—the theme is heard alone, then other parts enter one after another with that same theme. In other contrapuntal music, two or more melodic lines are present throughout the work. For children in elementary school, it is good to begin with pieces that are relatively short and that contain a familiar melody. The following contrapuntal works are appropriate for early listening experiences.

J. S. Bach:	Chorale Prelude on "In Dulci Jubilo"
	Fugue in G Minor ("The Little")
	"Gigue" Fugue
	"Fanfare" Fugue
Handel:	"For Unto Us a Child Is Born" from *Messiah*
McBride:	"Pumpkin Eater's Little Fugue"
D. Scarlatti:	"Cat's" Fugue
Thomson:	Fugue and Chorale on "Yankee Doodle"

Playing the Autoharp

The *autoharp* is an instrument with metal strings stretched across a frame. The player strums across the strings with one hand, and with the other presses one of several buttons to obtain the desired note combinations. The autoharp is usually laid on the lap or on a flat surface, with the long side toward the player. A seated player can cradle the instrument in an upright position in one arm and press the buttons with the same hand.

Each button allows a different chord to be produced. A *chord* is the sounding of three or more pitches simultaneously. When a button is pressed, it pushes a set of felts against the unwanted strings to stop their sound. When the D button is pushed, for example, only the pitches of the D chord are allowed to vibrate when the autoharp is strummed.

The number of chord bars shows how many chords are possible on the instrument. A 15-bar autoharp is recommended to accommodate the chords suggested for most children's songs.

An autoharp is tuned by comparing the pitch of one string with the same note on a pitch pipe, piano, or other instrument with

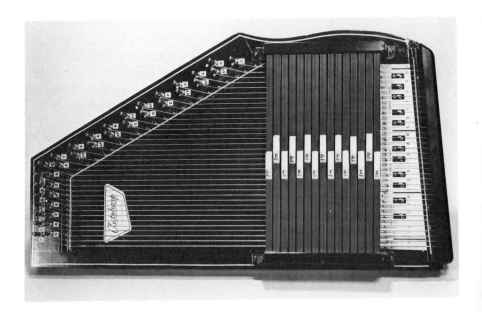

fixed pitch. A tuning wrench is placed securely over the tuning pin and slowly turned clockwise to raise the pitch, or counterclockwise to lower it. When one note has been tuned to its proper pitch, all strings of that name are then tuned to match it before the tuning proceeds to another note.

The tone of an autoharp can be varied by changing the type of pick used for strumming. A felt pick produces a softer and less metallic sound than a plastic pick. If neither is available, an eraser, rubber spatula, or paper clip can be substituted to vary the tone quality.

The style of strumming can be altered to produce further variety. Higher or lower strings can be emphasized in various phrases. For the heavier first beat of a measure, the low notes can be strummed more firmly, with the less emphasized beats being strummed more lightly on the higher strings.

The speed with which the strumming is repeated depends on the character of the piece. For a lively song, frequent strumming helps to maintain the brisk tempo. If the music is quiet and serene, less agitation (fewer strums) is more suitable.

To accompany songs with the autoharp when chord symbols are provided, a player simply pushes the button indicated and strums at a pace that seems appropriate for the music. If chord symbols are written only when a chord changes, several strums can occur following the appearance of only one symbol.

It is advisable for a player to strum with the most dexterous hand. If the instrument is positioned horizontally in front of a right-handed person, the player will need to cross the right hand over the left to strum midway along the length of the strings, where the best tone is produced.

The chord buttons are arranged in such a way that when the index finger of the left hand is placed over the button for the "home" chord, the next two fingers will be over the buttons for the next two most common chords in that key. This positioning of the fingers permits the player to sound the proper chords without looking at the instrument, and eliminates the need for fumbling and searching. The button arrangement for a 15-bar autoharp is pictured in Appendix C. That diagram shows that the three-finger position described above is applicable when playing in the keys of G, C, F, B♭, A minor, and D minor.

Chords

A *chord* is a combination of three or more tones sounding together. A *triad* is a particular type of chord: it consists of three tones that are each a third apart.

The *root* of a chord is the pitch on which the chord is built. The term "root" is not synonymous with the keynote or the first step of a scale, because any scale step can serve as the root of a chord. The root doesn't have to be the lowest-sounding pitch, either, because chord tones can be rearranged by assigning one or more to a different octave, and in this "scrambled" order the root may not be on the bottom of the stack. Whatever its position, however, it still retains its characteristic feel as the basic note of that chord.

An Arabic numeral such as 1, 3, or 6 refers to a single tone and describes its position in a given scale. A Roman numeral such as I, IV, or V refers to a complete chord and indicates the scale step on which it is built. The Roman numeral also suggests how a chord will function in a given key. A I chord, for example, sounds stable and final because it is built on step 1—the keynote—of a particular scale. A V chord, by contrast, sounds restless and active.

Certain chords appear more often than others, especially in the relatively simple songs sung by children. The three most common chords are called *primary chords*, and are shown here with their roots related to the scale, which in this case is C major:

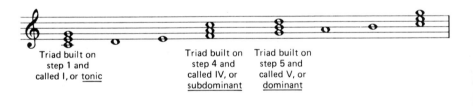

Triad built on step 1 and called I, or <u>tonic</u>

Triad built on step 4 and called IV, or <u>subdominant</u>

Triad built on step 5 and called V, or <u>dominant</u>

Harmony

Harmony is the simultaneous sounding of three or more pitches, and its primary function is to provide accompaniment, or background, for a melody. Because the autoharp offers an automatic way to play chords easily, the students themselves can play the simpler accompaniments with minimal teacher direction. The players can concentrate on the chords as units of

Primary chords in a minor key are derived in the same way, with one slight change. The dominant chord in a minor key sounds better when the seventh step of the scale (the middle note of the V triad) is raised one half step. With this alteration, the primary chords in E minor are:

A *seventh chord* consists of four pitches, each a third apart. The notes G B D F form a seventh chord with G as its root. This particular chord appears most often in C major, where the root of the chord (G) is the fifth or "dominant" step of the scale. A four-note chord built on that step is called a *dominant seventh* chord. The word "seventh" in this context does not mean that there are seven notes in the chord or that the root is step 7 of the scale. It simply refers to the interval between the root and the top note (G up to F).

The I or tonic triad acts as a "home base" from which the harmony moves and then returns. Almost all songs end on the tonic triad because the music seems incomplete if it is not sounded. The tonic triad is usually preceded by the dominant, because the chord progression V to I gives the music a strong feeling of conclusion.

sound, and they are freed from worrying about which notes go into every chord. The procedures for teaching harmony should enable the class to understand that the notes in the melody determine what chords are played and when they are played. The chord symbols appearing in the notation of a song are someone's decision as to the chords implied by that particular melody.

Harmonizing with a simple and familiar song like "Go Tell Aunt

Rhody" (p. 173) is a good way to make the students sensitive to the places where chord changes are needed.

> "Karl, take the autoharp, please, and strum a C chord on each beat of 'Go Tell Aunt Rhody.'" [Karl strums the chords feebly.] "Louder!" [He strums more forcefully.] "That's the way! Sing softly, class, so that you can hear the chords on the autoharp. Karl, keep playing that C chord until we tell you to stop, even if it sounds wrong to you. Class, when you think the C chord clashes with the melody, raise your hands. Karl will give us a C chord first so that we get the starting pitch. . . . Rea-dy, sing and play."
>
> [Karl strums vehemently while the class sings softly. A few hands go up in the third measure to indicate that the C chord needs to change. Uncertain students raise their hands in measures 4 and 5, in delayed imitation of their classmates.]
>
> "Listen again, so you can hear for sure when the C chord doesn't fit the melody." [The class sings the song again accompanied by the C chord.] "Okay, now we need another chord, the G7 chord. Joanne, you take Karl's place and strum the autoharp; we don't want to wear him out. Strum the G7 chord loudly." [Joanne starts strumming.] "Yes, like that.
>
> "All right, class, sing again and tell me when the G7 doesn't sound right any longer by raising your hands. We'll sing just the last two measures, where it says, 'old gray goose is dead.' Joanne will give us the chord so that we have the right starting pitch. . . . Rea-dy, sing." [The class sings, and on the last measure hands are again raised to indicate that a change of chord is needed.]
>
> "Trina, what chord do you think we might try on the last measure where a change is needed?"
>
> Trina shrugs. "The C chord is the only other one we've talked about so far," she guesses.
>
> [The teacher asks Joanne to try the C chord, and the class decides that it makes a good ending.]

By introducing the G7 so that it is played experimentally in the last measure, rather than earlier in the song, the class is more likely to hear the dissonance of that chord with the final sustained note of the piece. Judgments about harmony are easier to make when there is time to consider the chord, and no chord follows to distract the young listeners' attention. When the class has determined the chord order that sounds best with this melody, students can take turns accompanying the singing.

Harmony can be implied by vocal as well as instrumental accompaniments. After a little experience, students enjoy harmonizing simply by singing chord roots while others sing the melody. For "Go Tell Aunt Rhody," the class might first sing the chord roots with letter names, one note per measure, as follows: "C C G C, C C G C." The pattern can move from C to the G above or below it; there is no difference harmonically. In fact, the class should try the part both ways. When the singers feel secure with the chord roots, they can divide into two sections, one singing the melody and the other the root pattern. They should trade parts frequently, of course.

Learning to hear needed chord changes is a slow process for some students. It takes repeated practice over a number of months for them to learn to fit chords with a melody.

Chord construction

Although students in the upper grades of elementary school do not need to delve deeply into the subject of harmony, a basic knowledge of chord construction will help them find satisfaction in the harmonizing efforts of themselves and others.

Here is how a teacher might help the class discover the note pattern that is basic in chord construction.

"On the chalkboard I've written the letter names for every note in the F major scale: F, G, A, and so on. The letters are spread way out, and the note lineup extends for two octaves. You see three scales just alike.

"I'm going to tell you the notes that go into three chords. For each chord someone will come up to the board, mark the chord notes, and connect them together with a bracket. The first chord is built on F, and it has the notes F A C. Natalie, would you circle and connect those letters? Mark them from left to right, like the order in which I named them." [Natalie correctly circles the letters and draws the bracket.]

"Fine, Natalie. Gina, on the next line show us the B♭ chord. It's B♭ D F." [Gina draws the three circles and brackets the B♭ chord.] "B♭ D F. That's the way.

"Now, the last chord has one more note than the F or B♭ chords. It's the C7 chord, and its notes are C E G B♭. Jared, would you circle each of those letters on the board?" [Jared, working cautiously and in need of reminders, finally marks the four letters of the C7 chord and places a bracket above them. The scales look like this.]

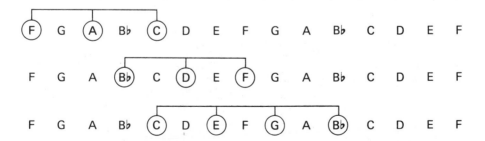

"Thanks, Jared. You see, class, why there's a two-octave scale on the board? Jared's chord won't fit into a one-octave scale unless we scramble the notes, and we don't want to mix them up yet. Sing the chord tones one at a time with me as I point to each note. Here's the pitch for F. . . . Letter names, rea-dy sing." [The class sings the pitches in the chords.]

"Now then. You're about to discover an underlying 'secret' of chords. Who sees or hears a pattern in each of these chords? Leanne?"

"They all use every other letter; they have a note and then they skip a note," Leanne observes.

"Yeah," Trent interrupts. "The notes go jump, jump, jump, like in checkers."

The teacher confirms their conclusion. "That's the secret combination, all right. That every-other-note arrangement is the basic pattern for almost all the chords you'll ever hear in music. What's the interval between those chord tones, class? . . . Sure, it's a third. Our system of harmony is built on thirds. Chords are built on what interval pattern? Everybody say it! *Thirds!*"

Learning about chords should be tied in as much as possible with actual music. Almost any song can serve as the context in which chord construction is examined and harmonization is experienced. "Down in the

DOWN IN THE VALLEY

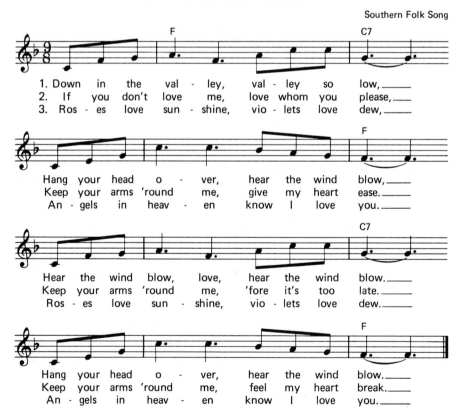

Southern Folk Song

Valley" is especially suitable because it involves only two chords and moves at a slow tempo.

The song "Hanukah" indicates the three chords that harmonize best with the melody. An autoharp accompaniment would be an appropriate addition after the class has learned the song. Assigning two children to the autoharp—one to strum and one to press the chord bars—not only will give more children a chance to play but will simplify the complexity of playing three different chords, particularly if the teacher gives finger cues to the child pressing the chord bars. The signals might be as follows: one finger held up by the teacher indicates a C chord, four fingers represent the F chord, and five fingers indicate the G[7] chord. Although young children do not need to know the significance of the finger numbers, the teacher may find it helpful to remember that in C major, the C chord is known as I, the F chord is IV, and G[7] is V[7].

Fitting chords to melodies

When the students can hear the implied changes of harmony in a melody, and when they have some understanding of chord construction, they can begin to consider why certain chords fit a melody and others do

HANUKAH

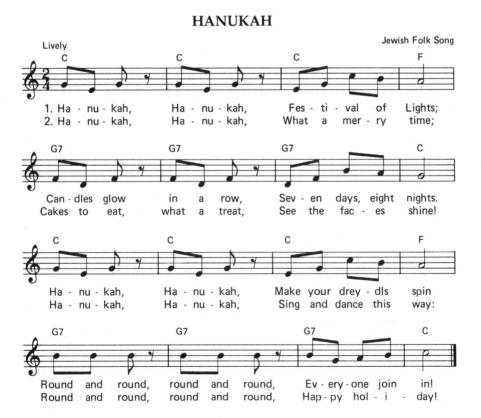

not. The clue to good chord selection usually can be found within the melody itself.

As the students learn to recognize thirds in chord construction, they become more sensitive to that pattern when they see it in a melody. For example, the first five notes of "Down in the Valley" (p. 200) are C F G A F, and four of those five notes are in the F chord, so that is the logical choice. (The G in that measure is merely a passing tone between F and A.) The first seven notes of "The Star-Spangled Banner" form an unusually extended chord outline. Chord selection is expedited in such a situation because the melody allows so few options.

By working with a round like "Dona Nobis Pacem" ("Grant Us Peace"), students can gain further insight into why certain chords do or do not fit well with a given fragment of the melody.

When the simultaneously sounding measures are aligned vertically, it is relatively easy for the class to see how harmony is achieved in a round. In the first measure, for example, the longest note values in each part form an F A C chord. Experienced students can go on to determine, with minimal

DONA NOBIS PACEM

Latin Hymn
Attributed to Palestrina

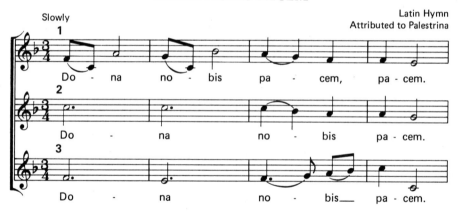

help from the teacher, that the basic harmonic progression for this round consists of one chord per measure, as follows: F C7 F C B♭ F C7 F.

"Dona Nobis Pacem" is longer and more complex than most rounds that children sing in elementary school. Short rounds like "Are You Sleeping?" and "Three Blind Mice" can be harmonized with a single chord, because when the phrases are short and entrances of the tune occur closely after one another, there is not enough time to accommodate different chords. The longer the phrases, the more harmonic variety is possible. Most songs cannot be sung as rounds because the harmony changes at a different spot in each phrase. To be successful, a round must have phrases that are equal in length, identical in harmonic background, and melodically different so that no two phrases will produce an extended unison passage when they are performed simultaneously.

A chord is not required on every note of a melody; only those notes that are longer or more important are harmonized. The meter of the song is also a factor in chord selection, because chord changes are more likely to occur on the strong first beat of a measure than on a weaker beat. A harmonic change occurring partway through a beat is rare.

Students in the upper elementary grades should become familiar with the two words that describe the relative degree of tension or restlessness in simultaneous sounds: *consonant* and *dissonant*. Most of the songs found in elementary music books contain few passages of extended dissonance in the voice parts. An occasional momentary dissonance adds zest to the music, and the singers can be encouraged to notice the way in which the dissonance resolves to a more consonant sound.

Review Questions

1. What is the basic difference between harmony and counterpoint?
2. Why are partner songs especially suitable for teaching the concept of counterpoint?
3. What is the relationship between a melody and its chords?
4. How can children learn to recognize when a change of chord is implied in a melody?
5. How can a teacher help a class to discover the pattern of notes found in almost all chords?
6. What is the main benefit of studying a round with its notation set in "layers," one part above another?
7. What are the three basic chords with which most elementary school songs can be accompanied?
8. What is the difference between the words "consonance" and "dissonance"?

Activities

1. From a music series book, select five songs in which a chord is clearly outlined somewhere in the melody.
2. Select a song with a descant or with two concurrent melodies.
   a. Sample the intervals between the two parts by identifying the interval on the first beat of every other measure. Write a one-sentence summary of your findings.
   b. Compare the amount of "activity" in each line, noticing whether the melodic motion generally alternates between the parts or occurs in each line simultaneously.

Skill Exercise

Decide which chords sound best as a harmonization for "Dona Nobis Pacem" (p. 202). Identify the chords that seem most appropriate for each measure by writing both the letter name and the Roman numeral for each chord. Check your selection of chords by playing your harmonization on the autoharp as you sing the melody.

C H A P T E R

14

Timbres of Voices
and Instruments

T he process of encouraging children to notice differences in tone quality continues beyond the primary grades. The concept of timbre and
its role in music is enlarged and refined as the students progress
through the upper grades.

Vocal Timbres

Opportunities for examining timbres are evident when the class decides on the type of singing tone that best reflects the mood of a song. For
example, should the singers try to achieve a mellow, warm sound? Should
they try to sound angry or joyous? How does a singer change the timbre of
his or her voice to achieve a desired effect? When the students listen to a
recording of a song or choral work, they should notice the vocal timbres
that result when the voice is varied for dramatic effect.

In the primary grades, the teacher encourages the children to notice if
the music is sung by a male or female. They should expand their powers of
observation in the upper grades by learning to recognize the differences in
timbre among the four basic divisions of adult voices. From highest to
lowest pitch range, the female voices are soprano and alto, and the male
voices are tenor and bass.

The ability to distinguish among voice types must usually be learned
by listening to recordings, because trained adult singers are seldom available to perform in elementary schools. It is especially helpful if the class can
compare recordings of the same piece sung by different types of voices.
Here is how such an example might be introduced:

> "The other day we listened to a recording of two songs that were sung
> by men who sing in different ranges of the male voice. The lower voice,
> I hope you remember, is called the 'bass' and the higher voice for the
> male singer is called the—what?" [Several class members volunteer that
> it is the tenor voice.] "Yes, the 'tenor.' There's a similar division in
> women's voices. Remember, the voices are women's voices, *not* girls'.
> Girls at your age have very similar singing voices, and none of you girls
> has an alto voice. Only a few of you eventually will, and not until about
> the time you finish high school.
>
> "To let you hear the two types of women's voices, I'll play a song in
> which both the *alto*—the lower of women's voices—and the *soprano*—
> the higher of women's voices—sing the same melody. As you might

guess, they sing it at different levels of pitch. Hunter, which woman's voice will sing the lower version of the melody—the alto or the soprano?"

"You said the alto," Hunter recalls.

"Right. The song is from the musical work *Messiah*, by George Frideric Handel. This particular song is called 'He Shall Feed His Flock.' It conveys the feeling of trust in a leader who will take care of his people as a shepherd takes care of his sheep. There's nothing flashy about the music; it just moves at a relaxed pace, sounding comfortable and confident."

The recordings that are provided with the music series books contain songs sung by men, women, and children with unchanged voices. By comparing the voices of adult sopranos and children, the students can learn to distinguish between the timbres of these two types of voices, even though they sing in the same general pitch range. Besides examples of solo singing, the students should hear choral groups such as boy choirs, women's and men's glee clubs, and mixed choruses, so that they can compare the tone qualities in these vocal ensembles.

A more subtle aspect of vocal timbre is the way in which slight changes suggest a different style of singing. As the children learn about other cultures in their social studies classes, they can also hear examples of singing from those geographical areas. They will begin to discover the differences among singing styles and vocal timbres in the many cultures of the world. Music series books for the upper grades usually include the music of various countries, and these experiences help the children to recognize the general characteristics of a culture's vocal music. Not only are there differences among cultures and ethnic groups; there are variables within them. The children can appreciate this diversity when they realize how many timbres are employed in singing the various types of music heard in present-day America—from country-western to opera.

Although words are inadequate to describe differences in tone quality, the students can try to find meaningful descriptions for the timbres they hear. They may decide that one timbre is "thin and pinched" and that another is "warm and easy." Finding the right word helps them to notice timbre, which is an aspect of music often neglected by the listener. It is revealing for the class to realize that their descriptions of timbre at a particular passage can almost double for descriptions of the mood at that moment, demonstrating again that there is an affinity between timbre and mood.

Instrumental Timbres

A good opportunity to promote awareness of timbre occurs when the children add an instrumental accompaniment to a song. Whether they reproduce an instrumental part recommended in the music book or create one of their own, they should consider the characteristics of instrumental sounds and the appropriateness of those sounds for a particular song.

Most music series books contain one or more units on orchestral instruments. These units include photographs and brief descriptions, along with recordings of musical works that feature particular instruments. Older children should become increasingly adept at recognizing instruments by sight and sound.

One work stands out for its musical quality and for the clarity with which it presents orchestral instruments. It is *The Young Person's Guide to the Orchestra* by the twentieth-century English composer Benjamin Britten. Not only does it feature each instrument and each section of the orchestra; it does so by means of finely crafted music that is interesting to every kind of listener—adult or child, musician or nonmusician. In many performances, narration is incorporated into the music, and written commentary is provided with almost all of the several available recordings of the work. Here is how a teacher might introduce it to the class.

> "Here's a piece of music for orchestra that's written to show you how the various instruments sound. You won't have any trouble knowing which instrument or section is playing, because the narrator on the recording tells you just before you hear the instrument. Listen for the theme-and-variation form. You'll hear a solid-sounding main melody, then many variations on it.
>
> "The music was composed by a man named Benjamin Britten, who lived in England in this century. For the theme he took the melody of a famous English composer named Henry Purcell, who lived 250 years earlier. I'll play the first half minute of it for you so that you can get the theme in your mind." [The teacher plays the first 30 seconds of *The Young Person's Guide to the Orchestra.*]
>
> "That's the theme. This time I'll go back to the beginning and we'll listen for about 12 or 13 minutes, so that you can hear each instrument play its solo variation. We can hear the rest of the music on another day."

The last three minutes of *The Young Person's Guide to the Orchestra* is a fugue, which is a type of music in which the main melody is presented by one part after another in follow-the-leader fashion. It is a rather distinct section, so for study purposes, either the theme and variations or the fugue may be heard alone without seeming to be incomplete.

In addition to music created for an entire orchestra, the class should hear music featuring particular sections of the orchestra. There are many fine works for string orchestra, for woodwind quintet, and for brass ensembles. Even the percussion section has been treated as an independent performing medium. Then there is the wind band, which has immediate appeal, especially when introduced through one of John Philip Sousa's famous marches. There are also several recordings of more sophisticated music for wind band, such as Symphony No. 4 by Alan Hovhaness.

As fine as recorded performances are, they are not as effective with children as live performances and personal demonstrations of instruments. In larger communities the local orchestra often provides children's concerts, which are a valuable addition to the children's musical and cultural education. Also of value, if well planned, are programs presented in the elementary schools by secondary school music groups. The students in these organizations benefit from performing before an audience, and the listeners benefit if the program includes music of quality and is not intended simply to entertain.

An effective way to teach about instruments is to plan classroom appearances by the children who play instruments. Such appearances create much interest in the class because they feature the children's peers, and they give the performer considerable status. The music performed need not be complicated or polished, but it should be played competently. Instrumentalists who study privately outside of school will probably have a few solos ready to play at any given time. Children are usually impressed just to hear a friend play on an instrument a song that they have been singing in class. The player can play the melody or learn the simple descants and accompaniments that most series books provide for student instrumentalists. An instrumental music teacher may be able to help the student prepare the music, but if that is not possible, an elementary school music specialist can do so.

Inexperienced instrumentalists may not realize that their pitches can differ from those printed for the singers. The pitch that comes from a transposing instrument such as a trumpet or clarinet is not the one that is seen on the page. Music for certain other instruments is written in clefs different from the treble clef that prevails in children's songs. The teacher, therefore, should remind young players to consider the factors of transposition and clef differences as they prepare their parts. This will prevent the dissonance caused by unanticipated pitch discrepancies, and will help to ensure a good experience in front of the class.

Creating Music with a Tape Recorder

Creating music by tape recorder is both very easy and very difficult. It is easy to record and "mess around" with a series of sounds. It is difficult, however, to construct a meaningful musical composition, whether with tape or through conventional media. Creating music with a tape recorder requires skill and judgment. In order for a tape composition to be meaningful, the sounds must have some logic and form. This is achieved, like the orderliness in all music, by conceiving patterns for the phrases and larger sections of the music, or by following the structure suggested by a "program" or story. The tendency of most young composers is to pour too many sounds and ideas into a short composition. Most students will be more successful in creating a work on tape if they are limited to only a few types of sounds for any one composition.

Working with a tape recorder is attractive to some students. For purposes of creating musical compositions with tape, a reel-to-reel recorder is required. A cassette recorder is adequate to record the sounds, but they must be transferred to a reel if anything is to be done with them.

To create music with a tape recorder, the students can manipulate the tape in three ways:

1. Splicing and editing of the tape requires a splicing bar or a cutting tool; scissors are safest if the work is done by the children themselves. The recording tape is cut at an angle, then a two-inch piece of splicing tape is placed over the cut ends of the newly joined recording tape.

2. A two-track recording requires these steps: cover one recording head with masking tape and record the tape on one track. Then wind the tape back to the beginning. Uncover the first head and cover the other. Record the tape again with different sounds. Rewind the tape to the beginning, and then play the tape with both heads uncovered. This will produce a counterpoint of two simultaneous lines of sound.

3. Sounds can be altered by changing the speed of the tape and recording the new sounds on a second tape recorder. Most reel-to-reel tape recorders allow for more than one speed. If no change is possible on a particular recorder, a hand held lightly on the feeding reel will slow down the speed and create a new effect.

Preparing tape recorder music is best done by individuals or very small groups, not by the entire class working en masse. The process consists of three phrases: (1) collecting the sounds on tape; (2) listening to the taped sounds and labeling them; and (3) organizing the sounds to create a composition. Here is how the process might be started:

> "Do any of you have tape recorders at home, either cassette or reel-to-reel? . . . A few of you. Good. I'll tell you people how to prepare tapes at home, but the rest of you need to listen because you'll do the same thing next Tuesday in class.
>
> "Here's the first step in making your own taped composition. Record some sounds on a reel or cassette that you can bring to school. Pick any five sounds that you think would be interesting in a composition. You can record your dog barking, a car starting—anything you want. Record each sound for three or four seconds.
>
> "When you've collected five sounds, write down on a piece of paper what they are. Then listen to your sounds on playback and write on the same paper the words that you think describe each one. You can use words like 'rough,' 'choppy,' 'delicate,' or anything else that means something to you.

"Bring your cassettes to class on Tuesday. We'll have machines here, so you don't need to bring any from home. We'll record your sounds onto another recorder through a patch cord. If you don't have a recorder at home, don't worry. You can use one of the school's recorders during class next Tuesday. Sorry, but we can't let anyone take the school machines home."

When tapes are prepared during the music period, it will save time if a few of the more reliable students can go with tape recorders into other areas of the building, or even outdoors, to collect sounds. As in a scavenger hunt, there should be a time limit on the length of their search. Allowing them to record outside the classroom will reduce the number of distractions, both for themselves and for those who are working on other projects in the room.

The third phase of the composing process is more challenging because it involves more equipment and long-range planning. Here is how the organizing of the sounds might be undertaken:

"Now, we've transferred all of your sounds onto this cassette. First your team will look over the master sheet of paper that lists the source of each sound, describes it, and tells where it is: the three-digit numbers shown on the tape counter indicate the distance from the beginning of the tape.

"Then make a plan in your mind or on paper about how you'll put the sounds together. Use at least three contrasting sounds. For instance, your main theme might be sound no. 2, which is listed as a 'wild wobble,' and sound no. 4, which is described as 'steady and dull.' Then find another sound to contrast with the main theme, say sound no. 7, which is a 'tapping effect.' For a balanced composition, repeat at least one theme—perhaps in the middle and again at the end."

[The teacher proceeds to describe a five-section composition that probably would last about 20 seconds. Since there is time and the class is attentive, the teacher demonstrates on two machines how the final tape or "composition" is developed.]

"Now we'll form teams of two people. You can work on the equipment whenever the two of you have time, like when you've finished your other assignments, or before or after school. If you compose during class time, you'll need to listen on the earphones so that you don't disturb others. And be sure not to shout when you wear the earphones! For some reason, people talk more loudly when they have earphones on.

"I think a week should give you enough time with the equipment so that each team can create the piece it wants. Now let's decide who'll be partners."

As the students evaluate their creative project, they may need to be reminded of certain fundamental aspects of the medium in which they have worked. Tape recorder music does not involve conventional music notation. A composer may assign symbols to certain aspects of an electronic piece, but these symbols are not music notation in the sense that someone could re-create the music by reading the symbols. Instead, they are like road maps or plans for the composition. Actually, notation is unnecessary in this medium. Because the final tape is the completed work, the music is performed merely by playing the tape. There is no performer serving as intermediary between the composer's intentions and the listener's perception of the piece.

When the students have completed their sound compositions and have shared them with the class, they will benefit from listening to examples of electronic music, to see how recognized composers handle nonconventional sounds. A short section of a work by Subotnick, Luening, or Babbitt should be played enough times so that the class can recognize what the composer is doing. The class members may wish to compare the composer's sound composition with the ones they themselves have created.

Review Questions

1. How can students be guided in learning to recognize the various types of singing voices and styles?

2. Although no words can adequately describe a timbre, why is it educationally worthwhile to encourage children to attempt to describe timbres?

3. What is one benefit of teaching children about tone quality through performances in class rather than through recorded music?

4. What are some ways in which live performances can be provided for elementary school children?

5. How can children be helped to realize that most instrumentalists use different timbres when playing different types of music?

6. How can different timbres and tonal effects be collected and formed into a composition on a tape recorder?

7. Why is music notation unnecessary for music created on the tape recorder?

Activities

1. Locate two or three recordings of songs that feature different types of voices. Briefly outline how you would present the recordings to a fifth-grade class.

2. Develop a short unit on teaching the instruments of *one* section of the orchestra to an upper-grade class. Mention specific pictures, recordings, and live demonstrations that are included.

3. In a music series book for the upper grades, find two songs for which the textbook authors have written simple descants or accompanying parts for instruments. Prepare to play or sing the parts for the class.

4. Prepare a short composition with tape recorder. Record five sounds from around the classroom. Re-record one sound at a different speed. Then create a short composition using the original and altered sounds.

C H A P T E R

15

Musical Forms

A lmost every piece of music has a design or plan, which is referred to as its *form*. Children in the primary grades are beginning to notice form when they discern that some phrases of a song are the same and others are different. A more specific study of form is often successful in the upper grades because the older students' ability to conceptualize helps them to remember and anticipate important structural features in the music they hear. The music itself is usually longer and more complex, and therefore presents more interesting formal patterns.

The understanding of form is predicated on an awareness of phrases which starts to develop in the primary grades. Unless the children can sense and identify the smaller units of a song, they will feel bewildered by the more advanced aspects of form. Because phrases are important to structure as well as to interpretation, children should examine them frequently, at every grade level, and learn to view them in the larger context of the entire piece.

Short Formal Patterns

"Sourwood Mountain" (p. 216) is a good song for introducing students to formal analysis. If the class in previous years identified phrases through the use of symbols like boxes, triangles, and circles, or through colors, the familiar system can be reviewed. If not, such symbolization can be taught in the upper grades. The form for "Sourwood Mountain" might resemble □ □ ○ ○, or "green-green-red-red," to indicate that the first two lines are the same, as are the third and fourth lines.

In the conventional identification system, phrases or short lines of music are labeled with lower-case letters and long sections are represented by capital letters. To introduce this system, the teacher may proceed as follows.

"This time as you sing 'Sourwood Mountain,' notice which lines of music are the same and which are different. That will help you find the form of the song. Listen for the music, remember, not the words." [The class sings one verse of "Sourwood Mountain."]

"Noah, are the first two lines of music the same?"

"Let me see . . . yeah, they are," Noah responds.

"Right. We'll label the first two lines with the letter *a*. Is the third line the same as the second, Angela?"

SOURWOOD MOUNTAIN

Appalachian Folk Song

1. Chick-en crow-in' on Sour-wood Moun-tain,⟩ Hey de-ing dang did-dle al-ly day.
2. My true love's a blue-eyed dai-sy, ⟩

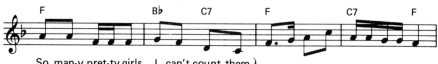

So man-y pret-ty girls I can't count them.⟩ Hey de-ing dang did-dle al-ly day.
If I don't get— her I'll go cra-zy. ⟩

My true love she lives in Letch-er, ⟩ Hey de-ing dang did-dle al-ly day.
My true love lives in the hol-low, ⟩

She won't come and I won't fetch her. ⟩ Hey de-ing dang did-dle al-ly day.
She won't come and I won't fol-low. ⟩

"No . . . but it's like the fourth line," Angela answers quickly, antic-
ipating the next question.

"Anyone disagree with Angela?" [Silence.] "You're right, Angela,
the last two lines are the same, but they're different from the first two.
Dulce, how should we label the third and fourth lines?"

"With a '3' and '4'?" guesses Dulce, taken by surprise during a moment of inattention.

"We're working with letters, Dulce, not numbers. Alexander, what
letter comes after *a*?"

"It's a *b*," says Alexander.

"Sure. The first segment is always some kind of A: little *a* for a short
phrase, capital A for a longer section. When you see or hear new material, call it B. Still more new material is C, and so on. 'Sourwood Mountain' divides nicely into four short sections, so the pattern will have four
letters in it. Tell me the form, class, so I can write it on the board. All
together, now: *a a b b*."

As the students become accustomed to finding the design of a song,
they can also learn a few terms for particular forms. The *a a b b* form in

"Sourwood Mountain" reduces further to *AB*, a form called *binary* because it implies two segments.

   Although lines and sections of music determine the form of a song, the class should continue to notice other elements that provide similarity or difference within the song. These features may not affect the form, but they help to give the song unity. In "Sourwood Mountain," for example, the fourth measures of each line are identical in words and music; the rhythm is the same in the third measures of each line; the rhythm in the first two measures of each line is similar, with only the sixteenth note added in the first two lines; the melodic contour of the second through fourth notes in each of the second measures is similar; and the melody ascends on the second beat of each third measure.

   Probably the most common structure for songs is *ternary* or *ABA* form, also called *song form*. (The term "song form" applies to instrumental as well as vocal music.) This is a balanced structure that achieves unity by ending on the same material with which it began. The logic of the pattern may explain why the form has been used so widely and has endured for so long. "Go Tell It on the Mountain" is one example of this form. The *A* segment goes through "born" in the third line, the *B* section goes from "When" to the end of the last line, and the final *A* section is a repeat of the first *A* section. Before singing the song, the class may need to be reminded about the D.C. or *da capo* mark at the end of the *B* section, which indicates a return to the beginning.

   As in "Sourwood Mountain," there are several elements that give a sense of unity to "Go Tell It on the Mountain." Measures 5 and 6 are almost exactly the same as measures 1 and 2, measures 9 and 10 are identical to measures 13 and 14, and so on. Incidentally, the song includes a second part that generally parallels the melodic line at the interval of a third or sixth. Syncopation is evident in measures 3, 4, and 7.

   When the students listen to instrumental music, they do not often have access to the notation, so they must rely on their listening skills to decide whether lines are the same or different. Instrumental works are usually much longer than songs. For example, on page 219 is the theme from the fourth movement of the Clarinet Quintet by Mozart. (A *movement* is a self-contained section of a long musical work.) The theme is a modified binary form, because the final line of the *B* section (the fourth line) is the same as the final line of the *A* section (the second line).

Types of Forms

   The theme from the Clarinet Quintet is only one among hundreds of examples of the fact that composers do not follow forms exactly. They are free to use a form if they wish, and to adapt it in order to create the musical results they want. The form of a work is extracted by analysis after the

GO TELL IT ON THE MOUNTAIN

Spiritual

day;   I   asked the Lord to help   me,   and   He showed me the   way.
wall;   And   if   I   am   a   Chris-tian,   I   am   the   least of   all.

composer has written the music; it is not binding on the composer during
the creative process. For this reason, there are almost no "perfect" or "textbook" examples of the various musical forms. For study purposes, however, these forms can be grouped into five broad categories or approaches
that composers seem to favor when they organize their ideas into a musical
work. The five types of organization may be designated as sectional form,
variation form, development, imitation, and free form.

Sectional forms

The first of these categories combines sections of music into a form. A
three-part sectional form, for example, most often consists of one section of
music followed by a contrasting section, which is followed by a return to

CLARINET QUINTET (Theme)

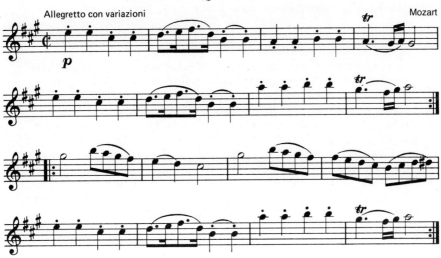

the music of the first section. The result is *ABA* or song form, which was mentioned earlier.

There may be any number of sections, presented in any order. A sectional form that is encountered in the last movement of many works by Mozart, Haydn, and Beethoven is the *rondo*, in which the main theme returns at least twice after its initial appearance. A typical pattern for a rondo is *ABACABA*, which is actually a balanced form, *ABA—C—ABA*. Other arrangements of rondo sections, such as *ABACADA*, are possible.

In the following situation, the teacher is adapting ideas from the Orff-*Schulwerk* method of improvisation presented in Chapter 9. Members of the class have devised several melodies of four measures in length.

> "Rachel, since you've worked out a melody on the bells, you can play the main theme—the *A* section. Beth, your melody can be the contrasting or *B* theme. Would you play it on the piano, please, so the tone will contrast with Rachel's bells. Kyle, what would you like to hear following Beth's melody in the composition?"
>
> "Rachel can play her melody again," Kyle decides.
>
> "All right. Yuval, do you want the piece to end there, or would you like to add something more?"
>
> "Well, Claire had a rhythm on the drum. If she wants to, she could play it next," Yuval suggests.
>
> "Good idea. Rachel, you can finish the piece by playing your melody one last time."
>
> Tanya whispers to a neighbor, "Rachel gets to play all the time." The teacher, overhearing, says, "Tanya, you're probably right in thinking

that more people should perform in this piece. If you're volunteering to play Rachel's melody, I'm sure she'll let you take the part at least for one section."

Tanya, looking surprised, shakes her head and admits softly, "I don't remember how it goes."

The teacher summarizes the compositional plan: "So there'll be five sections in the composition. Rachel's melody is first, third, and fifth. Beth will play the second section, and Claire will play the fourth section. You three players, come to the front and line up in order, A, B, and C parts. . . . That's right. Now raise your hands in the order you're going to play for section 1 . . . 2 . . . 3 . . . 4 . . . 5 . . . Good.

"By noticing the order of the sections, class, you can tell the form of the piece. Jose, what are the letters for this form?"

"*ABACA?*" Jose suggests.

"Right! When the beginning theme appears at least three times, with other material in between, the form is called a *rondo.*"

Variation forms

Another way to organize a musical work is to present the theme several times but to vary it with each appearance. The experience is like viewing similar pictures of the same subject, but seeing each one in a different light or from a different angle. Variation technique is applied more often in instrumental than in vocal music.

A good way to introduce children to variation in music is to play for them a set of variations based on a theme they already know. With the theme clearly in mind, they are better able to concentrate on the variations. Charles Ives' *Variations on "America"* is an excellent example that has a contemporary sound. The children can be invited to compare that work with the Beethoven composition for solo piano entitled *Variations on "God Save the King,"* which we know as "America."

Pieces of music with the word "variations" in the title are not the only compositions that feature variation technique. Some are constructed on bass lines or chord progressions that are repeated over and over, while new melodic material is heard with each appearance of the repeated bass line or progression. One such form is the *passacaglia,* while others are the *chaconne* and *basso ostinato* (literally, "obstinate bass").

Whatever work is selected for the students' listening, they will learn more about the concept of variation if they start with a simple, familiar theme and try to find out what the composer did to vary the music. If the students can hear a recording of a work in variation form while at the same time seeing its notation, they will be able to identify the changes more specifically.

In the music class described below, the teacher is preparing to play a recording of Mozart's *Twelve Variations on "Ah vous dirais-je, Maman,"* which we know as "Twinkle, Twinkle, Little Star." The students have been directed to look at the notated excerpts in their music series books.

> "I'll play the eighth variation again as you follow the notation in your books. Keep the theme in mind as you listen. Then decide how this variation differs from the theme. What exactly did Mozart do to vary it? Here's the eighth variation again." [The teacher plays a recording of the eighth variation.]
> "Vance, what's different about this variation?"
> "Well, it doesn't sound the same," Vance hedges.
> "Agreed. But *what* makes it sound different?"
> "I don't know exactly. . . . Um . . . It just seems 'darker,'" Vance tries again.
> "Okay, but what makes it 'darker'? Is the music lower, slower, in a different key?"
> "Yeah, I think it's in a different key," Vance responds quickly, seizing upon the concrete options that the teacher has suggested to him. "It could be in minor," he speculates.
> "It could be, and it is. What else is different about the variation?" [The teacher elicits from the class a few further observations about the eighth variation.]

Development

In writing variations, the composer takes a theme and recasts it by altering the harmony, melody, or rhythm. In writing music containing development of themes, however, the composer takes one or two themes and changes them more completely by dividing them into fragments, turning them upside down, putting them into different keys, and in other ways manipulating them. A variation generally accounts for each measure in the original theme, but a development section often extracts melodic fragments from the theme and treats them as new themes in themselves. Variations need not be musically complex, although they can be and sometimes are. Music with theme development tends to be longer and more intricate, because it is a sophisticated technique and a composer needs time in which to develop a theme. Although these comparisons only touch on the differences between development and variation, they do point out the main distinctions between these compositional approaches.

It is difficult in elementary school to delve into music that involves development. Class time is limited, and the children seldom have the musical background for such study. But they can be introduced to the idea that a theme in music exists not only for its melodic quality, but also for what the composer can do with it.

The symphonies and concertos of Mozart, Haydn, and Beethoven are good choices for studying development, because these earlier compositions usually are not as long as the works of nineteenth-century composers. Development also figures prominently in movements of chamber music, such as sonatas and string quartets from the Classical period. When deciding on selections for the class to hear, the teacher should of course check the length beforehand. But it is also advisable to notice whether there is an introduction. Particularly in early symphonies, the introduction is likely to move at a slow tempo and to present material unrelated to the theme that will appear after the introduction is completed. The hardest part of the teacher's preparation may be to locate the opening of the development section on the recording when it is played for the class.

Another consideration in the teacher's planning concerns the form of the first movement in many Classical concertos, if one is to be played for the class. The development section may appear to be delayed, because the composer often repeats the opening portion of sonata form, so that the first time the material is played by the orchestra and the second time it features an instrumental soloist with the orchestra accompanying.

Imitation

Many compositions achieve organizational unity by featuring melodic lines that imitate one another, which means that the music contains counterpoint. The *fugue* is the most notable contrapuntal form, but certain other types of music are likely to involve extended imitative passages, as well: the concerto grosso, choruses from oratorios, and motets and madrigals.

Through their singing of rounds, children are already familiar with the idea that lines of music can occur in imitation. The major difference between a round and the forms mentioned in the preceding paragraph is the complexity and length of the music. A round is a short song that maintains strict and continuous imitation, while the larger imitative forms are more complex and flexible, as seen in the fact that they include additional thematic material and occasionally modify the imitation. Here is how a teacher might introduce the fugue:

"You've been singing rounds for years now, so you know that the main idea of a round is that the same melody is sung by different groups starting at different times. The idea of imitation is also the basis for longer and more complicated pieces of music.

"Today we'll hear an imitative piece called a *fugue*. This one is for organ. It was probably written by J. S. Bach, and it's called the 'Fanfare' Fugue. Do you all know what a fanfare is?" [A few students demonstrate by humming into make-believe trumpets, while others offer verbal descriptions: "It's like a parade," and "You do a fanfare when you want to announce something important."]

"Right! You'll see how this piece got its name when you hear the music." [The teacher plays a recording of the "Fanfare" Fugue, which is quite short.]

EXPOSITION OF "FANFARE" FUGUE

J. S. Bach

"April, what instrument, besides organ, would sound good on this fanfare?"

"It sounds like what a trumpet might play," April responds.

"Yes, it does. And several of you demonstrated a few minutes ago that you know what a trumpet's like. But there's more for you to hear in this piece, so I'm going to play the recording for you again. This time, find out how many different lines are in this fugue. The lines of a fugue are called *voices*, even though the music is for instruments, not singers. You can find out the number of voices by listening at the beginning to the appearances of the theme." [The teacher plays the *exposition*, which is the term for the opening section of a fugue.]

"You're doing a good job of listening, class. The theme of a fugue is called the *subject*. So at the beginning of this fugue you heard the subject enter how many times?"

The students should realize that a fugue is not the only form that is based on imitation. They need to notice imitative passages in other works as well.

Free form

Many pieces exhibit no standard form. This does not mean that they are disorganized, but simply that they do not follow one of the recognized formal schemes. Most of these works are short and have a variety of titles such as "fantasy," "impromptu," "prelude," "nocturne," and so on. Many of them are for solo piano, and as their names imply, they are intended to create a particular mood and to sound improvised.

Program music. In this type of free form piece, the composer associates the music with a nonmusical idea or story, which is its "program." Musical sounds cannot in and of themselves tell a story; only words can do that. Yet program music is almost always instrumental, with no narration or song text to provide concrete meaning for the listener. The literal telling of a story, therefore, is not the purpose of program music. Its purpose is the same as that of most art music: to provide an interesting and satisfying listening experience through the skillful crafting of musical sounds. The program serves merely as a springboard for the composer's thoughts and as an extremely general idea to which the listeners may refer as they contemplate the music.

Danse Macabre by Saint-Saëns is one of the many program works that are interesting to children. It is a short imaginative piece with definite Halloween overtones. The title and 12 lines of poetry are the only nonmusical associations offered by Saint-Saëns, but the listener can easily imagine the dead rising from their graves and dancing wildly until the rooster's crow announces morning. There is even the tolling of the hour and the clanking of skeletons in a xylophone solo.

"Imagine that you're composers. You've been assigned to write a piece of music based on this poem. I'll read it for you, and as I read, think of what *musical* ideas it stirs up in your mind. You don't need to come up with a complete melody. Just share your ideas for sound effects, maybe, or special rhythms."

> Zig, zig, zig, Death in cadence,
> Striking with his heel a tomb,
> Death at midnight plays a dance-tune,
> Zig, zig, zig, on his violin.
> The winter wind blows and the night is dark;
> Moans are heard in the linden-trees.
> Through the gloom, white skeletons pass,
> Running and leaping in their shrouds.
> Zig, zig, zig, each one is frisking,
> The bones of the dancers are heard to crack—
> But hist! of a sudden they quit the round,
> They push forward, they fly; the cock has crowed.
> —Henri Cazalis, 1874

"Patrick, what musical ideas did you come up with?"

"I remember something in the poem about a violin playing a tune, and the story is about spooks and skeletons dancing, so maybe someone could play a scary tune on the violin," Patrick suggests.

"Good idea, Patrick. Who else can think of some special effects?"

Other recommendations follow quickly: "There's a line about bones cracking and skeletons jumping around, so I'd have some clanking and clinking sounds." "At the end the rooster crows, so someone should make that kind of sound."

[On hearing the last suggestion, a few of the more extroverted class members begin, without invitation, to audition for the crowing role. The teacher brings the brainstorming to a close.]

"You all have good ideas. As you may have guessed, I read these lines because a composer named Saint-Saëns has already written an orchestra piece that's associated with them. When you listen to it, you don't need to worry at what point in the music this or that happens in relation to the poem. Instead, notice how Saint-Saëns shapes the music into a good composition. As you listen, try to remember one or two things Saint-Saëns does, and we can talk about them after the piece is finished." [The teacher plays through *Danse Macabre* without stopping.]

Large Musical Forms

The word "form" has several applications in music. So far in this chapter, the term has referred to the overall pattern or design of a musical work. But the word "form" also denotes a type of music such as symphony, concerto, suite, and string quartet. When used in that broader sense, the term suggests both the particular performance medium and the longer nature of the work, which usually consists of several movements.

Time in elementary school music classes is too brief to permit detailed study of these forms, but children should be introduced to them and should know in general what they are. Students who attend children's concerts in the community are likely to hear a movement from a concerto or suite or other large form. It helps their understanding if they know ahead of time that a concerto features contrast between an instrumental soloist and the orchestra, that a concerto grosso contrasts a small group with a large group, and that a symphony is an orchestral work that has several movements (usually four). Above all, the children need to learn how to listen with concentration and openmindedness, whether the music is a short song or a long symphony.

Planning the lesson

In teaching children to listen more effectively, the teacher should keep in mind the points presented in Chapter 7 concerning repeated hearings and listening for specific points. Those suggestions apply to upper grade students as much as they do to younger children. The greater length and complexity of forms such as the concerto and suite require special planning. Fortunately, there is much music from which to choose, so it is rather easy to find an attractive piece of appropriate length for inexperienced listeners. A teacher may also decide to play only a portion of a work in a single class.

Whatever the listening selection, the teacher should give the class something specific for which to listen. That is what the teacher is doing in the following illustration. The listening selection is Haydn's Concerto in E Flat for Trumpet and Orchestra, third movement (p. 227).

> "Today we're going to listen to some music by Haydn. It's part of a concerto for trumpet and orchestra. Who remembers the main idea of a concerto? Paula?"
>
> "I think it's the contrast between small and large, like in a trumpet concerto between the trumpet and the orchestra," Paula explains.
>
> "Right. Now, as you listen, decide if the theme comes back or not, or if it ever goes away." [The teacher plays the opening 45 seconds of the third movement of Haydn's Trumpet Concerto. The theme does return, played by the trumpet, after a short section containing contrasting material.]
>
> "Rosa, did the theme go away, and if it did, did it come back?" Rosa reports "yes" to both questions.
>
> "That's right. Did the theme itself change, William?"
>
> "Yeah, I think the trumpet changed the theme," William answers.
>
> "What do you think, Jessica? Was the theme the same or different when the trumpet played it?"
>
> "It sounded the same to me," Jessica shrugs.

TRUMPET CONCERTO (Theme)

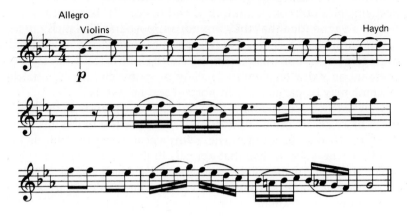

"There seems to be some disagreement here. We'd better listen to the music again, class, and see what actually happens to the theme." [The teacher plays the opening 45 seconds again.]

"What about the second appearance of the theme, William?"

"Well, it doesn't exactly change," William concedes, "but the trumpet makes the music sound different."

The class might go on to discover, through careful listening, that the movement is in rondo form. They might even notice that later appearances of the *A* theme are shorter, while the contrasting sections become longer.

In addition to orchestral forms such as symphonies, suites, and concertos, the students should hear examples of large works written for single instruments, as well as a representative sampling of chamber music. Young listeners are more likely to appreciate the qualities of chamber music when they understand that it is intended for performance in a room or "chamber" by a small group of musicians with only one person on each part. The more frequently heard combinations are the string quartet and the sonata. The latter form consists of piano and one other instrument, not in roles of soloist and accompanist, but as equal partners. The listeners should look for the clarity and interweaving of parts when they hear chamber music. They will be disappointed if they expect to hear the sweeping dimensions of a large group performance or the loudness of electronically amplified ensembles in the popular idiom.

Opera

Listening efforts in the elementary school should not be devoted exclusively to instrumental music, of course. Although school children in America sing for several years before they become involved in curricular instrumental music programs, most fifth and sixth graders know virtually nothing about art songs, oratorios, and operas. In fact, many children entertain a vague idea that they are not supposed to like such music, on the assumption that it is not intended to be understood or enjoyed by the average person. For this reason, teaching children to listen to vocal music presents an extra challenge. In view of many children's attitudes, such teaching may be particularly important and necessary.

A teacher can facilitate the students' acceptance of opera and other types of vocal art music by carefully choosing the works for study. Even though they may be good music, many vocal works are of little interest to children. The vocal music that appeals to them has something about it to which they can relate. Gian-Carlo Menotti's *Amahl and the Night Visitors* is an opera that fits this criterion very well. The two leads are a mother and her crippled son, Amahl, who is about twelve years old. He has several characteristics of a twelve-year-old, including enthusiasm, curiosity, a tendency to disregard what his mother says, and a flair for exaggerating the truth. Two other features make this work an attractive choice for young people: the opera is in English and is only about 50 minutes long. It was originally composed for television, and it has been restaged regularly.

The music series books contain abbreviated versions of musicals, operettas (which have spoken lines in addition to singing), and operas, including *Amahl and the Night Visitors*. These resources can help a teacher to identify the types of vocal music that are most appealing to young listeners.

Not only the choice of materials but the manner of presentation makes a difference in the students' acceptance of new forms. They should understand, first of all, that an opera is a drama set to music. They will grasp this point more clearly if they read the text as a play, with members of the class taking various roles. If they "walk through" the actions in a scene, the sequence of events will seem more concrete and vivid.

The students also need to realize that the music in operas and art songs is usually created to enhance the text, rather than to stand alone as a dynamic melody in itself. Here is how a teacher might demonstrate this concept to a class by referring to the song "How Far?" (p. 229).

> "We've been listening to *Amahl and the Night Visitors* and studying about it for a couple of class periods now. Look in your books at the music the three kings sing as they come nearer to the home of Amahl and his mother. They sing the same melody three times, and each time they sing it louder than before, to give the impression of an approaching sound.
>
> "You heard the music when we went through the opera the first time, but let's sing it over again now so that you can learn it a bit better. Here's the starting note. . . . Rea-dy, sing." [The class sings through the eight-measure excerpt.]
>
> "Zachary, would you say that's a good melody, one that we might sing for a concert or for the PTA?"

HOW FAR? (Excerpt)

Menotti

"How Far?" From Gian-Carlo Menotti, *Amahl and the Night Visitors*. Published by G. Schirmer, Inc., 1951, 1952. Used by permission.

"It doesn't seem real good, but then it doesn't seem real bad either," answers Zachary discreetly. Earl injects the opinion that the song is "kinda boring."

"You may be right, Earl. What is it about the melody that makes it seem boring?"

"Well, in the first line the notes wander around so much that you can't tell where they're going to settle down. The second line doesn't do much except go back and forth between two notes," Earl declares.

"Is there any reason for the melody to sound like that? I'll give you a hint: Where does it happen in the opera? Yes, Andrea?"

"The kings are wandering through the desert. They're probably lost, so the music should sound lost, too. Then on the second line, the rocking effect is maybe supposed to sound like walking along slowly for mile after mile," Andrea concludes.

Behind her, Dirk comments, "They weren't walking; they were riding on camels."

Andrea turns around to face Dirk and says, "Camels walk too, y' know." She turns to the front again while the teacher comments, "I like the walking idea. And how about the question in the second line? Class, what's the inflection in your voice when you ask someone a question? Does your voice go up or down?" [Several class members volunteer that the voice rises.] "Sure, it goes up at the end, just like the direction of the notes on the words 'How far?'

"And notice that the note values are longer in the second line, maybe to show that the kings are getting tired. By the end of the line, even the pitch doesn't move; it just stays the same.

"This song may not have a great melody, but it's just right for what the composer, Menotti, wants it to do; it helps set the mood of the situation. All through the opera, the music contributes to the sense of drama and enriches the meaning of the words and stage actions."

One stumbling block to full acceptance of opera in the mind of many people is the fact that the pacing of the stage action seems unrealistic.

Students in the upper grades are usually sophisticated enough to understand the reasons for this. Occurrences that would happen quickly in real life are often prolonged in opera so that the characters have enough time to articulate their feelings through music. Conversely, slow-moving events tend to be compressed in opera so that the action will move forward. This flexible attitude toward the time line of the story is of course characteristic of all theater, with or without music.

The impression of unreality in opera is heightened by its most basic and obvious feature—the fact that everything is sung, even the most mundane comments of the characters on stage. To an inexperienced listener the effect seems contrived, at best. So it is especially important for students to understand that opera is not trying to duplicate the realism of everyday life. Its purpose, instead, is to express emotions in a musical and dramatic setting.

Opera, with its blend of acting, scenery, singing, and orchestral accompaniment, represents the combination of several arts. Because the visual element is so important in opera, students are much more likely to understand the form and enjoy it if they can see a live performance. If that is not feasible, performances on film or television are available. Filmstrips with music and narration have been designed for use in the elementary schools, and the companies that offer such filmstrips are listed in Appendix A.

Students in the upper grades of elementary school do not need to know the details of particular musical forms. But when they hear the underlying organization of lines and sections of musical works, they are becoming better educated in music.

Review Questions

1. In what two ways is the word "form" used in music?
2. Why is the perception of musical phrases a prerequisite to understanding formal patterns in music?
3. What is the basic pattern for binary form? For ternary form?
4. How can a teacher reinforce the students' understanding of rondo form?
5. When a teacher is preparing to present the concept of variation, what is the advantage of selecting a work with a theme that is familiar to the students?
6. a. What are some ways in which a melody can be varied?
   b. How can a teacher help a class to notice more fully how a composer has varied a theme?
7. How might a teacher go about presenting a fugue for the class to hear?

8. Which is a more important focus of attention for a class listening to program music: to hear when events in the story are being represented, or to notice how the music is organized?

9. How might students be made aware of the fact that opera interprets events expressively rather than literally?

10. Suppose that no live performance of opera is available for the class to see. What can a teacher do to provide at least some of the visual element of opera?

Activities

1. Locate three songs in a music series book.
   a. Determine the form of each song.
   b. Study the songs for elements that give them unity.

2. Select an instrumental work, perhaps one mentioned in a music series book.
   a. Determine whether the form is basically sectional, developmental, imitative, variation, or free form.
   b. Develop a plan for teaching students about the form of the work.

3. Examine several of the music series books written for the upper elementary grades, and compare their presentations of art songs, oratorios, or operas. Select one unit or example and analyze it according to:
   a. the main points the children are to learn
   b. the method of getting the points across to the students
   c. the appropriateness of the material in terms of difficulty for the age and musical background of the class

C H A P T E R

16

Performing
Music

E very child should be encouraged to re-create music. Specifically, this activity implies singing and playing instruments, and often it involves the reading of music notation. Making music is important because it turns the learning experience into one of active participation rather than passive acceptance. Students learn the music better when they can perform it.

Improving Singing Skills

The goal of the singing experience in the upper grades of elementary school is to help the child to sing on pitch with a pleasant tone quality, and to engage in music-making with understanding and enjoyment. Singing is a skill, and skills are developed over a period of time, so continued work does not at all imply that the children's earlier instruction was faulty.

Voice quality

As children mature, their voices become gradually stronger. A ten-year-old's singing voice does not sound like an adult's, but it is noticeably more vibrant than it was at the age of five. The bigger vocal quality permits a greater range of loudness, which in turn permits more expressiveness in singing. The pitch range gradually increases, also. The average usable top note for first-graders is A on the second space of the treble staff, and the range appears to increase by about one note per year, so that by sixth grade the upper limit is about F on the top line of the treble staff. The range also expands slightly below the middle C cited for first-grade children to about A below the staff. Many children can force their voices higher or lower than their comfortable range, but the singing quality suffers when this is done.

The singing range seldom differs between boys and girls until after grade six. A small percentage of boys will begin to show signs of voice change in the sixth grade, especially if the average age of the group is higher than usual. The first indications of change are likely to be a characteristic huskiness and signs of strain when singing higher pitches. By the sixth grade, but prior to the voice change, it is not unusual for some of the boys' voices to acquire a brilliance and power that is not found in the girls' voices. This is the age of the boy soprano and boy choirs, a tradition more familiar in European churches than in America. A fine boy choir can achieve a quality of singing that is unique in the world of music.

Elementary music series books expect that the boys and girls will sing the same music, although songs in sixth-grade books occasionally include parts designated for boys. The pitch range of those parts is usually narrow.

Part singing

The most noticeable change from primary to upper grades in terms of singing is the addition of songs in parts. In a sense, work on part singing begins when the children first sing a round. Starting with a few songs in third or fourth grade, the teacher can introduce music with additional parts until about half of the songs at the sixth-grade level are of this type, sometimes with as many as three parts. In this way, part singing is introduced gradually over a period of years.

An effective first step in teaching part-singing has already been mentioned: singing rounds. A second step is the "echo" song, in which one part answers the other. "Follow Me" is such a song. It is like a round, but instead of a continuous melody, it features short statements or fragments. Simultaneously sounded pitches appear halfway through the song and at the end, but for only four beats each time.

A third step in teaching part singing is to present a song in which the second part is sung on one note or chanted. Such a part is easier to learn and to maintain than a second melody. "Chicka-Hanka" (p. 236) contains a line consisting of only one pitch. The words "chicka-hanka" are intended to imitate the sounds of an old steam engine puffing. The second part presents a rhythmic challenge, but if the singers start each phrase at the right time and accent the syllable "hank," they can sing it successfully. A few students can also perform the line on appropriate rhythm instruments such as sandblocks, woodblocks, or maracas.

Another way to introduce part singing is to insert a few pitches that move parallel to the melody at the interval of a third or its inversion, a sixth. (The added pitches will, of course, have to fit with the harmony that is implied by the melody at that particular point.) If the added part also has the same rhythm as the melody, it is relatively easy to learn. Initially, it may be wise to introduce a part in thirds or sixths for only a short portion of a song.

In "Marianina" (p. 237), the last few measures provide an optional part in small notes. Historically, phrase endings in music have been more ornamented than the rest of the phrase, and this remains a good way to inject part singing into a song.

The first and third lines of "Marianina" are identical, and the second and fourth are similar. Several phrases appear in *sequence*; that is, the same melodic pattern recurs at a different pitch level. Noticing such points of

FOLLOW ME

Traditional

similarity will help the students to learn the music more efficiently and to understand its structure.

When the class is comfortable singing the last few notes of "Marianina" in thirds, the children can be invited to sing the first five lines entirely in thirds, with the exception of the last note of line 2, where a fourth sounds better. A simple two-note part throughout most of lines 6 and 7 completes an attractive two-part song. When the class is ready, a three-part ending, incorporating the small notes of the first version, will sound good (see p. 238).

CHICKA-HANKA

Track Laborer's Song

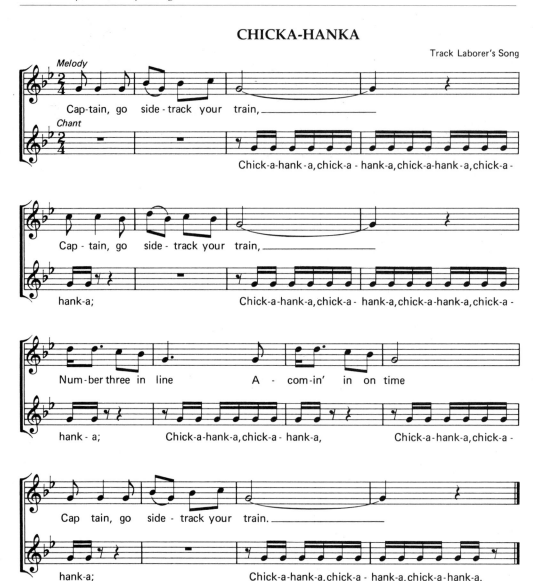

The second part of "Wonderful Copenhagen" (p. 240) contributes parallel thirds and a few sixths. It is rather easy to maintain when singing, because the rhythm of every syllable conforms exactly to the melody in the two-part passages. A slight emphasis on the first note of each measure will convey a feeling of rhythmic energy. The music is a waltz, and should "swing" with only one beat per measure.

Because there are only slight differences among children's voices in the upper elementary grades, all class members should learn both parts of a song, then trade parts occasionally. The only time when parts should be

MARIANINA

Words adapted by Mary Val Marsh

Italian Folk Song

From Mary Val Marsh et al., *Spectrum of Music*, Book 4. Words copyright © 1980 Macmillan Publishing Co., Inc.

assigned on a more or less permanent basis is when the song will be sung in public. In that case, the children can still learn both parts initially, but they should soon be assigned to a specific part so that they can learn it more thoroughly.

MARIANINA

Words adapted by Mary Val Marsh

Italian Folk Song

The melody is usually learned first because it is musically the more important line. But if the children then become reluctant to learn an additional unfamiliar part, the order of presentation can be changed, for variety and extra challenge. It is even possible to teach both parts together by alternating between them, one phrase at a time, but this interrupts the melodic flow of the music.

When the children are first experiencing two-part singing, the teacher can lend support by singing or playing one part on the piano while the entire class sings the other part. This gives them the solidarity and confidence of participating with a large group, and yet acquaints them with the total sound.

The children should learn to notice when the second part moves parallel to the melody and when it does not. The teacher might instruct them as follows:

> "Often in music a second part runs parallel to the melody, just as one rail of a railroad track runs parallel to the other. Where does parallel motion happen in 'Wonderful Copenhagen'?" [The students discover that most of the motion is parallel.]
>
> "So the second part moves parallel to the melody most of the time in this song, but not always. Where does it move in *contrary* motion—not parallel—to the melody? Cameron?"
>
> "Um . . . wait . . . Around the last part of the song, like on the words 'singing Copenhagen,'" Cameron finally answers.
>
> "Right, Cameron. Are there other places where the parts are not parallel?" [The class goes on to find more instances of contrary motion.]

Next in the general progression of difficulty are songs with a second part that is somewhat different from the melody. Perhaps its rhythm patterns or the words of the text differ. A *descant* is one such type of contrasting line. It is usually pitched above the melody, although the simple descant for "Sandy Land" on page 241 lies within the range of the melody. The similarity of range makes this song especially appropriate for the previously recommended procedure of letting the entire class learn both parts and then asking them to trade occasionally.

This song contains frequent repetition of melody, rhythm, and text patterns. The descant is also simple and repetitive. The first pitch of the first three phrases matches in both parts, which is a further help to young singers.

Parts are sometimes added to a song simply to provide a chordal background. Such parts are likely to be more difficult to learn than a descant or countermelody, because they lack melodic character of their own. They are more easily remembered in the context of the harmony than as an independent melody. Hearing the parts as harmony requires musical experience, which the children in elementary school are just acquiring.

WONDERFUL COPENHAGEN

Arranged by William Stickles

Words and Music by Frank Loesser

Won - der - ful, won - der - ful Co - pen - ha - gen, friend - ly old

Won - der - ful, won - der - ful Co - pen - ha - gen, friend - ly old

girl of a town,___ With her har - bor light, that she

girl of a town,___

wears at night, Like a gold - en, gold - en crown.__ Oh,

Like a gold - en, gold - en crown.__ Oh,

won - der - ful, won - der - ful Co - pen - ha - gen, sal - ty old

won - der - ful, won - der - ful Co - pen - ha - gen, sal - ty old

queen of the sea.___

queen of the sea.___ Once I sailed a - way, but I'm

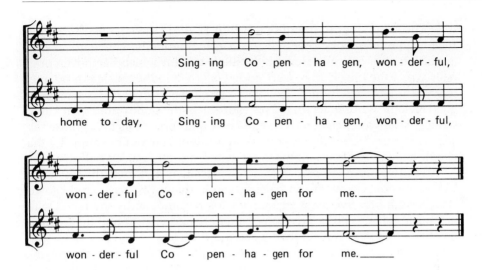

SANDY LAND

Oklahoma Folk Song

1. Make my liv-in' in san-dy land, Make my liv-in' in san-dy land,
2. Hoe-in' ta-ters in san-dy land, Hoe-in' ta-ters in san-dy land,
3. One more riv-er I'm bound to cross, One more riv-er I'm bound to cross,

Make my liv-in' in san-dy land, La-dies, fare you well.
Hoe-in' ta-ters in san-dy land, La-dies, fare you well.
One more riv-er I'm bound to cross, 'Till I meet my hon-ey.

Descant

San-dy land, San-dy land, San-dy land, Fare you well.

The song "Joyful, Joyful, We Adore Thee" is the famous theme from the fourth movement of Beethoven's Ninth Symphony. The words are not a translation of Johann Friedrich Schiller's text for which Beethoven originally wrote the music; they were added later when the music was adapted to serve as a church hymn. The melody itself seems to defy descriptions of good melodic writing: Its first 12 notes are all of the same duration, it moves by step within a range of only five pitches, and three of its four phrases are almost identical. Yet there is something intriguing about it—a quality that people have found fascinating for more than a century and a half.

The two harmony parts follow the persistent rhythm of the melody. A lack of melodic character can be observed in the lowest part, on the lower staff; for the first five measures it contains predominantly the note D. Yet the music conveys an impression of strength and vitality, and the frequent repetition of notes is an aid to inexperienced singers.

The more parts a class sings, of course, the fewer singers are available for each part. If a class of 28 divides into two parts, there will be 14 in each section. If it divides into three parts, there will be only 9 in each section, with an extra singer for one of the parts. There is a feeling of security when more singers are assigned to a part, but this can lead to mental laziness and may slow the development of independent singing.

In the following example, the teacher is trying to develop the children's part-singing skills while increasing their understanding of the music.

[The class has tried unsuccessfully to sing "Joyful, Joyful, We Adore Thee" in three parts.]

"You tried—good for you! I heard mostly melody, though—not much second or third part. You people on the lower parts seemed to 'run out of gas' as we went along. Try your two sections together without the words; just sing the notes on 'la.' Here are your pitches. . . . Rea-dy, sing." [The students on the second and third parts sing through the song on a neutral syllable without the melody. The portion in the fourth score with the D♯ and D♮ sounds insecure.]

"You're having some trouble on the words 'drive the dark of doubt away.' I'm not surprised; it gets tricky there. I'll play the song for you again. As you listen, concentrate on the parts below the melody, *not* on the melody itself. There's a certain logic to what Beethoven composed for the music at that phrase. He's suggesting a different key center—writing different harmony—to make the piece sound uncertain and more interesting at that spot. Listen." [The teacher plays the first verse of "Joyful, Joyful, We Adore Thee" on the record player, or on the piano.]

"Now let's have all three parts sing the two measures for 'drive the dark of doubt away.' We'll do it slowly so that you can notice how the music sounds. Here are your notes." [The teacher plays each starting note, then proceeds slowly, playing all parts at the piano as the children sing.]

"That's better. Now sing it again, this time a little faster and without the piano. Here are your notes. . . . Rea-dy, go."

JOYFUL, JOYFUL, WE ADORE THEE

Words by Henry van Dyke

Music Arranged from Ludwig van Beethoven

1. Joy - ful, joy - ful, we a - dore thee, God of glo - ry, Lord of love,
2. All thy works with joy sur - round thee; Earth and heaven re - flect thy rays,

Hearts un - fold like flowers be - fore thee, Open - ing to the sun a - bove.
Stars and an - gels sing a - round thee, Cen - ter of un - brok - en praise.

Melt the clouds of sin and sad - ness, drive the dark of doubt a - way.
Field and for - est, vale and moun - tain, flow - ing mead - ow, flash - ing sea,

Giv - er of im - mor - tal glad - ness, Fill us with the light of day.
Chant - ing bird and flow - ing foun - tain, Call us to re - joice in Thee.

There are other techniques for helping young singers learn music in three parts. The melody can be hummed while the other parts are sung with the words or a neutral syllable. Each part can be sung alone with piano accompaniment or with a recording. Various combinations of two of the parts can be tried at the same time. If the melody seems secure, more singers can be assigned to double the second or third parts, to give them more support.

Increased Understanding of Music

Certain aspects of music performance are more successfully introduced in the upper grades because a mastery of the concepts requires more maturity than most primary grade children possess. Among these concepts are expressive singing, phrasing, and songs as music literature.

Performing music expressively

The idea that not all songs should be sung in the same way begins appropriately in the primary grades, but efforts at furthering this notion should continue throughout elementary school. The point to emphasize in the upper grades is that the music and the text are combined to project ideas and feelings. The performers' role is to get "inside" the song and convey its intent.

A certain amount of sophistication is required to project the mood of "A Scottish Lullaby."

A SCOTTISH LULLABY

Scottish Folk Song

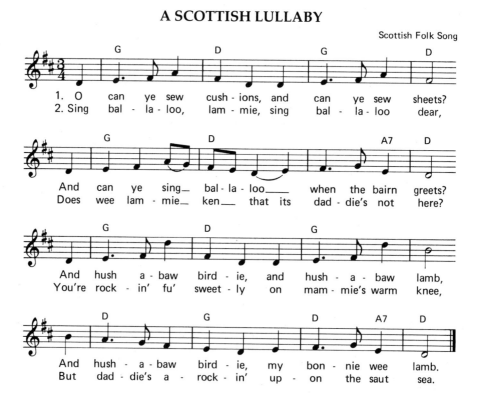

The Scottish words may need to be translated for the class. "Bairn" means "child," "greets" means "cries," "ken" means "know," "fu'" is the dialect sound for "full," and "saut" means "salt." Actually, the text of the song may be more profound than children can fully comprehend. The mother is thinking about the routines and hardships of life—the sewing of cushions and sheets, the rocking of a restless infant, and the long waiting when the father is away at sea. Even if the children do not understand the text fully, they can enjoy its beautiful melody and gain insight into one aspect of human experience.

Since the song is a lullaby, it should be sung tenderly and smoothly. The children's ability to control the flow of vocal tone will be challenged when they sing up a sixth to the syllable "baw" in the third line. The contour of the melody seems to require a moderate rise and fall of dynamic level within each line. The word "hush" suggests the gentle treatment that should permeate the entire song.

By contrast, "Wonderful Copenhagen" (p. 240) is a more boisterous, jovial song. Although it is like "A Scottish Lullaby" in meter and key, the two songs differ in spirit, and the children's singing should reflect this.

Phrasing

The phrasing and interpretation of a song are enhanced when the singers breathe together at certain places in the music. Students in the upper elementary grades can identify those moments rather easily, especially if they have learned to recognize the phrase as a logical unit of music and text. Nevertheless, the teacher may need to acknowledge that the practical—as well as the aesthetic—aspects of breathing must be considered if phrases are to be sung effectively.

> "Some of you are singing, 'Wonderful, wonderful Co- (breath) pen-hagen (breath).' What's wrong with that, Laird?"
>
> "It splits up the word?" Laird ventures.
>
> "Exactly. It breaks up the flow of the song. We should keep the melody flowing along until—where, Kirsten?"
>
> "Maybe after 'town,'" Kirsten replies.
>
> "Right. Why?"
>
> "Well, the word 'town' and the music sort of end a thought there," Kirsten continues.
>
> "Good, Kirsten. But that's a long way from the beginning. Some people may not be able to sing that long without a breath. If they can't, where would be the next best place to breathe? Heidi?"
>
> "I think it would be after 'Copenhagen,'" Heidi answers.
>
> "I agree. But let's try it, class, all the way to 'town' without taking a breath. Remember, don't waste air when you sing; we want sound, not air. All right, good breath, now. Rea-dy, sing." [The class tries singing to "town" in a single breath.]

Music literature

Students in the upper grades of elementary school perform with greater understanding when they know the background of a song. For example, "Wonderful Copenhagen" is from a motion picture about the Danish storyteller Hans Christian Andersen; "Marianina" is an Italian folk song; "Joyful, Joyful, We Adore Thee" is the melody from the fourth movement of Beethoven's Ninth Symphony; and "Sandy Land" is a folk song from the western United States. Whether performing or listening, students learn more when they are aware of the source of the song and the type of music with which they are involved. Geographical considerations are especially relevant when music is being integrated with social studies. In time, children can develop a sense of how Italian songs sound and how they differ from Irish songs, which in turn differ from Mexican songs. Children of this age can rather easily learn to identify different *types* of music, however—hymns and chorales, art songs, marches, waltzes.

Information should be provided to the students when they perform the music of a well-known composer. The process need not involve detailed biographical data; it is enough to mention some background about the times in which the composer lived, and perhaps pertinent information about the composing of the piece. The teacher's editions of the music series books usually provide such information. In short, the students should begin to acquire an understanding of the literature of music.

Improving Instrument Playing

Piano

Some elementary classrooms have a piano available to enrich the music experiences of the class. Classroom acquaintance with the instrument is in no way intended to replace private piano lessons for interested students. It will not equip them to play piano solos. Besides, most children whose families want them to engage in serious piano study have already started private lessons by the fourth grade. Children should perceive the classroom piano neither as a toy nor as a quick means to soloistic skill.

The value of a classroom piano lies rather in the fact that its keyboard is a fine visual tool for teaching pitch relationships. Because the pattern of black and white keys is tactile and clearly visible, it is easy to see and feel where the half and whole steps occur. By experimenting at the piano, the students can gain a greater awareness of how pitches are arranged in a song and on the keyboard. It does not matter if the children play the pitch pattern with one or two or more fingers; what matters is that they experience the pattern more fully when they hear, see, and feel it than when they only hear it.

"The Inch Worm" (p. 248) contains several patterns that can be understood better if they are played on the piano or on a xylophone-like instrument. Here is how the teacher might involve the children with piano as they learn the song:

"In 'The Inch Worm,' the notes of the melody are exactly the same the first time we sing 'two and two are four' and 'four and four are eight.' But the next two times we sing those words, they're changed so that the word 'are' is higher each time. Eric, come to the piano and help me play the note that changes each time." [Eric comes to the piano and is shown the notes B♭ and A. He practices them on cue, in the rhythm of the song, while the teacher sings softly with him, ". . . are four." The brief rehearsal continues with the same notes but with the teacher singing ". . . are eight."]

"Good, Eric! Now help us, class, by singing only 'Two and two (rest rest rest), four and four (rest rest rest).' Be really silent on the rest so you can hear Eric's part. He's playing a *half step*, where the notes are close together. Here's your starting note, class. . . . Rea-dy, sing."

[The class sings measure 1, the teacher and Eric perform measure 2, the class resumes at measure 3, and the teacher and Eric perform measure 4. The class participation is good, so the teacher decides to continue with measures 5–8.]

"Not bad! Now, Eric, play '. . . are four' on the notes C A, and '. . . are eight' on the notes D A, just as they occur in the song. Class, as Eric practices, notice that each set of notes gets farther apart than the half step he started with. Show them, Eric." [Eric plays the new notes on cue as the teacher points to them and sings them.]

"Okay, class, it's your turn to sing just 'Two and two (rest rest rest), four and four (rest rest rest)' as you did before. Start at the beginning, sing to the refrain, and listen to Eric's part as it changes during the 'resting' measures. . . ."

"Thanks, Eric. Stay here a moment, though. Someone else take a turn at the piano, now. Okay, Lori, come on up. Eric, teach her the pairs of notes. While you're doing that, you people by the windows come up and watch. Stand so that everyone can see the keyboard—that's better. Remember, those pairs of notes are called *intervals*, and they get wider as they go along in this song. . . . Nice going, Lori!"

In addition to melodic phrases, students can also play simple one-hand chords on the piano. Many songs in the series books contain symbols indicating chords. Even an inexperienced player can play the three notes of a triad. Here the class is learning a simple song in the key of G major.

"How many different chord symbols do you see in the song, class, and what are they?"

"Two: G and D," answers Alison.

"Right! Keith, come to the piano and find the notes G, B, D, which make up the G chord. I'll help you. . . . Good. Stay right here, Keith. Mario, come to the piano and find the notes D, F♯ and A, which make

THE INCH WORM

Words and Music by Frank Loesser

Slowly

Two and two are four, four and four are eight; That's all you have on your busi-ness-like mind. Two and two are four, four and four are eight; How can you be so blind?___

Refrain

Two and two are four, Four and four are eight,

Inch worm, inch worm, mea-sur-ing the mar-i-golds,

Eight and eight are six-teen, Six-teen and six-teen are thir-ty two.

You and your a-rith-me-tic, you'll prob-a-bly go far.___

Two and two are four, Four and four are eight,

Inch worm, inch worm, mea-sur-ing the mar-i-golds,

Eight and eight are six-teen, Six-teen and six-teen are thir-ty two.

Seems to me you'd stop and see how beau-ti-ful they are.

up the D chord." [The teacher helps the players find their respective triads so that the roots lie in the octave above middle C.]

"Here's a music book for you. When you see the symbol for your chord in the music, play the chord and hold the keys down for one measure. If you see no new symbol, then play your chord again for the next measure. Be sure to move your hand away to let the other player have a chance when it comes his turn. Practice the entire piano part, now. I'll help you by pointing to you when your turn comes." [Keith and Mario practice the part.] "Good. The accompaniment's ready to put with the singing now, class. Here's your starting note. . . . Rea-dy, sing." [The class sings the song with the block chord accompaniment played on the piano.]

It is suggested that the chords first be played within the children's singing range, for two reasons. The youngsters are accustomed to hearing and producing musical sounds at that level, so their aural pitch discrimination will be more acute within that range. Further, if the chord tones are written out on staff paper for the "pianists," or are written on the board for the class to see, the notation will look more familiar, just like the notes the children have been seeing in their books.

For variety of pitch level, however, it is good to let the piano-playing students occasionally move their chords to the octave below or above the central range, remaining at the new location for perhaps one verse of the song. This acquaints them with the "geography" of the keyboard and provides the class with an opportunity to make musical judgments as to the accompaniment range that sounds best with a particular song.

Most activities that can be done with the piano can also be performed on the bells and similar keyboard instruments. Even chords can be performed by using mallets in both hands or by involving additional players in the activity.

Recorder

The recorder is introduced in many upper elementary classrooms. It is especially well suited for music instruction because it can be inexpensive, is simple to play, and can sound most of the pitches that the students sing. (Its notes sound an octave higher, but they are notated within the children's singing range.) The recorder also possesses a light and gentle tone quality. In fact, if a player blows too hard on it, no sound will be emitted. Its sustained tone is more like singing than are the diminishing sounds produced by the piano and bell-type instruments.

When the students have learned several notes on the recorder and have mastered the essentials of tone production on the instrument, they will be able to play as well as sing most of their songs, especially those that are in easy keys such as G, F, and C. Recorders sound especially good on descants and other types of added parts.

There are a few practical obstacles to overcome in teaching the recorder. The children will learn more effectively when the class is no larger than about 10 or 12 students. Storing and keeping track of instruments may present a problem. If the children keep the instruments with their other school materials in the classroom, there is more risk of breakage and loss. But if the teacher keeps them, the children are less likely to practice and improve their playing skills outside of class time. If possible, they should buy their own recorders. This increases the children's sense of responsibility, and they can keep the recorders when they are through using them in school. If the school owns them, the instruments need to be cleaned before they are passed on to other children.

Music Reading

Music reading is a skill in the sense that eye movement must be coordinated with physiological reactions to produce the sounds specified on the page of music. As is true of so many skills, appropriate physical response to visual stimuli depends on knowledge as well as on successful past experience in similar situations, making exercises in music reading particularly well-suited to the upper elementary grades.

In the song "Wonderful Copenhagen" (p. 240), the students will read more accurately if they understand the accidentals and notice the points of similarity in the music. Here is one way in which the teacher might help them apply what they have learned.

[The class is looking at "Wonderful Copenhagen" for the first time.]

"Before you try to sightread this song, you should be prepared for some of its features. Who can find some measures that are alike? Better use measure numbers. Marcie?"

"Measures 1 and 2 are alike, and . . . um . . . 5 and 6 . . . (pause). . . . And later it goes like the beginning again."

"Right, Marcie. Now, are there some measures that are a lot alike but not exactly? Adam?"

"It seems like 'With her harbor light' and 'that she wears at night' are nearly the same," Adam volunteers.

"Yes, they are. Later in the song, the same is true for the words 'Once I sailed away' and 'but I'm home to stay.' What about the musical symbol on the second note of the song? Megan?"

"That's a sharp, I think," answers Megan, a bit unsure of herself.

"Good thinking, Megan. What does a sharp mean?"

"It says to make the note a little higher than it was," Megan replies.

"That's the idea. It's not just a little higher, but exactly one half step higher. All right, we have several repeated places and a number of sharps. Be on the lookout for them as we sing through the song with all of us on the top line of each staff, which is the melody. Since this is the

Recorder

The *recorder* is a simple wind instrument made of wood or plastic. Of the several sizes available, the soprano recorder is the most practical for classroom use.

Although not difficult to play, the recorder takes time to learn; it cannot be mastered in a couple of minutes as an incidental music activity. Some of the music series books devote a few pages to learning the recorder, and inexpensive method books for the instrument are available commercially. A fingering chart for recorder is presented in Appendix D.

The recorder is played by inserting it slightly between the lips, holding it at a 45-degree angle to the body, and with the tongue against the back of the upper teeth, starting the sound gently with the syllable "doo." This is called *tonguing*, and it produces a clear start or "attack" for the tone. A *slur* is produced by playing two or more different pitches with one continuous breath after the initial tonguing action.

The left hand is placed on the upper portion of the recorder. By covering the holes completely with the ball (not the tip) of the finger, the player prevents the air leaks that cause wrong notes or no sound at all.

first time, we'll sing it without the words. Sing it on 'loo.' Here's the starting note . . . Rea-dy, sing." [The class sings through "Wonderful Copenhagen" on a neutral syllable.]

The amount of help the teacher needs to give a class in reading a song of the difficulty of "Wonderful Copenhagen" varies depending on the previous experience of the children. Sounding a note here and there at the beginning of a new phrase or at the more tricky passages is often all that is needed. The teacher should not habitually sing or play the entire melody along with the class. If this is done consistently, the students, instead of reading, will merely become adept at following what they hear someone else doing. In this version of "Wonderful Copenhagen," in the seventh line, the melody is briefly given to the second part. If the entire class is singing the top part, the children can simply count out the measures silently. While this practice breaks the flow of the melody, it is good training for the children because it makes them more conscious of the beat.

The words need not always be omitted on the first reading of a song, but it does make the task of music reading easier because there is one less factor requiring attention. Also, it relieves the singer of having to coordinate an up-down motion of the eyes to read the two lines of words and music, in addition to the left-right motion normally required for reading.

Reading music is a complex skill involving not only mental comprehension but also prompt and finely developed physical responses. If children are going to learn to read music, they need to do it often, and in an organized sequence of difficulty. They need to practice to develop the mental comprehension and the muscle responses that transform a printed code—music notation—into sound. In the upper grades it is a good idea to provide this practice by encouraging the children to sight-sing most of their new songs. Music-reading exercise material is also useful, and can be found in some of the music series books.

Opinions differ among music teachers as to the value in the upper grades of pitch syllables and numbers. If the students are well-grounded in these systems and seem to profit from them, the use of syllables or numbers may be continued. Older children, however, should gradually begin to discard these reading aids.

If students can understand notation and read it with some degree of fluency and accuracy, they can learn a piece of music faster, and music will be more enjoyable for them. Although the enjoyment of music does not depend on the ability to read music, this skill enables a person to grow as a performer, and performing contributes to a person's growth as an appreciative listener. Children in the upper elementary grades want and need the active and varied musical experiences that are possible through music-making.

Review Questions

1. How do the quality and range of children's voices change during the elementary school years?

2. What differences, if any, exist between boys' and girls' voices in the upper elementary grades?

3. a. How may part singing be introduced to elementary school children?
   b. What order of difficulty is recommended in presenting the various types of part songs?
   c. What is a descant?

4. Suppose that you are teaching a three-part song. The children singing the second and third parts are experiencing trouble with their parts when the entire class sings. What teaching procedures might help them?

5. What steps can a teacher take to encourage the class to sing more expressively?

6. What factors in the music and the text guide singers as they determine where a breath should be taken?

7. What are the benefits of including the piano as an aid in the teaching of music?

8. To what extent should pitch syllables or numbers continue to be used in the upper grades as an aid to reading music?

9. What are some effective ways to help students increase their music-reading skills?

Activities

1. Examine one of the music series books designed for fourth, fifth, or sixth grade. Randomly select six songs and study each for the following features:
   a. What is the pitch range?
   b. Is the song written in parts, and if so, how many parts are indicated?
   c. Are any of the parts specifically designated for boys or girls?
   d. How would you rate each part song as to difficulty? Give reasons for your ratings.

2. From the six songs studied for the previous activity, or from another source if necessary, select a part song and prepare to teach it to the class. Consider the following steps in your preparation:
   a. Learn the song thoroughly, both the text and all vocal parts.
   b. Determine what expressive qualities should be projected in the song.
   c. Decide what the singers should do with the tone quality, dynamic level, tempo, and style to help bring out the expressiveness of the music.
   d. Anticipate the phrases that may cause difficulty for the singers.
   e. Notice any repeated melodic or rhythmic patterns.
   f. Decide on the places where a breath will create the most effective phrasing.
   g. Decide what you can teach the class about the song as a work of music literature.

3. Learn to play an accompaniment of three-note triads on the piano for one of the songs in the elementary music series books.

4. Learn to play two simple melodies on the recorder.

Skill Exercise

Practice the following melodies on the recorder.

C H A P T E R

17

Improvising and Composing

The principles for guiding music classes in creative experiences at the upper grade levels are generally the same as those discussed in Chapter 9 for children in the lower grades. Usually it is individuals, not classes or committees, who think up musical ideas. Every successful effort to manipulate sound contributes to the child's musical growth and feeling of competence.

Altering Existing Music

An easy introduction to creative efforts is to take a piece of music that already exists and modify or alter it. The existing music provides a structure from which the children can work, and the number of options is less bewildering than when they start from scratch. They can change the music in several ways.

Instrumentations

A good way to encourage creative thought about music is to devise instrumental accompaniments to songs the children know. They need to decide which instruments will be used and in what way. The type of song often suggests appropriate instruments, as it does in "La Conga."

Sometimes it is helpful to give the players a few ideas for an accompanying pattern. They certainly should not feel required to use another person's suggestions but many children appreciate an idea or two. The song often contains a rhythm or melody pattern that seems especially adaptable for an instrumental part.

Before the instrumentalists attempt to play their parts with the song, they should perform alone once to make sure that their rhythm patterns fit well with "La Conga." The parts the students develop might be:

LA CONGA

Moderately

Brazilian Folk Song

1. When you hear ma - ra - cas_ "boom-chick, boom-chick, boom - chick!"
2. When you hear this rhy - thm_ played up - on a bon - go,_

And you hear the cla - ves_ tap - ping "click - a - click - click!"
Then you know it's time for_ all to do La Con - ga!_

One, two, three, kick!_ That's the way you do it!___

One, two, three, kick!_ There is noth - ing to it.___

After the players have tried their parts, the class can evaluate each rhythm as to its appropriateness for the song. In that way, the entire class can share in the creative efforts.

"Arirang" (p. 258) is a Korean folk song. If the children are sensitive to the qualities of this music, they will choose accompanying instruments and rhythms quite different from those they selected for "La Conga." The teacher might guide the class in this way:

"You know 'Arirang' well enough now so that you can add instruments to it. Velonda, could you go over to the table and name off some of the instruments that we have there? Point to one thing at a time and name it, then call on someone to tell us whether they think it would sound appropriate for an oriental love song like 'Arirang.' They have to give you a reason for their answer, too, Velonda."

[Velonda begins her instrument identification.] "Claves. Martina?"

"Um . . . no. Claves always sound Mexican or some country like that."

"Finger cymbals. Valerie."

"They seem sort of gentle and I think they might be nice with an oriental song," Valerie decides.

"Bongo. Heath."

ARIRANG

Korean Folk Song

1. A - ri - rang,— A - ri - rang,— A - ri - rang,— A - ri - rang,—
2. A - ri - rang,— A - ri - rang,— A - ri - rang,— A - ri - rang,—

A - ri - rang,— A - ri - rang,— A - ri - rang fair.
A - ri - rang,— A - ri - rang,— A - ri - rang fair.

Through the pass___ I watch you___ go___ there._____
Here I wait for you, wait, wait___ and___ stare._____

A - ri - rang,— A - ri - rang,— A - ri - rang fair.
A - ri - rang,— A - ri - rang,— A - ri - rang fair.

"Nah. Too loud." [The selection process continues, and the following instruments are chosen: temple blocks, gong, small drum, triangle, and finger cymbals.]

During this decision-making process the teacher should be sensitive to the reactions of any students who appear to be in disagreement with a friend's judgment. The merits of a particular instrument can be discussed briefly to hasten consensus.

Chants

Another way to use an existing piece of music as a springboard for creative effort is to add a *chant*—a rhythmic line with little variation in pitch, so that the style resembles speech. "This Old Hammer" suggests the relentless monotony of tools, machinery, and hard work—an appropriate setting for a repetitious chant.

THIS OLD HAMMER

Here is one way to help the children develop a chant:

> "You may have noticed that 'This Old Hammer' has a persistent, machine-like quality about it. Here's an assignment for you: make up a chant that a few of you can repeat over and over while others sing the melody. Your chant doesn't need to have a pitch to it at first—just a strong rhythm and a word or two. Keep it short. We'll sing through the song again, so you can get ideas for a short phrase that might make a good chant for this song. Here's the pitch. Rea-dy, sing." [The class sings "This Old Hammer."]
>
> "Who has an idea for a chant? When you have one, say it for us in a rhythmic, energetic style. Travis?"
>
> "How about '*Ham*-mer, *ham*-mer, *ham*-mer,'" Travis recommends, illustrating with steady eighth notes and a nod of his head on each beat.
>
> "Sounds good. Let's try it: you six people closest to Travis, say his chant with him. The rest of you sing the song. Here's your pitch . . . Rea-dy, go." [The class divides and sings the song with the suggested chant, to the obvious pleasure of Travis.]

The teacher, after a few subtle hints to the class, may be able to elicit from the group another chant, spoken at first, then pitched as follows:

The pitch D is a good choice because all phrases of the song begin and end on that pitch, so the one-note chant is likely to be successful. The momentary dissonance between the chanted D and the E in the next-to-last measure of the song is not offensive. In fact, it gives good emphasis to an important word, and can well be accented for dramatic effect.

Chants seem more effective when the song is not fast and when the melody contains a few long notes during which a listener's attention can pass to the chant for a moment. The main problem in performing a chant is that young singers tend to rush the tempo. They must maintain a steady beat if the chant is to be convincing.

A chant, performed alone at the beginning and end of the song, makes a fitting introduction and *coda* (concluding section). It sets the mood at the beginning of the song and reinforces it at the end. When combined with well-controlled changes in dynamic level, the chant has a dramatic effect.

Ostinato parts

A chant must be spoken or vocalized in some manner, but an *ostinato* can either be played on an instrument or sung. Its characteristic feature is its persistent repeating of a rhythmic or melodic pattern. (The word "ostinato" in Italian literally means "obstinate" or "stubborn.") An ostinato can be created in the same way as other accompanying parts. A simple figure derived from the song is effective, and choosing a pitch level is easy if the harmonic structure is straightforward and uncomplicated. In "Swing Low, Sweet Chariot," the note C is selected to predominate in the ostinato because in the key of F major, C is common to both the tonic chord (F A C) and the dominant chord (C E G).

Although an ostinato must be limited in pitch range to minimize dissonance with the chord changes in the song, this restriction is helpful in guaranteeing that the part will be easy to sing or to play on an instrument. An ostinato, like a chant, can serve as both an introduction and a coda to the song. Or, the last repetition of the ostinato may be altered, to sound more final. In "Swing Low, Sweet Chariot," for example, the part can conclude in any of the following ways: "Swing low, chariot, swing_____," or "Swing_____ swing_____ low_____," or "Comin' to take me home_____," ending on the tonic note.

Variations

The theme and variation technique has a long history in music. For centuries, composers have been intrigued by the possibilities of devising variations on a melody. Students will find that simple, familiar songs are the easiest to vary. Here is how a teacher might help a class create variations on "Yankee Doodle."

"You all know 'Yankee Doodle.'" Well, now it's time for you to change it some to make it truly *your* song. How can you change it? Let's list some

SWING LOW, SWEET CHARIOT

of the ways here on the board." [The teacher explains each point while writing "Change pitches in the melody. . . . Decorate the melody. . . . Change the rhythm. . . . Combine two or more of the above techniques. . . ."]

"For now, we're going to change only one feature of the song. Don't try to do a combination yet! Now, people sitting by the windows, you try to vary 'Yankee Doodle' by changing just a few pitches. Each one of you by yourself think of a few changes, but not too many, please.

"You people here in the center of the room, try to make a few changes in the rhythm, like lengthening some notes and shortening others. You people by the door, think of some decorative notes that you can work into the melody of 'Yankee Doodle.'" [The teacher gives an example of decorative or ornamental notes.]

"We'd better sing the song together once, in case someone has forgotten how it goes." [The class sings the song.]

"Okay, take a couple of minutes to think quietly. Decide how you want to demonstrate your ideas. You can play your variation on an instrument or sing it. Don't worry about the words. Just sing with any syllable you want. Ready? Start planning your variation."

It is helpful to have the music for "Yankee Doodle" written on the chalkboard or on large sheets of paper, so that the children can see the notation as they plan, and so that their changes can be added later with colored chalk or felt marker. If the teacher cannot notate what the students perform, a tape recorder can be used to preserve their creative efforts.

Some of the students' variations will probably contain ambiguities of rhythm and key. But the children are learning from the experience of manipulating musical sounds, and the teacher should be supportive of every child's effort.

The teacher should encourage the class to sing each child's variation. This will have to be undertaken on a neutral syllable, since the original song words will not accommodate the addition or deletion of notes, or the shifted accents caused by a change of meter. Obvious mistakes can be smoothed over as the creative effort is reproduced by the class. The group participation involves everyone in supporting the novice "composer," and is a means of keeping performance alive in an area that can quickly become merely an intellectual exercise.

New words

There are hundreds of melodies that have been associated with more than one set of words. Many patriotic songs and church hymns originally had words other than the ones to which they are sung today. At the upper grade levels, students can progress beyond simply substituting humorous words as suggested in Chapter 9, although the occasional writing of a non-sensical text is certainly acceptable.

The value of writing new words for a song is that the activity makes the child notice heavy and light beats, and it requires attention to the way in which word patterns are arranged to conform to those beats. Simply stated, stressed syllables should occur on the beat. When words are written to accommodate the music, the arranger should experiment until the language is as natural as possible, while at the same time supporting the nuances of each musical phrase. Fortunately, older children are generally sensitive to rhythm in both music and language, and they will know when their arranging efforts are comfortable to sing.

Children often assume that song words must rhyme at the end of each line. In fact, however, rhyme is one of the least relevant considerations in selecting words for a song. Rhyme, with its similar-sounding words, may to some extent reinforce the similar-sounding notes at phrase endings in the music. But rhyme is essentially an artificial contrivance that too often leads to trite expression and garbled syntax. Since the purpose of song words is to convey ideas and feelings, children should be encouraged to write with a natural flow of language so that they can communicate more fully and accurately in their music.

Creating New Music

Changing someone else's melody does not require the degree of originality that is demonstrated when a composer creates an entirely new piece of music. It is more difficult to develop the original work, because the composer must choose from among so many options of procedure and content. The teacher will need to provide discreet guidance so that the children do not feel overwhelmed by their own inexperience and the array of choices before them.

Providing structure

When students first attempt to create original music, the teacher should provide structure by specifying rather fully the conditions and requirements of the project. Initially the students can be asked to compose a piece involving only the element of rhythm (perhaps a pattern for drum or a one-pitch pattern on some other instrument) or the element of tone quality (probably a series of sounds derived from various vibrating objects). Rather than limiting the students' creativity, such restrictions seem to inspire inventiveness.

When children in the upper grades are successful in developing one-element pieces, they can begin using more than one element at a time. The specifications can involve pitch and can be more varied, like the following:

1. Write a melody eight measures long, in $\frac{2}{4}$ meter.
2. Use only quarter, eighth, and half notes, and end with a half note.
3. Begin and end on the same pitch.
4. Indicate two changes of loudness.
5. Make the music smooth and songlike.

As the children gain experience in writing according to specifications, the amount of structure can be reduced.

The work on composition assignments need not be done in class. Children should be encouraged to try out their music by singing it or by playing it on any instrument they wish. The performing media most likely to be chosen are the more familiar classroom resources such as bells, piano, recorder, and voice.

Many children do not know notation well enough to transcribe what they sing or play into music notation. In such cases, they can perform their songs for the music specialist to write down, or they can record the music on tape, either at home or at school, for playback at a later time. The inexpensive cassette tape machines that many children own generally fail to convey the clarity and tone quality of a good music performance, but they are satisfactory for the purpose of preserving the children's compositional ideas.

Another solution to the notation problem is for the teacher to accept "homemade" notation systems. That is, the child can devise any set of symbols that serves as a personal reminder of the previously constructed melody. Such a system may not be intelligible to another individual, but it is commendable because it represents the child's ingenuity in solving a problem. Of course, a child can simply remember a melody that has already been thought out, and perform it whenever invited to do so. But for accuracy and permanence, conventional notation is the best way of encoding musical sounds.

Setting poetry to music

For centuries, people have been setting poems and other texts to music. That is generally what happens when a composer writes an art song or opera: the literary aspects are developed first, then music is composed to enrich and enhance the words.

Some children in the upper grades of elementary school can devise music to express a text. Such an endeavor integrates music with language study and builds on the children's previous experience with creative activities in music.

Straightforward poems with clear imagery or distinctive moods are best for the initial efforts at writing music for a particular text. "Who?" by Edith Savage is such a poem. Its first verse is:

> With great yellow eyes
> Staring through the night
> The dark owl watches . . . watches . . .
> All night he cries
> Who? Who?
> I wish I knew.

The teacher might introduce the creative effort like this:

"All the words of 'Who?' are important, but some seem to require more attention than others. For instance, in the first line, which is more important, 'with' or 'great'? Nancy?"

"'Great,' it seems like," Nancy answers.

"Yes. And what about 'staring' and 'through'? Andrew?"

"'Staring' is more important," Andrew decides.

[The class continues to look for the more significant words. The teacher concludes as follows.]

"This poem isn't strongly rhythmic like some we've read. It doesn't make you want to tap your foot. But there's a kind of rhythm to it.

Imagine that you're going to mark the words or syllables that receive more emphasis. Let's read the poem through together, so you can notice the places that you would mark for emphasis."

Determining the rhythm of the words is important, but it is only one step in preparing a musical setting. The mood of the words is also significant.

"Let's read the first verse of 'Who?' together again. This time, think about the expression, the feeling projected by the words. The poet is trying to communicate something to you." [The class reads through the verse together expressively.]

"What kind of music should go with that poem? For now, don't try to decide if your ideas are good or not. Just 'brainstorm.' Brian?"

"Since it's sort of moody and talks about night, I don't think the music should go very fast," Brian comments.

Holly adds, "You could make 'watches, watches' more important by having a little silence after each one."

"If the owl 'cries,' then you would make that word special," Wendy suggests. "You could make it louder than the other words, and maybe higher, too."

"And when an owl says 'Whooo, whooo,' he makes it long and smooth, sort of slide-y," Paul offers, enhancing his bird call by putting his hands in his armpits and flapping his elbows, while looking around at his neighbors for encouragement.

After the class has exchanged ideas and considered suggestions, individuals can begin to set the poem to music. When sufficient time has elapsed, they can present their finished songs in front of the class. The group is *not* asked to approve or disapprove of musical phrases as the teacher puts them on the chalkboard. Consensus is unnecessary because there is not going to be a final amalgamated version composed by the class. Instead, there should be several compositions, each valued because it represents individual creative effort. The class should listen attentively to each version and comment on the following factors:

Does the music reinforce the mood of the poem?

Does the beat of the music fit easily with the rhythm of the words?

Do the phrases of music seem to belong together, so that the song sounds unified?

Is the song attractive and interesting?

Because the children's musical inventiveness may exceed their ability to write down their ideas, this is a good opportunity for the teacher to extend their understanding of notation. They will see a need for learning the written symbols, and they will be able to use this knowledge immediately, in a personal way, as they try to preserve their compositions.

Composing with tape recorders

This technique, in which taped sounds are manipulated to form a composition, was discussed in Chapter 14. Such compositions present fewer problems in terms of notation and performance, but require the necessary equipment.

Improvisation

The line between composing and improvising is by no means clear. Essentially the difference is that composing takes place over a period of time, during which revisions and trial-and-error procedures are expected. *Improvisation* means making variations on a melody or on certain chord tones, with the music performed spontaneously so that it appears to be made up on the spot.

Improvising is a dual skill, then, because the improviser must be a competent performer as well as an inventive arranger. Both talents are woven together during performance. It is rare to find a student in elementary school who can effectively demonstrate this combination of musical abilities, but many children in the upper grades are intrigued by the process.

Class members who thought up variations on "Yankee Doodle," and were able to sing or play their altered arrangements, have had an initial experience with improvisation, especially if there was minimal time lapse between the idea and the child's performance of it. Most students in the upper grades of elementary school cannot go much beyond that level of improvisational competence, however, unless they receive outside help. There is just not enough time in the typical twice-a-week music class to teach the necessary skills, among which is a good knowledge of harmony.

But all children, even those who were uncertain in their modifying of "Yankee Doodle," can experience the feeling of improvisation by participating in the statement-answer technique suggested in Chapter 9. Although this is not sophisticated improvisation, the use of a short rhythm or melody pattern as a statement provides a structure for which the answering child can provide an immediate response. In addition, the temporary nature of the answer—if it is not notated, recorded, or previously planned—may help to put at ease those children who are uncomfortable with the more formal creative activities. They will probably enjoy spontaneously completing a musical phrase like the following:

Comments on a child's musical "answer" might discuss how well it matched or contrasted with the style , contour, and dynamics of the opening phrase, and whether it had a sense of finality.

If children enjoy the experience of creating music, the benefits will be both psychological and practical. Their self-esteem will be enhanced, they will be motivated to improve their musical skills, and they will understand music better.

Review Questions

1. When children have had little previous experience in creating music, what are the advantages of asking them to add their own ideas to existing pieces of music, in contrast to composing entirely original works?

2. Name a factor that a class should consider in deciding which instruments to assign to a song accompaniment.

3. What qualities in a song make it a good choice for the addition of a chanted part?

4. What is an ostinato?

5. Describe how children can be guided to create variations on a melody that they already know.

6. What words or syllables in the text of a song should coincide with the beats in the music?

7. How can structure be provided for children in the initial efforts to create original music?

8. a. How can children be helped to discover the more important words in a poem they are setting to music?
   b. How can a class be encouraged to become more aware of the mood of a poem?

9. Many children cannot put their musical thoughts into notation. What are some ways of overcoming this problem?

10. How can improvisation experience be introduced and implemented in a school music class?

Activities

1. Examine one or more of the music series books designed for grades 4, 5, or 6. Select a song for which you can create a simple accompaniment involving two instruments. Either tape record your instrumental parts or write them in music notation.

2. Make a few melodic variations in the song you selected for activity 1. Then make a few variations in the rhythm of the song.

3. Write a different set of words for the song you selected, keeping the music in its original form.

4. Select four lines of a poem you find in a music series book, and create a melody that expresses that text. Evaluate your efforts according to the questions raised on page 265. Either tape record your song or put it into notation.

PART
IV

Other Aspects of Teaching Music in the Elementary School

The fourth and final section of this book consists of three chapters on topics that are relevant to teachers involved with music instruction. Unlike the preceding fourteen chapters, these topics do not relate to specific aspects of music. Instead, they discuss the content and methods of music instruction that occur in special situations in the elementary school.

Chapter 18 explores ways in which children can be helped to understand music in terms of its cultural setting.

Chapter 19 deals with the teaching of music as a fine art. Again, the emphasis is on practical application, not on philosophical positions.

Chapter 20 discusses ways to teach music to special education students. The ideas can be applied in the children's own special classroom or in a mainstreamed setting.

C H A P T E R

18

Music and Culture

M

usic does not develop in a vacuum unrelated to the people who create it. It reflects the larger culture and its customs and accomplishments. The relationship of a musical work to its culture can be viewed from two perspectives: time and place. Like other expressions of culture, music changes from one historical epoch to another, and reflects the attitudes and practices of a particular time. It also differs from one area of the world to another, and may even differ significantly within a rather small geographical area.

Students in the upper elementary grades learn in social studies about the life and customs of the United States and other countries of the world. This gives them a certain amount of geographical and historical background for instruction dealing with music in a particular culture. A classroom teacher is well equipped to teach this area of study. He or she knows the students' background in social studies, teaches the subject, and has expertise in that area. Such a person is in a good position to integrate social studies and music.

Openness to Other Cultures

To appreciate more fully the significance of music in different cultures, both within the United States and around the world, students need to become receptive to unfamiliar sounds and customs. An attitude of openness and curiosity is more likely to be engendered if the teacher helps the class understand the following points.

1. Music is not a cultural manifestation that is limited in time, like the custom of writing with a quill pen, or in location, like the traditional Japanese tea ceremony. Instead, music is a part of every culture throughout the world, and has been throughout the history of the human race. As was pointed out at the beginning of Chapter 1, this fact is an important reason for including music in the school curriculum.

2. Music differs from one culture to another. Just as the people in various parts of the world have different languages, styles of dress, types of housing, religious beliefs, and culinary preferences, they also have different kinds of music.

3. No culture or its music is superior to another. The languages of other countries are as useful and valid for those countries' citizens as the English language is for Americans. The music and dance of other cultures are as interesting and beautiful to those peoples as the art forms of Western civilization are to Americans.

Because no culture is better than another, the class should be encouraged to develop an attitude of respect for the music of other cultures. Sometimes people unconsciously adopt the view that in effect says, "If it's different from what I know, something must be wrong with it." Instead, the attitude should be, "If it's different, I want to find out more about it." Although the students should acquire information about the different kinds of music around the world, their attitudes toward unfamiliar types of music may, in the end, be more important than information.

Attitude and knowledge, however, are related. People tend to like what they know, and to be skeptical about what is unfamiliar. They are uncomfortable in situations in which their lack of information makes them feel inadequate, so they tend to develop attitudes of prejudice and dislike toward the unfamiliar area. Increased knowledge, on the other hand, contributes to an attitude of increased respect and curiosity, which in turn encourages a person to want to know more. It is important not only to know that there are many different types of music but also to know what makes the types of music different. Students in the upper elementary grades are advanced enough to learn, for example, that the music of India is improvised, is based on a melodic formula called a *raga* and a nonmetrical rhythm pattern called a *tala*, has no accompanying chords, and is played on instruments such as the sitar and tambura.

Resources for Teaching about Culture and Music

Although the music series books differ in the depth and method of presenting information about music of other cultures, most of the books contain song material and pictures, and there are recorded music examples in the supplementary record albums.

Some music series books present material in units, while other books take a one-song-at-a-time approach. Generally, more lasting and effective learning occurs when the material is presented as a unit. The teacher will probably cover fewer types of music, but the presentation is usually more thorough and therefore more likely to be remembered.

A recording can present all the subtle inflections and nuances of pitch, rhythm, and timbre that are important in a particular style of music. Most of these nuances cannot be rendered in music notation. Even in the case of an American folk song, it is important to listen to a version performed in an authentic style. For example, a song from the Appalachian mountains is best performed by a folk singer from that area. The recordings available for use with the music series books contain a number of authentic versions of the music—both Western and non-Western—presented in the textbook. As a further aid to teachers, packages of supplementary material can be purchased from the sources listed in Appendix A.

Teaching the music of different cultures lends itself well to making exhibits. An attractive bulletin board about the life and music of a particular culture or country draws attention to the topic and helps the students learn. Some of the commercially prepared study units have pictures that can be posted, and more general pictures are available from travel services and other sources.

A few residents of the community may be persons from another country. They can talk to a class about their native land, and in some cases even perform some of its music. If such persons are available, they should by all means be invited to share their culture with the class.

One's teaching colleagues can also be approached for ideas and materials. The natural alliance between music and social studies facilitates a pooling of assets among the teachers involved. When a class is studying about Africa in social studies, that is a logical time for the music teacher to introduce African music and for the classroom teacher to emphasize its cultural implications. Communication and cooperation between music specialist and classroom teacher are needed to bring about the most effective learning in both music and social studies.

The total content of the music instruction should not be determined by what is covered in social studies, however. While some integration of the two subjects is desirable, many aspects of music are quite unrelated to other curricular areas. The subject of music needs to be taught systematically, and that is not possible when the music curriculum is organized according to the teaching plan for another subject area.

Teaching the Music of a Particular Culture

Students do not gain much when a teacher simply says, "This song is from France" and points to France on a map. They need to investigate what makes the song French. Is there a characteristic rhythmic pattern, melodic style, instrument, or text?

Singing a song from another culture makes a greater impact on the students than just listening to a recording of it. The amount of satisfaction that they derive from their involvement will depend partly on the syntax of the new sounds. American young people can easily learn to perform music from western Europe and Latin America in a rather authentic style, because it is not too different from the music they already know. But in the case of oriental, Indian, Arabian, and African music, it is unlikely that the singing by Americans is very close to the way the music should actually sound. When the style of music is so unfamiliar, the amount of listening to recordings should be increased and the amount of performance reduced.

The students can still benefit from attempting to sing in the new idiom, but they should understand that the effort is being undertaken for their own experience, rather than as a rehearsal for eventual public performance. They need to realize that the nuances and inflections which they are *not* duplicating may be a more distinctive characteristic of the style than the obvious notes and rhythms they are trying to imitate.

Although African music is presented in this example, the same basic approach of exploring distinctive characteristics is possible for music of any culture.

"Here's a recording of a piece of African music. Listen and see what you think makes it sound African. It's dance music from the Shona tribe in Zimbabwe."

[The teacher plays *Kalanga Dance*,* which features drums and rattles.]

"Bruce, what do you think gives that music an African sound?"

"I guess the drums are different. At least they don't sound like the drums we hear in America. . . . And the rhythms are different, too," Bruce responds.

"That's right. We've talked about the importance of drumming in African culture. What was one of its purposes?"

"Oh, I know!" Several hands go up, and Barbara explains, "The people communicated to places far away through drum language, like a code."

"And was this kind of speech pretty easy, Amanda, or was it complicated?"

"It was complicated. At least I'd never be able to understand it," Amanda says, to which Philip declares, "Sure you would, if you lived there."

Amanda pauses, then agrees, "Yeah, I guess I would."

"Good point, Philip," the teacher says. "We get so used to our own culture that it's hard to imagine ourselves in some other time and place."

To show the class how an African drummer might feel when playing complex rhythms, the teacher can involve several students at a time by handing out five rhythm instruments and assigning two students to each instrument—one person to play and the other to help the performer count the rhythm. A large rhythm score like the one below, prepared ahead of time by the teacher and displayed prominently, will help the drummers.

"Notice that you have only eighth notes and eighth rests. There are how many eighths in each measure, class?" [Benjamin volunteers that there are 12.] "Yes, 12. Count them with me at this tempo: 1 2 3 4 5 6 7 8 9 10 11 12." [The class counts together.] "Good. Are any of the five parts the same? No, they aren't. So you people in the teams

*Recording for *Silver Burdett Music*, Book 5 (Morristown, N.J.: Silver Burdett, 1974).

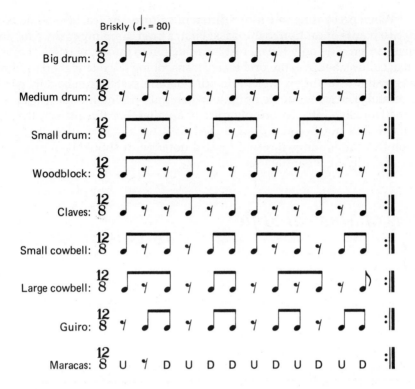

had better take a minute and look at your parts carefully. Then take another few minutes and practice your part softly by tapping out the notes as you count. All right, practice."

[The teams work quietly together, with occasional giggles and signs of impatience as errors are made. After about two minutes, the teacher hears each line separately, counting aloud for each, in tempo.]

"Now I think you're ready to put the piece together. Above all, keep the rhythm steady."

[The class attempts to reproduce the rhythm in organized fashion, beginning with one line. Other lines are added one at a time. There are several false starts, however, and the class begins to lose its sense of serious effort. The teacher brings the activity to a close and the players return to their seats.]

"If you had been sending a real message, what would it have been?"

"I don't know," comments Ryan, "but if the next room sends us a message back, they're gonna tell us to quit this and get back to something we know how to do."

Experience with a multi-linear drumming pattern is likely to convince even the most casual student that African rhythm is complex, especially when its intricacies are supposed to be shaded with speech-like nuances.

When presenting music of a different culture, the teacher should convey two points of caution to the class. First, a brief sampling of rhythms and songs can provide only the merest introduction to the many types of music in that culture. Second, the problem of transcribing the pitches and rhythms of African music, for example, into our notation system can be only partly successful. The same problems exists when transcribing the speech sounds of one language into the orthography of another. For this reason, the students should not become preoccupied with the notation of such music. When their attention is directed toward notation, it should be for the purpose of clarifying what they see and hear.

Eras of Musical Style

History is not usually taught as such in elementary school social studies, although American history receives attention at about the fifth-grade level. For this reason, upper grade students are likely to have had little experience in viewing events from a historical perspective. The music teacher may introduce the usual name for a stylistic period (Renaissance, Baroque, and so on) as the class encounters music of that style, but a detailed survey of music history has little meaning for children whose sense of time span is not well developed and whose experience with different musical styles is still severely limited. With most children it is premature to attempt to convey the sweep of music history.

What may provide them with a better understanding is to relate a style of music and culture to a person. For example, Haydn and Mozart composed during the time of George Washington and the American Revolution, and Johannes Brahms was composing his first works just before the American Civil War. Associating styles with a few important composers may present a somewhat distorted view of music history, but it helps the children begin to organize their impressions into an orderly time sequence, and it reminds them that history is, after all, a record of human events.

Here is a music class in which the teacher is centering attention on the music and times of Joseph Haydn.

> "In your books you'll find some information about Franz Joseph Haydn. His name is pronounced *High*-din. You'd better say it with me, class: Haydn. The book points out that Haydn lived about 200 years ago. Who was alive and important in America 200 years ago? Kalayna?"
>
> "Well, the Revolutionary War was about then, so George Washington and Benjamin Franklin were pretty important," Kalayna reports.
>
> "That's right. In fact, Washington and Haydn were born in the same year, 1732. Of course, Washington was born in Virginia and Haydn in a country named Austria in the middle of Europe, so they never knew each other.

"The work that we'll hear by Haydn is part of a string quartet called 'The Bird.' It's played by two violins, a viola, and a cello. The viola, remember, is a little bigger and lower in sound than the violin. Here's the first movement of Haydn's quartet. As you listen, follow the music themes printed in your books and try to think of a word or two that you might use to describe the style of the quartet. Is it 'clear,' 'light,' 'dark,' 'emotional,' or what?" [The teacher plays the first movement of "The Bird" Quartet in C major, Op. 33, No. 3.]

"Patricia, what word do you think best describes this music?"

"Chirping," suggests Patricia. "You said the name of the quartet is 'The Bird,'" she explains.

"Good thought. Kurt, what word do you think describes the quartet?"

"Clean; everything seemed exactly in place and not cluttered up with a lot of stuff," Kurt decides.

[The teacher elicits other students' ideas about the quartet. Most of the descriptive terms suggest that the music is good-natured and logical.]

"The words you've come up with like 'direct' and 'clean' are good ones for Haydn's music," the teacher summarizes. "In a way, his music is logical like the style of Washington and Jefferson and the other Americans who drew up the Declaration of Independence. For a document that was declaring freedom, it is quite 'cool' and logical. That was the style of art, music, and literature during the classical period. People wanted their art works to be very controlled."

On subsequent days the class can discover other features of Haydn's "The Bird" Quartet, including the form and the short, tuneful patterns of the melodies. The class might hear another work by Haydn, perhaps the second movement of his Op. 76, No. 3 ("Emperor") Quartet. That movement is a good choice because it is an example of theme and variations in which the melody is present in all variations. The melody itself is the national anthem for Austria and is sung in churches today under the title "Glorious Things of Thee Are Spoken."

GREENSLEEVES (ROCK VERSION)

Arranged and Adapted by Buryl Red

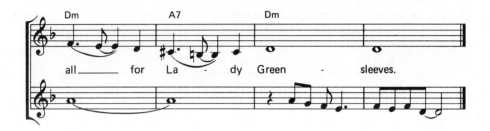

Popular Music

The students should be encouraged to examine popular music as well as folk and art music. Some music series books for fifth and sixth grade include songs and units on rock and other types of popular music. Whatever type of popular music is studied, the attention should be on learning about music, not on just having fun. The students can engage in that kind of activity on their own outside of school. Both the students and the teacher should approach the music with a "Let's learn about it" attitude.

A good way to encourage the students to think about the musical qualities that make up a type of music is to compare two versions of the same song. The song "Greensleeves" was presented in its original form on page 183 in the discussion of interpretation in singing. The version of "Greensleeves" on pages 278–79 is essentially the same melody but arranged in a rock style. In addition to helping the children sing the song, the teacher can guide them in comparing the rock version with the original.

> "We've now sung two versions of 'Greensleeves': the original version from hundreds of years ago and the rock version from our time. How are they different? Emily?"
>
> "The old one is in $\frac{6}{8}$ and the rock is in $\frac{4}{4}$," observes Emily. "And the rhythm has been changed a lot," Lewis adds.
>
> "You're both right. But what's different about the rhythm in the rock version?"
>
> "It 'swings' and is off the beat," Stephanie volunteers. "I think it has some syncopation." "And the rock version has a second part with sounds on 'bah' instead of words," Nicholas contributes.

"You're right. But there's another difference that doesn't appear on the pages of the books. Listen as I play the recording of the rock version." [The teacher plays the recording from the album accompanying the series books.]

"Brent, can you name another difference between the old and the rock versions, one that you could hear?"

"They sound different . . . but I don't know why."

"Were there some instruments in the rock version that weren't in the original version from England that we listened to a couple of days ago?"

"Drums?" Brent tentatively suggests.

"And what do the drums and other instruments add to the rock version?"

"Well, they made the rock version seem pretty jumpy. It's like two different songs. I think the old version was nice and smooth and sort of peaceful."

As with many songs, a simple instrumental accompaniment can be added to the rock version of a song like "Greensleeves." There may be students in the class who have studied electric guitar, and they can bring their instruments to school and add much to the accompaniment. They can be asked to create a part for their instrument. Other classroom instruments can also contribute to an accompaniment. For example, the autoharp can play the chords indicated in the music with this pattern:

A drum or tambourine can play:

Such parts can make the students more aware of the emphasis on the second and fourth beats in rock music.

No type of music should be ignored in school music classes; the only limitation should be the time allotted to any one type. No music, whether art or popular, exists apart from the larger culture. A musically educated person knows about the varied types of music, and has some understanding of where a piece fits, geographically and historically, into the world of music.

Review Questions

1. What three points should students remember if they are to be receptive to unfamiliar music?

2. How are knowledge and attitude related?

3. Where can a teacher locate materials on music from various countries and cultures around the world?

4. Why will Americans usually sing a German folk song better than they sing a song from Turkey or Indonesia?

5. a. Why is it useful to sing songs when learning about other cultures?
   b. Why is it important to listen to recordings of authentic performances of such music?

6. The integration of music and social studies is desirable up to a point. Why is a combining of the two subjects not recommended for the entire music curriculum?

7. Why is a unit of study recommended instead of a single-song approach when a class is learning about a particular culture?

8. How can students be helped to gain an initial understanding of historical eras in music?

Activities

1. Examine several of the music series books prepared for grades five and six. Find a unit, or combine several pieces of music to form a unit, on any type of non-Western art music. Then develop a plan for teaching the following with your unit:
   a. The features and characteristics of the music
   b. The cultural setting in which the music was created

2. Using the same unit, write a description of how you would incorporate the music into an appropriate social studies unit.

C H A P T E R

19

Music and the Fine Arts

A well-balanced education in music requires attention not only to the subtleties of sound but also to the fact that music is only one type of artistic endeavor. Sculpture, painting, dance, drama, poetry, and music are areas of human achievement referred to as the *fine arts*. Although each art exists in its own medium—poetry in words, music in sounds, painting in color and shapes on a two-dimensional surface, and so on—the fine arts fulfill a basic human need. They are valuable not for the practical benefits they offer but for the psychological satisfaction and stimulation they provide. They make life richer and more interesting. They provide human beings with a mode of thinking and a type of experience found nowhere else in life.

The fine arts often reveal the similar viewpoints that have prevailed at various times and places in human history. The blurred outlines in impressionistic paintings result from the same approach to art works that influenced Claude Debussy's impressionistic music. Admittedly, there are differences among the arts because of the techniques that each employs; the painter Monet worked with paint on a flat surface, while Debussy organized sounds to be heard within a span of time. But aside from the obvious differences in the media of expression, the arts at times have shared a similar outlook.

Because the arts are characterized by a common purpose and a shared view of time and place, the study of one art medium can be enriched by an examination of the others. A comparative study of this nature makes the students more sensitive to the expressive properties of sound, color, and form. The fundamental mode of thought needed for understanding the arts is reinforced and enlarged, and the students become more conscious of the qualities that distinguish artistic endeavor from the more functional forms of human activity.

There are two basic approaches for correlating music instruction with the fine arts. One approach is to supplement the music study by alluding to other arts at appropriate places in the music curriculum. The other approach is to combine all the arts, and sometimes the humanities as well, into an integrated program of study. These two approaches merit further explanation and discussion.

Enrichment with the Arts

At first glance, any distinction between the "enrichment" approach and the integrated study may seem negligible. Their basic premises, however, are different. In the enrichment type of teaching, music study is enhanced by including aspects of other arts where appropriate *for music.* Music has first priority, and the other arts are consigned to second place. In the integrated approach, instruction is organized around a unifying factor other than music, and that makes a considerable difference in what is taught.

The main virtue of the enrichment approach is that music is taught systematically and as thoroughly as time permits. This outcome is necessary if music is to be a significant part of the elementary school curriculum.

The negative aspect of an enrichment format is that the other fine arts are not taught in a systematic way. While the music educator may be pleased to have other arts contribute to music instruction, an art teacher or dance instructor may feel, justifiably, that such minimal coverage in his or her area is completely inadequate, especially if it is the only education the children will receive in that area during elementary school. This problem is alleviated if art is taught as a subject in itself, and if physical education experiences stress free movement as well as games and sports.

There are several ways in which music can be enriched by references to the other arts. In the following example, the teacher is referring to architecture to help the children understand the concept of form.

"You've been learning about form in music, and you know how to analyze it by assigning letters to the lines of songs and sections of pieces. Today let's consider form from another point of view, and see what form is like in architecture. In your books, look at the pictures of the two buildings. One is the Cathedral of Notre Dame in Paris, France, and the other is a modern office building.

"Concentrate first on the Cathedral. Who can point out something about the design or form of it? Joshua?"

"It has two towers, one on each side," Joshua reports, "so they give the building balance."

"That's right; the Cathedral is evenly balanced. Monica, what do you see in the center of the Cathedral, about halfway up?"

"Well, it looks like a big round window," Monica says.

"Yes; it's called the 'rose window.' What about the doors and doorways, Julio?"

"The middle door looks like it's a little bigger . . . and the doorways have lots of decoration around them . . . and they're shaped like an upside-down 'U' with a point at the top," Julio concludes.

"Okay. Now what about the up-and-down form of Notre Dame? Molly?"

"It has sort of three levels or layers, and then the towers are on top of that," Molly decides.

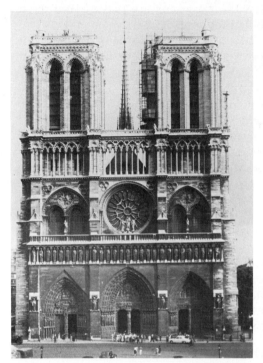

Notre Dame

Seagram Building

"Good. You're all very observant, and you've recognized that there's a design to the Cathedral of Notre Dame. Is its form anything like the forms we've learned about in music, Ethan?"

"Some of our music forms have three parts."

The teacher nods. "Which three-part form is like the three sections of Notre Dame, Ethan?"

"I guess the *ABA* form. It's got the tower, a center part, and another tower," says Ethan.

"That's a good comparison. Class, notice that the *ABA* form and the three-section form of Notre Dame are similar, even though the *ABA* form happens in a period of time, and the three-part structure of Notre Dame exists in space. Both show planning, and both have a logical balance of two parts with something different in between. Now, what about the modern building? Does it have form?" [The teacher helps the students to contrast its form with that of Notre Dame.]

The music series books offer several other examples of enrichment, like the picture of the Balinese performers shown on page 287. Typical of the classical dances of Bali, India, and other countries of southeast Asia is the attention given to facial expression and the position of the hands and fingers. By noticing such distinctions, children learn that the artistic dance in Bali differs in several ways from ballet in the Western world. They can also observe the instruments that the musicians are playing and try to imagine the timbres that each would produce.

Other musical concepts can be enriched through the use of poetry. In this example the teacher asks the class to read the poem "Everyone Sang" by Siegfried Sassoon.

> Everyone suddenly burst out singing;
> And I was filled with such delight
> As prisoned birds must find in freedom,
> Winging wildly across the white
> Orchards and dark-green fields; on—on—and out of sight.
>
> Everyone's voice was suddenly lifted;
> And beauty came like the setting sun:
> My heart was shaken with tears; and horror
> Drifted away . . . Oh, but Everyone
> Was a bird; and the song was wordless; the singing will never be done.

"Craig, does the poem have a form?"

"Well, it has two stanzas. Is that form?" Craig wonders.

"Could be, but keep looking. What do you notice about the first two lines of each stanza?"

"They're sort of alike. Both lines have the words 'everyone . . . suddenly.' Um . . . and both of the second lines begin with 'and,' so I guess there's a plan," Craig discovers.

"Okay. Now, Claudia, are there any lines where the sounds of the words or first letters of words contribute to the effect of the poem?"

"Ah . . . you have three 'W' words where it says 'winging wildly across the white,'" Claudia says.

"Good for you. Another way to unify a poem is through rhyme. Is there some rhyme in this poem, Naomi?"

"Yeah. In the first stanza the last words of a line sometimes rhyme, like 'delight,' 'white,' and 'sight'. . . . And the same thing happens in the second stanza," Naomi notices.

"So the poet is thinking about the sound of the words as well as their meanings. Is there anything similar about what a poet and a composer do when they work? Vanessa?"

"Music is sounds, and a poem is partly sounds, so I guess they do some things the same," Vanessa answers.

The teacher can point out an even more basic similarity between the two arts: Good music and good poetry both invite the listener to return to the work and explore its fuller meaning. The initial attractiveness is not an end in itself but a promise of further reward as a person probes for the deeper significance of the experience.

Most of the music series books realize the value of enriching music with poetry, dance, and art, so they often provide appropriate materials.

Copies of many excellent art works from the National Gallery of Art are available in inexpensive reproductions. In many cities the public libraries loan pictures in much the same way they loan books. In recent years several programs funded from federal and state sources have made dancers, poetry readers, film makers, and other artists available for performances in schools. A live performance by a qualified artist is a stimulating experience for children. The ways of enriching music instruction through the arts are many and varied.

Combined Arts Programs

As was mentioned earlier in this chapter, a second way to correlate the fine arts in the elementary school is to combine them into a single program. Such an integrated course of study is usually organized around a unifying aspect other than music. One example is an approach called "three arts" or "allied arts," which combines art, music, and dance through the study of common elements such as line, rhythm, form or design, and so on. Some combined programs present the arts from the standpoint of style periods like Baroque, Classical, and Romantic, although this organization is probably too advanced for elementary school children.

A somewhat different type of combined course involves not only the arts but also philosophical concepts such as truth, love, and freedom. This combination is often called a "humanities" program, since it involves more than just the arts.

Bringing several areas together in this manner clearly overarches the traditional subject-matter boundaries. It enables children to think about an idea in a way that is seldom possible in the subject-matter classes. Love and truth are topics that transcend arithmetic, spelling, punctuation, and music.

There are limitations to the combined approach, however. When such programs are examined from the perspective of what is learned in music, the results are disappointing. There is little systematic study of the subject, and virtually no development of skills such as playing the recorder or singing. The main problem is lack of time. It is nearly impossible to do justice to five subject-matter areas in a single course of instruction unless one has an hour or more each day to devote to the program. When there is only so much time available, adding more subjects simply means reducing the amount of time for all areas.

There are other problems, too. One concerns the training and interests of the teacher. It is a rare teacher indeed who is competent to teach art, music, dance, drama, and poetry. If a teacher tries to do so, almost always one area receives more attention than the others. It is possible to form a team of teachers for the program, if there are specialists available for the school. But teaching in a team is a bit like teaching by committee. The venture requires much time and patience on everyone's part if it is to be successful. Sometimes team teaching is little more than "turn teaching." Each teacher takes a turn with the class, but there is little integration of the various areas.

Another problem involves the false parallels that are sometimes drawn between one art and another. For example, the fact that the word "line" is found in both music and painting does not indicate that they refer to the same thing. A line or melody in music evolves rather slowly because it is a series of pitches occurring consecutively through a span of time; a line in art is seen within a millisecond. A musical line cannot be duplicated in physical space, and a visual line cannot be duplicated in a time span. (It is possible to draw a picture of a clock, but that it not the same as a picture of time. Nor is notation a picture of music. It is a blueprint for reproducing sound, not a substitute for aural experience.)

Looking for parallels between the temporal and spatial arts only confuses the children. Comparisons should not suggest that a chord in music is like a pillar in a building, or a clarinet tone is like a certain color. Children can see that dance involves both time and space in a continuously evolving motion that casts the dancer as a design-maker within three-dimensional space. And they can see that drama involves literary elements in addition to time and space manipulation. But the distinctive advantages and limitations of each medium should not be compromised to make them appear interchangeable. Each art form stands by itself without direct support from any other. In fact, any attempt to establish direct relationships only detracts from each art.

What does all this mean for the teacher who is considering the feasibility of a combined approach? First, because it does not include the teaching of music in much depth or order, the integrated program should not be the only music instruction the children receive. There should be a good program of music study before a combined course is added to the curriculum.

Second, the teacher will need to devote extra effort to the planning and teaching of an integrated program. Such instruction is not everyday fare in elementary school, so most teachers have had little experience with it. Furthermore, it requires a greater amount of subject-matter preparation, and few materials are available.

Third, the other teachers, administrators, and parents may not have a clear understanding of what the combined instruction is trying to accomplish. There is no problem in explaining the need for instruction in reading or arithmetic, but the advantages of learning music are more difficult to pinpoint, and the benefits of fine arts or humanities programs seem even more obscure. Telling a principal or parent that the instruction "seeks to make the students into better human beings" does little to clarify the goals. This fact does not mean that integrated arts or humanities programs should be avoided. It does indicate that the teacher should develop the course in such a way that it can be explained adequately to everyone.

Enriching Other Subjects with Music

This chapter has discussed bringing other arts into the music instruction to enrich it, and combining the arts into a single program. There is another practice: taking the arts into other areas of the elementary school curriculum. The idea of infusing the rest of the curriculum with the arts has been promoted in recent years by several foundation and governmental grants, one of which was the IMPACT project mentioned on pages 6–7. Although the objectives of some of the projects have been fuzzy and the claims of success exaggerated, the idea has merit if handled carefully. A curriculum infused with the arts is more interesting for the students, which means that more learning is likely.

Because the infusion process is one of bringing the arts into other areas of the curriculum, it must be done by the classroom teacher, and not by the music specialist who teaches only one subject and who sees a classroom for only a limited time each week. The specialist can help by offering ideas and materials appropriate to the topics the class is studying. The more the classroom teacher and the music specialist work together in this undertaking, the better will be the educational results.

The enrichment of social studies with music was mentioned in Chapter 18. It is the area in which infusion is most easily accomplished. Other areas can be enriched with the arts, too. The combining of poetry and songs is another logical choice, since almost all songs have texts and many poems have been set to music. If one of the objectives of the reading program is to have children read "with expression and meaning," then a poetry-music study can be valuable.

Even science can be enriched with the arts, if the teacher is alert to the possibilities. In this example, the class has been studying the solar system, and the teacher is building on that study by playing a movement of Gustav Holst's *The Planets*.

> "You've learned a lot of scientific things about the planets and the solar system. Now let's switch to a different way of thinking about them. Listen to how the idea of the planets influenced a composer named Holst. He wrote this piece in 1915 and called it *The Planets*. It has seven sections or movements, one for each planet.
>
> "Why seven instead of nine planets? Because he left out Earth, and Pluto wasn't discovered until 15 years after Holst wrote the music.
>
> "Anyway, Holst wasn't interested in telling us how many miles away a planet is, or what kind of atmosphere it has. Instead, he was attracted by the names of the planets, which come from the names of ancient Roman gods. One of the sections of *The Planets* is called 'Mars, the Bringer of War," and another is called 'Mercury, the Winged Messenger." Usually you see pictures of Mercury with wings on his helmet and his feet; he's the character you see in the ads for telegraphing flowers.
>
> "Holst wanted these sections of *The Planets* to give a sense of the Roman gods for whom they were named. See if you can sense the quality of these two movements. I'll play one of them, but I won't tell you which one. Listen carefully, then decide which it is." [The teacher plays the movement titled "Mercury."]
>
> "Duane, which movement was that: Mars or Mercury?"
>
> "The music goes pretty fast, so I think it was Mercury," Duane answers, moving in his seat as if dancing vigorously.
>
> "You're right, it was Mercury. In a day or two we'll hear the Mars movement of *The Planets*."

The teacher may want to introduce some works of art and literature related to the planets. The children can attempt to create musical compositions or draw pictures based on the idea of the planets and their names.

The main reason for infusing the study of planets with music and art is to provide enrichment and variety. Holst's *The Planets* does not try to give factual information about the solar system. Instead, it demonstrates the inventiveness of a human mind that was stimulated by the idea of the planets to create a fascinating musical composition.

The arts have much to offer, both as subjects for specialized study in themselves and as components of other areas of the elementary school curriculum. They stimulate the imagination and make the school day more interesting and richer for the children. Such benefits are reason enough to look for ways to integrate the arts and subject-matter areas in the classroom.

Review Questions

1. What are two fundamental points that the fine arts have in common?
2. a. What is the basic difference between the "enrichment" approach to including the other arts in music instruction, and the combined or integrated approach?
   b. What are the strengths and weaknesses of each approach?
3. Why is it desirable to enrich music instruction with the other arts in elementary school?
4. What are some sources of pictures and poems with which a teacher can enrich the study of music?
5. What is the difference between a fine arts program and a humanities program?
6. Why is it so demanding on the teacher to instruct in a fine arts or humanities program?
7. a. What are "false parallels" among the arts?
   b. Why should they be avoided in teaching the arts?
8. a. What are some ways of infusing the arts into other curricular areas in the elementary school?
   b. Why is the classroom teacher in a better position than the music specialist to infuse the arts into other areas of the curriculum?

Activities

1. Select a music series book and examine it for the amount and type of enrichment it contains from the other arts. Prepare a report on your findings.
2. Develop a plan for a music lesson into which another art can be incorporated.
   a. State the objective of the instruction.
   b. List the materials needed.
   c. Describe the teaching procedure.
3. Select a topic from any area of the elementary school curriculum except the fine arts. Then select two items from music, art, or poetry to infuse into the non-arts learning. Develop a short plan to describe how the material will be integrated.

20

Music and Special Learners

rate & scope

Almost all children can learn to enjoy music and to participate in it to some degree. In fact, music can be of particular value to children who are handicapped in their ability to hear, see, think, move, or respond.

The federal government has mandated a "free appropriate public education" for all handicapped children. Since the passage of Public Law 94-142 in 1975, these children are not only involved in a school setting, but are being placed in "the least restrictive environment"—that is, with non-handicapped children of comparable age and ability. This practice is called *mainstreaming*. For this reason, most classrooms are likely to include one or more handicapped learners.

Music Education for the Handicapped

The basic goal of music instruction for all children, including those with handicaps, is to educate them to be sensitive to music, knowledgeable about it, and somewhat skilled in its performance. Enjoyment is also a legitimate outcome of good music instruction.

When alterations in the program are needed for special learners, the changes most often involve the *rate of learning* and in some cases the *scope* of what is learned. The handicapped child may take significantly longer to accomplish the same amount as the nonhandicapped child. Nor can every handicapped child succeed at every task. Blind students cannot read printed music, although they can be taught Braille notation. Children who cannot walk will not be able to march with the music, but they can keep time in other ways. Retarded children may never be able to conceptualize some aspects of music, but most are able to participate in music and enjoy the experience.

The mentally retarded

Several terms have been devised to classify varying degrees of mental retardation, but they all refer to below-average intellectual ability. The mentally handicapped children who are mainstreamed into regular classrooms are likely to be only mildly retarded, and they can do many things in music.

They learn more slowly and in smaller increments, however, and they require more repetition. Their attention span is short. Because they are less able to generalize, concrete learning experiences are more effective. Their language ability is limited, so work with a book or written notation is not successful in most cases. Despite these limitations, a mentally handicapped child who is mainstreamed into a music class should be placed with students who are close to his or her chronological age. A social problem can be created if the age difference is too great, and the words of songs enjoyed by young children may not be suitable for the older retarded student.

Mentally handicapped children are usually quite receptive to music, and a teacher can enhance their enjoyment by keeping these points in mind when teaching them, whether in a homogeneous class or in a mainstreamed situation:

1. Choose songs that have repetition in words and music, and a text that has concrete imagery and relates to the children's experiences. Include American folk music and selected popular songs for older students, to give them a social bond with their non-handicapped peers.

2. Base the learning on active participation. A song with motions requires the child to attend to the words, and helps the teacher assess the extent of the child's understanding.

3. Keep verbal directions and explanations short and to the point.

4. Change songs and activities frequently, to accommodate short attention spans.

5. Praise each child frequently, by name, for specific accomplishments, but do not be effusive or dishonest in the commendations.

6. Do not confine instruction to simple tasks that the students can always do; they need to be challenged at times.

Improving self-image through names.   Mentally handicapped children need to hear their names often. Severely retarded children who are unable to speak or to maintain interest in activities around them sometimes show momentary alertness when their names are spoken. The teacher may need to speak or sing the name directly in front of the child, and bend down or touch the child lightly to make contact.

Names can be incorporated into music class in several ways. A simple procedure is to substitute a child's name for other words in a song. To the melody for "He's Got the Whole World in His Hands," the class can sing, "He's got Gloria Porter in his hands," or "He's got Joyce and Stewart in his hands." If the class members each want a turn as a subject of the song, the latter version, referring to two children at a time, is a good way to move through the class quickly. In fact, each verse can accommodate several different names, but it is better to limit the number in each verse, and then repeat them. In this way, the children will be more likely to notice when their names occur, and they will derive more pleasure from hearing their names repeated.

Names can also involve a directive for each child. In the song "Michael, Row the Boat Ashore," the class can sing "Gordon plays upon his drum, Hallelujah!", or "Nicole, shake your tambourine, Hallelujah!" Again, a full verse should be devoted to one child so that the slower responses can be accommodated.

The song "Little David, Play on Your Harp" can be similarly altered to allow for specific names and actions. The teacher may want to eliminate the word "little" in the substitute phrases because it connotes small stature and immaturity. Names can be incorporated into "Little David, Play on Your Harp" in several ways, while still retaining the characteristic syncopation of the music: "Here's Howard clapping his hands," or "Christina, smile as you sing," or "Neil Johnson, tap with your foot."

Children who can associate their names with letters will enjoy the song "Initials." Songs of this type should provide an early clue to the children that this is "their" verse, so that they have sufficient time in which to recognize the initial letter and stand. The words should be adapted, of course, to accommodate the needs of children with limited mobility.

INITIALS

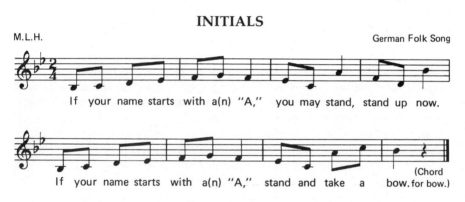

Body awareness. Mentally handicapped children need to have their sense of self enhanced not only by hearing their names frequently but by knowing the names for the parts of their bodies and how they work. The song "If You're Happy and You Know It" (p. 41) is one of many good songs for increasing the children's awareness of their bodies, and it can be done from a seated position if necessary. Further motions for the song may include directives such as "pull your ear, blink your eyes, touch your nose, wave your hand, pat your hair, nod your head, bend your knee, show your teeth, make a fist."

The physically handicapped

Sometimes called "orthopedically impaired," these children are limited in mobility and may lack control of gross or large muscle movements, which means that they have trouble moving their arms, legs, or entire body.

They may lack fine motor skills, which involve the use of small muscles and the manipulation of objects with the hands and fingers.

Physical activity in music may be altered to accommodate orthopedic handicaps, but it should not be eliminated. A child in a wheelchair can participate by moving rhythmically while others march with the music. Musical instruments can be adapted for playing, too, even to the extent of hitting a bell with a beater held between the teeth. In such a case the instrument's height may have to be adjusted, or other arrangements made for the child's comfort. Most physically disabled children who are not in other ways deficient are ingenious in thinking up ways to overcome their disability. With a little help they can do nearly everything that other class members do, but sometimes their participation takes a different form.

The visually impaired

Students with vision problems are usually able to function well in music classes, probably because their condition has forced them to listen attentively and to remember what they hear. Sight-impaired persons also depend heavily on tactile sensations, as well as on hearing.

Their limitations in music involve reading printed music and other visual materials. Braille, an international system of reading through the fingertips by feeling embossed dots on paper, has a code for music as well as for letters and numbers. Reading Braille music is no easy matter, however, and few children in elementary school have mastered that skill. Even an experienced blind performer who knows the Braille system for music notation must painstakingly figure out the dots in terms of each particular piece, so sightreading at tempo is not possible in the sense that it is with sighted persons.

Another area in which children with sight limitations encounter difficulty is in moving to music. They cannot see how others move, so they cannot imitate movement. They must also contend with the ever-present possibility of physical injury when they move in an unfamiliar situation.

The teacher should keep these points in mind when teaching children with sight impairment:

1. Remember not to rely on instruction by visual means; explain verbally for sight-impaired children.
2. Encourage the children to identify instruments by touch as well as by sound.
3. Label bells and autoharp buttons with tactile symbols or Braille letters. The student may be able to make the letters if the teacher does not know them.
4. Prepare raised-line drawings if special duplicators are available.
5. Use wide-lined staff paper and large print to help partially sighted children read music notation.

6. Arrange for vision-impaired children to practice parts on an independent basis so that they are prepared ahead of time for the music class.

7. Assign a sighted partner to help a sight-impaired child in activities that involve moving about the room.

8. Do not ask visually impaired children to cover their ears.

hand motions

Visual perception.   Some children find it difficult to discern the visual properties of objects, distinguish between a figure and its background, relate symbols to objects, remember visual images, and judge distance. In the above situations, the problem often lies not in a physical disorder of the eye but in faulty perception. Perception is the brain's ability to interpret and evaluate the stimuli that come to it. Flaws in visual perception impede a child's educational progress because so much of what is learned is obtained through the sense of sight.

A child with visual perception problems may require more time in which to grasp the symbolic aspects of music notation. The teacher can help direct the child's visual attention by making hand motions, either to indicate pitch levels, or to produce the hand signs associated with the Kodály method. The child may also benefit from seeing a particular shape or color affixed to different bells, so that the correct sound can be played when that symbol shows up in notation.

As the child becomes more sensitive to musical sounds, the visual symbols that represent those sounds are likely to become more meaningful.

The hearing impaired

In clinical diagnosis, "deaf" refers to profound hearing loss, while "hard of hearing" describes less severe impairment. Very few children hear nothing at all. Some are unable to hear pitches in certain ranges, while others cannot hear soft sounds. With the improvement of hearing technology, the trend today is to develop whatever hearing potential the child has, rather than to rely completely on lip-reading or signing. Fewer than 50 percent of speech sounds are visible, so lip-reading is limited in effectiveness, and signing is limited by the small number of persons who can communicate in that way.

A hearing aid amplifies the sound entering the ear, and must be fitted to the individual by a specialist in that work. The teacher needs to know the child's hearing ability with the aid, because it is with the aid that the student will be functioning in class. Although it is a remarkable invention, the hearing aid is limited in terms of the distance at which it can pick up sounds and its fidelity for reproducing timbres. Like listening to music over the telephone, hearing through an aid provides less richness of timbre than normal hearing does. Loud sounds must never be produced directly into a hearing aid, because the device has already been adjusted to provide the best sound level for that child's needs. Further amplification can be a painful experience for an aid-dependent person.

Although most sounds are transmitted to the brain through the ears, vibrations are also felt through other parts of the body, as anyone can report who has stood by a bass drum when it is struck. The tactile sense complements the ear, and it is for this reason that children with hearing problems are encouraged to touch sound sources. Hearing-impaired persons can learn to feel a difference between high and low pitches, and this helps them to sing. Often singing is aided by experience with blowing wind instruments such as kazoos and commercial devices such as Pianicas. Hearing-impaired children have been taught to play conventional wind instruments such as the clarinet and saxophone, on which pitches can be located without careful hearing.

As might be expected, hearing-impaired children exhibit poor speech development as a result of their auditory limitations. Often what they try to say is difficult to understand and lacking in inflection. They require much work on language development, even in music class. The teacher should point out rhymes, explain words, and employ chants to develop lively speech that has rhythmic drive. It is likely that some deaf children are not surrounded by language in the home because their families mistakenly think that the spoken word is of no use to the deaf. But they can respond to sound vibrations in parts of the body other than the ear, and the social benefits of being involved in some form of language communication are incalculable.

Many hearing-impaired children are tense and lag in motor development, perhaps as a result of overprotection, lack of socialization skills, or their inability to receive information about the environment that surrounds them outside their immediate field of vision. They need music activities that provide relaxation and self-confidence in both bodily movement and social situations.

The teacher should remember these points when teaching children with hearing problems:

1. Do not startle the children by touching them after approaching from outside their range of vision.

2. Do not speak when turned away from the class, as when writing on the chalkboard.

3. Speak directly to the child, even if it means bending down in the case of small children. They cannot see the facial expression or lips well when looking in an upward angle.

4. Speak clearly, with normal fluency and inflection, but do not talk loudly.

5. Encourage the children to talk, not merely to gesture. Feel free to correct their speech or to admit that you do not understand what they said, but do so in a positive and constructive manner.

6. Use visual as well as verbal symbols to indicate the beginning of a song

and similar activities. For example, the children might respond to a stop-and-go sign previously prepared with appropriately colored paper on opposite sides of a stick.

7. Do not expect a high degree of timbre discrimination.

8. Encourage hearing-impaired children to touch sound sources directly, so that they can feel the vibrations and sense the beat.

9. Do not ask hearing-impaired children to close their eyes.

Auditory perception.   Deficiencies in auditory perception include an inability to identify sounds, locate the source of a sound, relate sounds to visual cues, remember what is heard, organize sounds, and pay attention to a particular sound while others are heard at the same time. The last-named disability involves a flaw in figure/ground perception, which causes sounds to assail the brain in a confusing jumble. Children with this perceptual problem need help in learning to discern which sounds are important and which ones may be disregarded.

Because music instruction teaches students to listen more carefully, it contributes significantly to alleviating problems in auditory perception. Whatever the class activity, it should call for a response from the perceptually impaired children so that the teacher can note individual progress and ensure that music is not regarded as a passive experience. As the children improve in auditory perception, they will be able to move from playing an instrument, which is relatively easy because of tactile and visual reinforcement, to singing, which involves subtle internal bodily actions and requires a mental impression of each sound before it is produced. Eventually the children should be able to devote complete attention to a music listening experience, sorting out the complexity of sounds with both knowledge and enjoyment.

A teacher can further auditory perception by introducing activities such as the "Stretching Song" on page 300. The rhyming words are emphasized by being sustained for a longer time in the song. Such combinations as tall/small/ball, wide/hide/side, and high/lie/sky help hearing impaired children to discriminate among words with different initial sounds, and their concreteness helps the children to respond appropriately. The teacher can then assess the children's understanding of the words by observing their actions.

The speech impaired

Communication disorders are evident in poor articulation, stuttering, voice irregularities, unnatural pitch range, and use of faulty word sequence. The fact that music helps overcome stuttering and stammering was mentioned in Chapter 1. Music is helpful in aiding over 92 percent of all such

STRETCHING SONG

Words and Music by Eunice Boardman

1. I'm stretch-ing ver - y tall,   And now I'm ver - y small.   Now tall!
2. My hands I stretch out wide,   Be - hind me they will hide.   Now wide!
3. My hands I stretch up high,   Now on the floor they lie.   Now high!
4. Now with my head I shake,   Now not a move I make.   Now shake!
5. Now all the girls and boys   Don't make a sin - gle noise!   Sit down!

1. 2. 4. 5.   **3.**

Now small! Now I'm a ti - ny ball.
Now hide! I put them at my side.
Now lie! Now   way up to the sky.
No move make! Now my whole bod-y I shake.
No sound! And dream of man - y toys.

From E. Boardman et al., *Exploring Music,* Book 1. Copyright © 1975 by Holt, Rinehart and Winston, Publishers.

problems—an extremely high success rate.[1] Perhaps it is successful because vocal music treats speech in a way that differs from the students' usual experience with language. In singing, vowels are sustained, and the rhythmic flow of the music encourages fluency of expression. Some songs require the performer to simulate animal noises, whistles, wind, and other nonverbal sounds. Other songs contain echos, which are beneficial in providing phrases to be imitated. All of this attention to mouth-sounds makes children more sensitive to spoken language. Needless to say, all musical experiences related to speech for nonproficient children should be undertaken in a relaxed and nonthreatening atmosphere.

To encourage inflection in speech, the teacher may engage the class in activities that focus on rhythm (fast/slow), pitch (high/low), and sound level (loud/soft)—all of which are aspects of expressive nuance in speech as well as in music.

The learning disabled

This category as defined in the 1977 *Federal Register* includes any "disorder in one or more of the basic psychological processes involved in un-

[1]Richard M. Graham, comp., *Music for the Exceptional Child* (Reston, Va.: Music Educators National Conference, 1975), p. 35.

derstanding or in using language, spoken or written, which may manifest itself in an imperfect ability to listen, think, speak, read, write, spell, or to do mathematical calculations."[2] These children are of average or above-average intelligence, although at times they exhibit characteristics of mental retardation. It takes them longer to organize information that comes to them from two or more senses, and they are slower in making judgments, evidently because they are trying to process information that has become distorted before they can sort it out. Some of them have trouble judging distances and direction, so they cannot play catch with a ball. Some cannot use two senses at the same time, so they cannot simultaneously sing and walk. Others have a poor concept of time, so they have little sense of past or future. Still others fail to remember for more than a few seconds.

Children with learning disabilities often have one sense that is stronger than the others, and some are quite talented in music. When possible, the teacher should work with the stronger capability to build the child's confidence, then seek to improve performance in the weaker areas. The child should learn one point thoroughly before attempting another—that is, learn to sing a song well before adding an activity such as clapping. These children do not profit from repetition to the extent that mentally retarded children do, because the same drill may elicit a different response each time.

The teacher should follow these guidelines in teaching learning disabled children:

1. Get the child's attention before trying to communicate.

2. Present only one directive at a time.

3. Limit the number of choices offered to the child.

4. Use visual materials that are uncluttered with distracting images or printing.

5. In action songs, be ready to help the child identify the right and left sides, or recall the sequence of motions, when these patterned responses are required in the music activity.

6. Expect short attention spans, or overattention, as when the child seems unable to break the spell of interest in a prior activity and move on to something new.

7. Do not pressure a learning-disabled child for a response before he or she is ready to respond. If there has been a pattern of responding impulsively, encourage the child to take time to think.

8. Praise the child for specific accomplishments, especially in matters involving attentiveness, sequencing, and problem-solving.

9. Maintain order and consistency in classroom operation.

---

[2]*Federal Register,* Vol. 42, No. 163 (121a.5), August 23, 1977, p. 42478.

The emotionally disturbed

This handicap is manifested by an inability to learn that cannot be explained by intellectual, sensory, or health factors. Emotionally disturbed children exhibit inappropriate types of behavior or feelings under normal circumstances, and are unable to work well with others. Their antisocial behavior may take the form of withdrawal, hyperactivity, clowning, defiance, or aggression. Children who are antisocial generally have a poor opinion of themselves and feel insecure, despite frequent displays of bravado. Their self-control is tenuous, and they appear to have little regard for the future benefits or discomforts that are likely to result from their present actions.

Music instruction can help both withdrawn and aggressive children. Music by its nature is a different "language." Furthermore, music periods are relatively short and are often taught by someone other than the classroom teacher. For these reasons, music instruction frequently suggests a different atmosphere from the classroom setting, which the disturbed child may perceive as frustrating. Music class is not a retreat, however, because music instruction also takes place in a social setting. Part-singing, playing instruments, moving to music, and sharing ideas are accomplished in conjunction with other students. The benefits of responsible social interaction are available to the troubled child in music instruction as well as in other areas of the curriculum.

The teacher can reinforce a child's progress toward emotional stability in several ways.

1. Choose songs with texts that contribute to a positive self-image and encourage sensitivity to others. The child may be quite sophisticated intellectually, so choose relevant materials that do not talk down to the student.

2. Plan activities to accommodate a short attention span.

3. Limit the number of choices available to the child. An emotionally disturbed person often feels more secure when simply told what to do, and following directions provides an orderly focus for behavior.

4. Plan carefully for any activities involving movement. An emotionally vulnerable child may feel threatened when surrounded by persons engaged in free movement.

5. Provide orderliness by establishing procedures that are expected when the child distributes and collects materials such as instruments.

6. Recognize that the child will have good days and bad days for no apparent reason. Expect swings of mood but do not cater to them.

7. Try behavior modification techniques, which reinforce desirable behavior through a system of rewards.

8. Find time to help the child on a one-to-one basis, since individual attention is often what is needed and wanted by the child.

The health impaired

A child's educational performance can be adversely affected by chronic health problems. Any condition that limits the strength, vitality, or alertness of a child must be taken into account by the teacher. Music activities can be adapted to meet the special needs of the ill child. In many cases, approaches designed for the handicapped will apply equally well to children who are disabled for health reasons.

To help every child feel relaxed and confident in the learning situation, some teachers teach their classes a "welcome song" which is sung for each new child who enters the group, handicapped or not. It is a valuable social gesture for every incoming child, but especially so for handicapped youngsters, who may feel particularly fearful and insecure as they try to join into a new situation. The song is equally appropriate as a welcome to adults and other persons who visit the room. In conjunction with the "welcome song," a few of the class members may shake hands with the new student or guest. Children like to do this, and they benefit by learning to become more compassionate and caring.

The task of helping handicapped children is demanding and difficult. Even with good support services in terms of counseling and materials, the responsibility falls largely on the teacher, who must be knowledgeable, patient, understanding, and inventive. The teacher's positive attitude may be the most important factor in ensuring that the music experience will be exciting and productive for both the teacher and the students.

Review Questions

1. What is the goal of music instruction for handicapped students?
2. In what ways does music instruction for handicapped students differ from that given nonhandicapped students?
3. Describe three techniques for teaching music to mentally retarded students.
4. What limitations in music do sight-impaired children have, besides being unable to read music?
5. What activities associated with music instruction will help to develop children's visual perception?
6. What are the limitations of a hearing aid in terms of music?
7. Describe three techniques for teaching music to hearing-impaired children.
8. In what way does music help children learn to speak better?
9. Describe three techniques for teaching music to children who are learning disabled.
10. What is the principle of behavior modification techniques?

Activities

1. Decide whether you wish to concentrate on aiding the children's visual perception, auditory perception, or speech. Then select a song or music activity to help you toward that goal. Plan a short lesson in which you use the material.

2. Observe a music class with one or more handicapped children in it. Answer the following questions from your observation.
   a. Were the handicapped children easily noticeable?
   b. What handicaps were evident?
   c. What special procedures did the teacher use to help the handicapped children?
   d. Were the handicapped children able to participate successfully in the class?
   e. What were the attitudes of the other children toward the handicapped students?
   f. What was the teacher's attitude toward the handicapped students?

Appendix A
Additional Resources

Elementary School Music Series Books

Holt, Rinehart & Winston, 383 Madison Ave., New York 10017. *The Music Book.*

Macmillan Publishing Co., Inc., 866 Third Ave., New York 10022. *The Spectrum of Music.*

Silver Burdett Company, 250 James St., Morristown, N.J. 07960. *Silver Burdett Music.*

Books on Aspects of Teaching Music in the Elementary Schools

GENERAL

Adler, Marvis S., and Jesse C. McCarroll, *The Elementary Teacher's Music Almanack* (West Nyack, N.Y.: Parker Publishing Company, 1978).

Andress, Barbara, et al., *Music in Early Childhood* (Reston, Va.: Music Educators National Conference, 1973).

Aronoff, Frances W., *Music and Young Children* (New York: Holt, Rinehart & Winston, 1969).

Athey, Margaret, and Gwen Hotchkiss, *A Galaxy of Games for the Music Class* (West Nyack, N.Y.: Parker Publishing Company, 1975).

Baird, JoAnn, *Using Media in the Music Program* (New York: Center for Applied Research in Education, 1975).

Batcheller, John M., *Music in Early Childhood* (New York: Center for Applied Research in Education, 1975).

Bramscher, Cynthia S., *Treasury of Musical Motivators for the Elementary Classroom* (West Nyack, N.Y.: Parker Publishing Company, 1979).

Carabo-Cone, Madeleine, *A Learning Theory and Music Methods for Teachers of Elementary and Pre-School Children: A Sensory-Motor Approach to Music Learning* (New York: MCA Music; or Melville, N.Y.: Belwin-Mills). Four books.

Crews, Katherine, *Music and Perceptual-Motor Development* (New York: Center for Applied Research in Education, 1975).

Gingrich, Donald, *Relating the Arts* (New York: Center for Applied Research in Education, 1974).

Graham, Richard M., compiler, *Music for the Exceptional Child* (Reston, Va.: Music Educators National Conference, 1975).

Graham, Richard M., and Alice S. Beer, *Teaching Music to the Exceptional Child* (Englewood Cliffs, N.J.: Prentice-Hall, Inc., 1980).

Hardesty, Kay W., *Music for Special Education* (Morristown, N.J.: Silver Burdett, 1979).

Hotchkiss, Gwen, and Margaret Athey, *Treasury of Individualized Activities for the Music Class* (West Nyack, N.Y.: Parker Publishing Company, 1977).

Konowitz, Bert, *Music Improvisation as a Classroom Method* (New York: Alfred Music, 1973).

Landis, Beth, and Polly Carder, *The Eclectic Curriculum in American Music Education: Contributions of Dalcroze, Kodály, and Orff* (Reston, Va.: Music Educators National Conference, 1972).

Marsh, Mary Val, *Explore and Discover Music* (New York: Macmillan, Company, 1970).

Monsour, Sally, *Music in Open Education* (New York: Center for Applied Research in Education, 1974).

Mulligan, Mary Ann, *Integrating Music with Other Studies* (New York: Center for Applied Research in Education, 1975).

Nash, Grace C., *Creative Approaches to Child Development with Music, Language, and Movement* (Port Washington, N.Y.: Alfred Publishing Company, 1974).

————, *Today with Music* (Port Washington, N.Y.: Alfred Publishing Company, 1973).

Nocera, Sona D., *Reaching the Special Learner Through Music* (Morristown, N.J.: Silver Burdett, 1979).

Nye, Vernice, *Music for Young Children* (Dubuque, Iowa: William C. Brown Company, 1975).

Nye, Vernice T., Robert E. Nye, and H. Virginia Nye, *Toward World Understanding with Song* (Belmont, Calif.: Wadsworth Publishing Company, 1967).

Palmer, Mary, *Sound Exploration and Discovery* (New York: Center for Applied Research in Education, 1974).

Reeder, Barbara, and James A. Standifer, *Source Book of African Materials for Music Educators* (Reston, Va.: Music Educators National Conference, 1972).

Willman, Fred, *Electronic Music for Young People* (New York: Center for Applied Research in Education, 1974).

Zimmerman, Marilyn P., *Music Characteristics of Children* (Reston, Va.: Music Educators National Conference, 1971).

DALCROZE

Driver, Ethel, *A Pathway to Dalcroze Eurhythmics* (New York: Thomas Nelson and Sons, 1963).

Findlay, Elsa, *Rhythm and Movement: Application of Dalcroze Eurhythmics* (Evanston, Ill.: Summy-Birchard, 1971).

Gell, Heather, *Music, Movement and the Young Child* (Sydney, Australia: Australian Publishing Company, 1969).

KODÁLY

Choksy, Lois, *The Kodály Method: Comprehensive Music Education from Infant to Adult* (Englewood Cliffs, N.J.: Prentice-Hall, 1974).

Choksy, Lois, *The Kodály Context* (Englewood Cliffs, N.J.: Prentice-Hall, 1981).

Daniel, Katinka S., *The Kodály Approach* (Belmont, Calif.: Fearon Publishers, 1973). Three books.

Lewis, Aden, *Listen, Look and Sing* (Morristown, N.J.: Silver Burdett, 1971). Four books.

Richards, Mary Helen, *Threshold to Music* (Belmont, Calif.: Fearon Publishers, 1964). Four books.

Szabo, Helga, *The Kodály Concept of Music Education* (New York: Boosey and Hawkes, 1969).

Szönyi, Erzsébet, *Kodály's Principles in Practice*, trans. John Weissman and Raymond Alston (New York: Boosey and Hawkes, 1974).

Wheeler, Lawrence, and Lois Raebeck, *Orff and Kodály Adapted for the Elementary School* (Dubuque, Iowa: William C. Brown Company, 1972).

ORFF

Keetman, Gunild, *Elementaria*, trans. Margaret Murray (Melville, N.Y.: Belwin-Mills, 1974).

Keller, Wilhelm, *Introduction to Music for Children* (Mainz, West Germany: B. Schott's Söhne, 1974). Obtainable from Belwin-Mills, Melville, N.Y.

Nichols, Elizabeth, *Orff Instruments Source Books, I and II* (Morristown, N.J.: Silver Burdett, 1970).

Orff, Carl, and Gunild Keetman, *Music for Children* (Mainz, West Germany: B. Schott's Söhne, 1950). English edition adapted by Margaret Murray; obtainable from MMB, Inc., St. Louis, Mo. Five books.

Wheeler, Lawrence, and Lois Raebeck, *Orff and Kodály Adapted for the Elementary School* (Dubuque, Iowa: William C. Brown Company, 1972).

Sources for Music Teaching Materials

Because the producers of materials to be used in teaching music in the elementary schools frequently add and delete items, it is suggested that interested persons contact the company to secure the current catalog.

GENERAL ENRICHMENT

Bowmar, 4563 Colorado Blvd., Los Angeles, Calif. 90039. Recordings and enrichment units, especially of music of various countries.

Children's Music Center, 5373 West Pico Blvd., Los Angeles, Calif. 90019. Enrichment material on American Indians.

Keyboard Publications, 1346 Chapel St., New Haven, Conn. 06511. Recordings and enrichment units on various types of music; also publishes a magazine for students, *Man and His Music*.

FILMS AND FILMSTRIPS

American Book Company/Keyboard Publications, 7625 Empire Drive, Florence, Ky. 41042.

BFA Educational Media, 2211 Michigan Ave., Santa Monica, Calif. 90404.

Churchill Films, 622 North Robertson Blvd., Los Angeles, Calif. 90069.

Educational Audio Visual, Inc., Pleasantville, N.Y. 10570.

EMC Corporation, 180 East 6th, St. Paul, Minn. 55101.

Film Associates, 11559 Santa Monica Blvd., Los Angeles, Calif. 90025.

Franson Corporation, 225 Park Avenue South, New York, N.Y. 10003.

National Geographic Society, Washington, D.C. 20036.

Prentice-Hall Media, 150 White Plains Road, Tarrytown, N.Y. 10591.

Shetler, Donald J., ed., *Film Guide for Music Educators*, Music Educators National Conference, Reston, Va. 22091.

Society for Visual Education, Inc. 1345 Diversey Parkway, Chicago, Ill. 60614.

INDIVIDUALIZED LEARNING

Macmillan Publishing Company, Inc., 866 Third Ave., New York, N.Y. 10022.

MuGin Publications, P.O. Box 36528, Los Angeles, Calif. 90036.

KODÁLY METHOD

Boosey and Hawkes, Oceanside, N.Y. 11572.

MUSIC READING

Shawnee Press, Delaware Water Gap, Pa. 18327.

ORFF METHOD

MMB, Inc., 10370 Page Industrial Blvd., St. Louis, Mo. 63132.

SPECIAL EDUCATION

Abingdon Press, 201 8th Ave. So., Nashville, Tenn. 37202.

Educational Activities, Inc., Freeport, N.Y. 11520.

Kimbo Educational Records, Box 246, Deal, N.J. 07723.

MMB, Inc., 10370 Page Industrial Blvd., St. Louis, Mo. 63132.

Myklas Music Press, P.O. Box 929, Boulder, Colo. 80306.

Appendix B
Common Dance Terms

Address, honor—bow to another dancer

Balance, as in *balance* polka, *balance* waltz—perform the steps in place

Caller—the person who gives the square dancers verbal directions that duplicate the rhythm of the music and are often in rhyme

Clog—a dance in which the performers beat strongly audible rhythms on the floor as if wearing clogs (heavy wooden-soled shoes)

Corner—in a square dance set, the nearest person on the side away from one's partner

Do-si-do (from *dos a dos*, "back to back")—a movement in which two persons approach one another, pass right shoulders and then left shoulders, and return backward to place, keeping arms folded across the chest

Grand chain, or Grand right and left—in a single circle with others, partners face, clasp right hands and pass right shoulders, then give left hands to next dancer and pass left shoulders, proceeding in this manner to original positions. Instead of grasping hands, the dancers can swing once around each new person.

Grand march—an opening procession in which all the dancers participate with simple changes of pattern

Head couple—in a square dance, the partners standing with backs to the music

Longways dance—a dance in which the basic formation is two lines formed by partners facing each other

Polka—a lively duple dance of Bohemian origin, characterized by three quick steps and a pause

Promenade—a square dance figure in which the couples walk counterclockwise, usually with hands crossed in skating position

Schottische—a dance in duple meter like a polka, but slower and characterized by three steps and a hop

Set—the formation of dancers at the start of a dance

Shuffle—the style of square dance walk in which the dancers slide their feet in a relaxed manner instead of lifting them

Skating position—a folk dance position in which partners are side by side with right hands joined under joined left hands

Square dance—a type of American folk dance in which four couples form the four sides of a square and move with a variety of steps and figures.

Swing or buzz step—a square dance step in which the partners face in opposite directions with right sides together to form an axis around which they turn. The right foot steps in place on each beat, and the dancers pivot to the right by pushing off with the left foot on the "and" of each beat. The movement is also called "swing your partner."

Virginia reel—an American longways dance in duple meter characterized by the swinging of partners, lines circling around themselves, and the forming of arches under which other dancers pass.

Waltz—a couple dance in fast triple meter, characterized by a "step slide step" movement and frequent turning

Appendix C
Autoharp Chord Bars

	D Maj.		Gm Min.		A7 Sev.		Dm Min.		E7 Sev.		Am Min.		D7 Sev.	
E♭ Maj.		F7 Sev.		B♭ Maj.		C7 Sev.		F Maj.		G7 Sev.		C Maj.		G Maj.

Appendix D
Recorder Fingering Chart

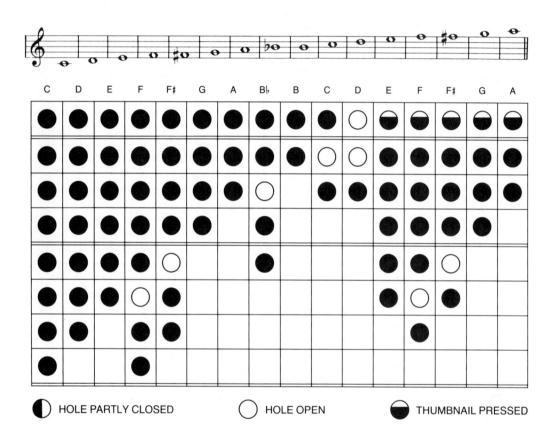

C	D	E	F	F♯	G	A	B♭	B	C	D	E	F	F♯	G	A

◑ HOLE PARTLY CLOSED   ◯ HOLE OPEN   ⬒ THUMBNAIL PRESSED

Glossary of Music Terms

accent   sudden loudness at the beginning of a tone, followed by an immediate reduction in dynamic level

accidental   a sharp (♯), flat (♭), or natural (♮) used within a composition to show a pitch not indicated by the key signature

acoustics   the science of sound

action song   a song that can appropriately involve body actions in addition to singing

alto (or contralto)   the lowest women's singing voice

art song   a song composed to achieve an expressive unity of text and music

autoharp   an instrument with metal strings stretched across a frame. The player strums with one hand and with the other presses one of several buttons to obtain the desired chord.

bar   a measure, which is the notation for a meter pattern

barline   the vertical line that separates each bar or measure from the one adjacent to it

baroque period   in music history, the period extending from about 1600 to 1750; characterized by the stabilizing of harmony into major and minor keys, music written for specific instruments in a solo role, much composition for organ, and dramatic choral works. The style is exemplified in the music of Bach, Handel, Vivaldi, and Telemann.

bass   in vocal music, the lowest men's singing voice

bass clef   the clef in which the F below middle C is positioned on the fourth line from the bottom of the staff, between the two dots of the bass clef sign

beam   a straight, heavy line connecting the stem ends of consecutive notes that would otherwise have individual flags

beat   the recurrent throb or pulse in music, and the unit by which the passing of time is measured

bells   metal strips arranged in keyboard fashion on a supporting frame and struck with a mallet. In some sets, the bells can be removed for individual use.

binary form   a musical structure consisting of two segments, identified as *AB*

borrowed pattern   a rhythm pattern in which the note values represent durations different from those indicated by the meter signature. Such patterns are identified by a slanting numeral that tells how many notes of irregular length are involved, and the patterns may also be marked with a horizontal bracket.

canon   a contrapuntal composition, usually instrumental, in which the imitation between two or more lines of music is not always at the same pitch level

cantata   a composition for chorus, vocal soloists, and orchestra; often on a religious subject and somewhat dramatic in style, but not intended to be acted or staged

castanets   two small wooden cup-shaped pieces struck together against the leg or palm of the hand, or held in one hand and tapped together with the fingers, or (if attached to a handle) struck together by a whip-like motion of the wrist

chaconne   a composition featuring melodic variations on a chord pattern that is repeated throughout the work

chamber music   instrumental music intended for performance in a small room or "chamber" by an ensemble involving only one person on each part

chant   a repeated phrase spoken rhythmically, with strong accents; also, in sacred music, a single line sung with subtle nuances in pitch and rhythm, to imitate the inflections of speech

chord   a combination of three or more tones sounded simultaneously

chord function   the role of a chord in a particular key. In one key a chord will seem active and restless, but in another the same sound will give a sense of repose and finality. The effect or function of a particular chord is indicated by the Roman numeral that matches the scale step number of the chord root.

chromatic notes   notes altered on the left side by a flat, sharp, or natural sign to indicate a departure from the prevailing key signature

classical period   in music history, the period extending from about 1750 to 1825; characterized by well-defined forms, controlled emotional content, and standardization of orchestral instrumentation and chamber ensembles such as the string quartet. The style is exemplified in the music of Haydn, Mozart, and Beethoven.

claves (*clah*-vays)   two cylindrical wood blocks, one of which is supported lightly in the palm of one hand and struck with the other block

clef   a sign placed on the staff to show the exact pitches of the written notes

coda   a concluding section that is not essential to the form of a piece of music

composing   developing and notating an original musical work over a period of time

compound meter   meter in which the beat subdivides into three background pulses

concerto   an extended musical work, usually in three movements, for an instrumental soloist with orchestral accompaniment

concerto grosso   a musical work for a small ensemble of instrumentalists—one on a part—in contrast to the accompaniment provided by a larger instrumental group

consonance   the effect of simultaneous sounds that the listener considers agreeable or pleasant

contour   the "shape" of a melody, evident in the way its notes ascend and descend in pitch

contrary motion   melodic lines that move in opposite directions at the same time

countermelody   a melodic line designed to occur simultaneously with another melody and in contrast to it

counterpoint (the adjective form is **contrapuntal**)   the simultaneous sounding of two or more equally important melodies

crescendo (cresc.)   becoming gradually louder

"cuckoo" call   the descending interval of a minor third found in many children's songs throughout the world

cymbals   large metal discs struck together, or suspended singly and hit with a mallet or brush

da capo (D.C.)   a term directing the performer to return to the beginning of the music

Dalcroze method   techniques devised by the Swiss music educator Emile Jaques-Dalcroze to refine the physical experience of body movement and rhythmic response

decrescendo (decresc.)   becoming gradually softer

descant   a decorative line performed with a more important melody, generally in a higher pitch range than the basic melody and in contrast to it

development   manipulating a musical theme by changing its intervals and/or rhythm, extracting fragments for special treatment, inverting its melodic direction, and altering it in other ways

diminuendo (dim.)   becoming gradually softer

dissonance   the effect of simultaneous sounds that the listener considers discordant

dominant chord   the chord built on the fifth step of the scale

dominant seventh chord   a four-tone chord built on the fifth step of the scale and encompassing the interval of a seventh from the root to the top note of the chord

dotted note   a note followed by a dot that increases the duration of the sound by one-half of the note's value

drum   an instrument consisting of a skin or membrane stretched over a frame and struck with the hand or a beater

dynamics   the varying levels of loudness and softness, as indicated by the basic Italian words *piano* (*p*) and *forte* (*f*), with their qualifying terms, and by other symbols

echo-clapping, echo-singing   performing a musical task by immediately imitating another person's performance of it

eighth note   a note written as a solid head connected to a stem with one flag. It lasts only half as long as a quarter note.

ensemble   a group of musicians; also, the effect of unity achieved when they perform together

exposition   the opening section of a fugue

fine arts   the body of subjects, including music, painting, sculpture, dance, drama, and poetry, that are pursued not for their functional benefit but for their aesthetic qualities

finger cymbals   two small metal discs struck against each other on their edges to produce a high-pitched, bell-like sound

finger plays   a series of finger, hand, or arm motions performed rhythmically to depict the images suggested by a song or rhyme

flag   the short curved line extending from the open end of a stem that is part of an eighth note or a note of shorter duration

flat   a symbol (♭) indicating that a pitch should be lowered by one half step; also, the sound of a note that is performed below its proper pitch

form   the design, plan, or structure of a piece of music; also, the type of work as suggested by a particular performance medium (concerto, string quartet, and the like)

free form   a musical structure that does not follow an established pattern

frequency (of pitch)   the number of vibrations per second that occur when a sounding medium is activated, with a faster frequency producing a higher pitch

fugue   a musical form in which the theme or subject is presented by one part after another in imitative style; it may include additional thematic material as well

glockenspiel   small metal strips arranged in keyboard fashion and struck with a mallet

grace note   an ornamentation which is performed very fast and is followed immediately by a more important note of the melody. The grace note is printed in smaller size than the regular notation, and a slash goes diagonally through its stem and flag.

guiro (*gwee*-roh)   a notched gourd scraped with a stick

guitar   a flat-bodied six-stringed instrument that is plucked to produce notes in a range of more than three octaves

half note   a note written as an open head connected to a stem. It lasts twice as long as a quarter note.

half step   the smallest pitch interval possible on a keyboard instrument

hand signs   a system of signals in which various hand positions represent the different pitch syllables

harmonic minor scale   a minor scale in which step 7 is raised so that it is a half step away from the upper keynote

harmony   the effect created when pitches are sounded simultaneously

humanities   the branches of learning, such as fine arts and philosophy, that deal primarily with culture and avenues of human expression

improvisation   varying a theme while performing it spontaneously without benefit of notation

instrument families   a categorizing of orchestral instruments according to their method of tone production, with the three most basic groupings being the winds, the strings, and the percussion instruments

interpretation   the style of musical expressiveness in a performance

interval   the distance from one pitch to another. The name of an interval is determined by the number of letters it includes, counting the lower tone and the higher tone.

inversion   turning a melody upside down so that an ascending interval descends, or vice versa; also, rearranging the notes in an interval or chord so that they occur in a different order

irregular meter   asymmetrical beat patterns within a measure

jingle bells   small spherical bells attached to a strap or frame and shaken

key   the effect created when several tones are related to a common tonal center. If these notes are rearranged to form a scale, the starting note of the scale (step 1) is the name of the key.

key center   the tonic, which is the pitch on which a scale is built and toward which the music tends to gravitate

key signature   the group of flats or sharps at the left of the staff in a musical work. The key signature indicates that certain notes should be consistently raised or lowered by one half step.

keyboard   an arrangement of five black and seven white keys that is repeated in several octaves to encompass a wide range of pitches

keynote   the tonic, which is the pitch on which a scale is built and toward which the music tends to gravitate

Kodály-Hungarian Singing School   techniques devised by the Hungarian composer Zoltan Kodály to develop musicianship by emphasizing good vocal tone, freedom of musical expression, and music reading

locomotor activity   actions that require movement from one place to another

leger lines   short horizontal lines indicating the pitch of notes too high or too low to be placed on the staff. Leger lines extend the range of the staff.

major key   the effect created when steps 3-4 and 7-8 are a half step apart

major scale   an eight-tone scale with a half step between steps 3-4 and 7-8

maracas   rattles, often in pairs, that are shaken to produce the sound of moving pellets

measure   the visual representation of meter; specifically, the notation for one meter pattern, separated from adjacent patterns by vertical barlines

melodic minor scale   a minor scale in which steps 6 and 7 are raised one half step when the notes ascend and lowered when the notes descend

melody   a series of consecutive pitches that form a cohesive musical entity

meter   the grouping of beats according to their relative heaviness or lightness

meter signature   the two numbers, or their symbols, occurring at the beginning of a piece of music to indicate the meter pattern by telling how many beats are in each measure and what kind of note lasts for one beat

metronome   a mechanical device for producing repeated taps, the tempo of which can be regulated to mark any beat speed

middle C   the C nearest the middle of the piano keyboard, and the note that is written halfway between the treble and bass staffs

minor key   the effect created when the third step above the keynote is lowered

minor scale   an eight-tone scale that in its natural form has a half step between steps 2-3 and 5-6

minuet   a slow dance in $\frac{3}{4}$ meter, characterized by frequent bowing and toe pointing; also, music in the style of that dance

mixed meter   the changing of meter within a musical work

modulation   changing key while the composition is in progress, usually without a break in the music

motive   a short melodic or rhythmic fragment that is important because of its frequent appearances in a musical work

movement   a sizable and self-contained section of a long musical work

music   the art of organized sound; the combining of vocal or instrumental tones into an aural experience that reveals structure and continuity

music consultant   a music specialist whose role is not primarily to teach but to provide help for classroom teachers and others who do the actual music teaching in a school district

music literature   the body of music that has been created through the ages

music reading   the ability to look at music notation and to translate its symbols into sound

music specialist   a teacher who holds certification in the subject area of music, and whose function is to teach music to children and help classroom teachers provide appropriate music experiences

music supervisor   an administrator with certification in music, who provides leadership for the music program and serves as liaison between music teachers and the central administration of the school district

music theory   a study of the way in which musical sounds are organized

natural   a symbol (♮) that cancels a sharp or flat previously applied to a particular note

natural minor scale   a minor scale in which there is a half step between steps 2-3 and 5-6

nonlocomotor activity   actions that do not require movement from one place to another

note   a sign placed on the staff to indicate the pitch and duration of a musical sound

note value   the duration of a particular musical sound, determined in relation to the beat

octave   the interval between a note and the nearest pitch with the same letter name

opera   a sung drama involving staging, costumes, acting, and orchestral accompaniment

oratorio   a musical work based on a religious or biblical subject and involving chorus, vocal soloists, and orchestral accompaniment, but not acting, costumes, or staging

Orff-*Schulwerk*   techniques devised by the German composer Carl Orff to develop musicianship by involving the child in movement, speech, rhythm, singing, and playing specially designed instruments in an improvisational manner

ostinato   a pattern of rhythm or melody that is repeated persistently

parallel major and minor keys   a major and a minor key that share the same keynote but require different key signatures. C major and C minor, for example, are parallel keys.

parallel motion   melodic lines that move in the same direction at the same time

partner songs   two or more songs that can be sung simultaneously because they are identical in key, harmonic structure, and length

passacaglia   a set of variations over a melodic ostinato that occurs in the lowest part and is repeated throughout the work

Patsch (German; plural is *Patschen*)   a thigh slap

pentatonic scale   a five-tone scale in which every note is either a whole step or 1½ steps away from its neighbor, like the black keys of the piano

phrase   consecutive sounds that belong together as a musical thought, like a phrase in language

piano   a large keyboard instrument capable of producing 88 pitches, each sounded by the action of a hammer hitting the strings

pickup note   an unstressed note, usually less than one beat in duration, that begins a musical phrase

pitch   the highness or lowness of a musical sound, as determined by the number of vibrations per second

pitch syllables   the Latin syllables—*do, re, mi, fa, sol, la, ti, do*—traditionally applied to pitches to show their relationship to a key center

polka   a lively duple dance of Bohemian origin, characterized by three quick steps and a pause; also, music in the style of that dance

polymeter   several meters occurring simultaneously

polyrhythm   several rhythms occurring simultaneously

primary chords   the chords most commonly used in a major or minor key. They are the tonic or I, the subdominant or IV, and the dominant or V.

program music   instrumental music associated with a story or other nonmusical ideas

quarter note   a note written as a solid head connected to a stem. It is the note value that is most often assigned to represent the beat.

range   the upper and lower pitch limits of a voice, an instrument, or a piece of music

recorder   a wind instrument, generally of wood, on which notes are produced by covering finger holes. The songflute, flutophone, and tonette are similar to the recorder, but they are made of plastic and are of simpler construction, with a smaller range.

register the general pitch level of a song, taking as a standard the range of the voice or instrument performing it

relative major and minor keys a major and a minor key that share the same key signature but start on different keynotes. G major and E minor, for example, are relative keys.

Renaissance period in music history, the period from about 1450 to 1600; characterized by small vocal ensembles with independent voice lines sung in imitation, instruments few in number and confined to an accompanying role, a quality of intimacy and restraint, and a gentle rhythmic flow to the music. The style is exemplified in the music of Palestrina, di Lasso, and Byrd.

repertoire music that has been prepared for performance by an individual or group; also, the body of music that has been created for a particular medium, such as the "piano repertoire"

rest a period of measured silence in music. For every note value there is a rest with the same name and duration.

rhythm the sense of orderly motion that occurs as music progresses in terms of time

rhythm syllables a word system that assigns a certain syllable to a particular note value, to aid in the recognition and performance of various note durations

romantic period in music history, the period extending from about 1825 to 1900; characterized by rich harmonies with much chromaticism, extremes in mood and dynamic level, large orchestras, program music, disinterest in formal structures, a strong sense of nationalism, and much piano composition. The style is exemplified in the music of Chopin, Liszt, Mendelssohn, Dvorak, Grieg, Tchaikovsky, Berlioz, and Wagner

rondo a piece of music in which one melody returns several times, with other musical ideas interspersed between its various appearances

root the note on which a chord is built, and the note that gives the chord its name, whether the identification is by alphabet letter or by the numeral that reflects its position in the scale

rote learning by imitating another person

round strict imitation occurring between two or more lines of music throughout the song

rubato a performer's slight deviation from strict rhythm, for expressive purposes; tempo fluctuation that is intentional and controlled

sandblocks flat metal or wood surfaces over which sandpaper is stretched to create a scratching sound when two are rubbed together

scale a series of pitches ascending or descending according to a prescribed pattern of intervals

score music notated in such a way that the parts for different performers appear vertically, one above another

sectional forms music in which unity is achieved by balancing contrasting sections with material heard earlier, as in the forms *ABA* and *ABACABA*.

sequence the immediate repetition of a musical phrase at successively higher or lower pitch levels than the original phrase

seventh chord a chord of four pitches, each a third apart. The most common seventh chord is the V7, or dominant seventh chord.

sharp a symbol (♯) indicating that a pitch should be raised one half step; also, the sound of a note that is performed above its proper pitch

sightreading the ability to look at music notation and translate its symbols into sound without first hearing or studying the music

simple meter meter in which the beat subdivides into two background pulses

singing game a structured group activity in which the players perform similar motions in a particular formation, often a circle

sixteenth note a note written as a solid head connected to a stem with two flags. It lasts only one fourth as long as a quarter note.

sleigh bells small spherical balls attached to a strap or frame and shaken

slur a curved line connecting two or more notes of different pitch, indicating that there should be no separation between them; in vocal music, a slur also connects notes that are to be sung with a single syllable of a word in the text

solfeggio (Italian) or **solfège** (French) use of the *do, re, mi* syllable system for identifying pitches

sonata a multi-movement work of chamber music performed by one instrument alone, or by piano and one other instrument as equal partners

sonata form a movement of three sections, the second of which is called the "development" section because of its intricate treatment of thematic material

soprano the highest women's singing voice

staff the five lines and four spaces on which notes are placed

step an interval in which one note is adjacent to the other both in alphabet letter name and in the position of their note-heads on the staff; also, any of the specific pitch levels in a scale

stick notation a simplified form of rhythm notation in which unnecessary symbols, such as note-heads, are eliminated in the early stages of teaching rhythmic reading

subdominant chord the chord built on the fourth step of the scale

subject (of a fugue) the theme of a fugue

suite a multi-movement instrumental work that is usually a collection of dances or a collection of music from a ballet or opera.

suspension a dissonant tone that was consonant in the preceding harmony and that eventually resolves downward to become consonant in the present harmony

symphony an extended orchestral work of several movements, usually four

syncopation an impression of shifting metrical accents, most often achieved by staggering the starting of tones so that they begin and end between the beats rather than on them

tambourine an instrument having a skin or membrane stretched across a wooden hoop rimmed with metal discs that produce a jangling sound when the instrument is shaken, struck on the center, tapped with the fingers, or played with mallets

temple blocks wood blocks struck with a mallet to produce a hollow, resonant sound

tempo the rate of speed at which the beats recur

ternary form a musical structure consisting of three segments; also called *ABA* or song form

tenor the highest men's singing voice

terraced dynamics distinct levels or planes of loudness and softness, with no gradual increase or decrease from one level to the next

theme a melody that is structurally important because it is the basis for a long work of music

theme and variations   a composition in which a theme is presented in different ways

third   the interval from one note to another when there is only one alphabet letter missing between the names of the two notes, as in the interval C-E. The third is basic to the harmonic system because it is the interval used in constructing triads and almost all other chords.

tie   a curved line connecting two or more notes of identical pitch to indicate that they should be combined into one continuous sound

timbre (*tam*-ber)   the tone quality of an instrument or voice

time signature   the meter signature, which consists of the two numbers, or their symbols, occurring at the beginning of a piece of music to indicate the meter pattern by telling how many beats are in each measure and what kind of note lasts for one beat

tonal center   the tonic, which is the pitch on which a scale is built and toward which the music tends to gravitate

tone color   the tone quality of a voice or instrument

tonic   the pitch on which a scale is built and toward which the music tends to gravitate

tonic triad   the chord built on step 1 of the scale

tonguing   using the tongue to start and stop the sound on a wind instrument

transposition   changing the key of an entire piece so that it is performed at a higher or lower pitch level than the original version

treble clef   the clef in which the G above middle C is positioned on the second line from the bottom of the staff

triad   a chord of three pitches, each a third apart

triangle   a three-sided suspended metal frame struck with a beater to produce a clear metallic tone. The impression of a continuous sound is achieved by repeated strokes occurring in rapid succession and alternating between adjacent sides of an inside corner

ukulele   a small four-stringed guitar popularized in Hawaii for accompanying songs and dances

unison   the musical result of two or more sounds produced simultaneously at exactly the same pitch level

upbeat   an unstressed note, usually the last beat of a measure, that begins a musical phrase

value   the duration represented by a particular note

variation forms   music in which a theme is changed with each appearance. The three most common variation forms are theme and variations, passacaglia, and chaconne.

waltz   a couple dance in fast triple meter, characterized by a "step slide step" movement and frequent turning; also, music in the style of that dance

water bottles   a set of glass containers, each holding a level of water that will produce a specific pitch when the bottle is tapped

whole note   a note written as an open head with no stem. It lasts four times as long as a quarter note.

whole step   an interval as wide as two half steps

wood block   a block of wood struck with a mallet to produce a hollow, resonant sound

xylophone   wooden bars arranged in keyboard fashion and mounted on resonating devices that enhance the tone when the bars are struck with mallets

Index of Songs

Index of Music Recommended for Listening

Subject Index

Sweatshirt
  1/2 yd. Material (cotton)
  Sweatshirt paint (color paint)
  heat-n-bond
  Scissors
   pencil

                                    Hall's
                        9:45

  Drinks